READING STRATEGIES FOR SECONDARY SCHOOL TEACHERS

Lou E. Burmeister
University of Texas at El Paso

ADDISON-WESLEY PUBLISHING COMPANY
Reading, Massachusetts
Menlo Park, California · London · Amsterdam · Don Mills, Ontario · Sydney

To my mother, Alyce, and Thad
and John W. McFarland,
all of whom made the writing of this book possible

This book is in the
ADDISON-WESLEY SERIES IN EDUCATION

ISBN 0-201-00739-8
DEFGHIJKL-MA-798765

CONTENTS

READING AND THE SECONDARY SCHOOL TEACHER

All teachers want students to learn. To promote this goal, almost all teachers use printed materials—books, pamphlets, magazine and newspaper articles—in the classroom. The present book has been written to help teachers and pre-service teachers both choose and utilize printed materials to promote optimal student learning and enjoyment. Throughout the text, the teaching of reading skills and the selection of appropriate reading materials are viewed as means toward helping each student achieve his full cognitive and affective potential.

Learning to read, study, and select appropriate reading materials are viewed in this book as continuous processes rather than as skills which can be achieved at one period of time, such as in the elementary grades. The blocks laid and molded into a meaningful base during a person's earliest years form the foundation for an ever-evolving skill structure. Even when students leave our care—upon graduation—they have just begun to develop. At colleges and universities, in the business world—whatever their job—or at home, they must continue to grow. We can help provide a strong background so that they are able and willing to do so.

Those teachers who are most interested in having their students master content—be it science, math, literature, social studies, or anything else—will find that there is in reality no dichotomy between teaching reading and teaching content. When fused with the teaching of content, the teaching of reading skills and the selection of materials appropriate for each student make it possible for students to understand content.

Content area teachers are not expected to teach reading skills in isolation, but they will find that learning is facilitated if they teach those skills which are necessary for understanding their materials. This they can do at the same time that they teach content.

ORGANIZATION OF THIS BOOK

To guide the reader's thinking along these lines, this book has been written. It is divided into four units. Unit One, titled "Adjusting Reading Materials for All Students," deals with such topics as understanding how well students read, judging the difficulty of reading materials, and devising classroom strategies which are helpful in finding the appropriate level of materials for each student and finding materials of interest to each student.

Unit Two, titled "Developing Classroom Strategies for Reading in Content Fields," deals specifically with classroom teaching and organizational strategies which can be used to promote learning and interest. Unit Three, titled "Improving Learning Through Reading Development in Content Fields," deals with specific ways of developing needed tools for such strategies. And Unit Four, titled "Utilizing School-wide Resources and Staff," deals with strategies for using school resources and extending the program to encompass the whole staff in a cooperative effort.

COGNITIVE AND AFFECTIVE DEVELOPMENT

Two unifying concepts permeate the book. One is concerned with the cognitive development of students; the other, with affective development. *Cognitive development* is intellectual development, the kind of thing teachers have always been interested in. The *cognitive domain,* or intellectual realm, has recently been analyzed, and its components have been arranged in levels according to the degree of intellectual activity necessary at each level. According to Benjamin Bloom, there is a hierarchical continuum of cognitive skills ranging from memory (recall) responses at the lowest level to highly intellectual, critical (analytical)-creative (synthetic)-evaluative thinking at the highest levels.[1]

Affective development relates to the development of a value system, interests, and involvement. The *affective domain,* as delineated by David Krathwohl, describes behavior ranging from simple awareness of an idea at the lowest level to complete internalization of the idea, demonstrated by a state of "characterization," whereby an idea or value permeates a person's whole being.[2]

Although often discussed separately, cognitive and affective behavior normally interact. The processes of valuing, being interested in, and involved with an idea frequently spark a higher level of cognitive understanding or response to the idea than would otherwise occur. This higher-level intellectual response may, in turn, cause increased affective involvement, and so on.

USE OF THIS BOOK AS A TEXTBOOK FOR A COLLEGE COURSE

This book consists of 12 chapters. In a college class, perhaps one chapter could be studied each week; slightly more time might be spent on some chapters and less on others. Basic related references for further study are listed at the end of each chapter. Also included are suggested activities for students who may wish such guidance. This schedule also provides ample time for giving and discussing two or three examinations.

Relate Reading in This Book to a Content Field Book of Your Choice

It is recommended that the reader of this book have at his side one or more content area textbooks of his choice, at the grade level of his choice. Assignments within some chapters and the suggested activities at the end of chapters can be applied to such texts. Doing such assignments concurrently with the reading of this book should help prepare the student for the implementation of suggested principles and techniques in future teaching.

NOTES

1 Benjamin Bloom, *et al. Taxonomy of Educational Objectives: Handbook I, Cognitive Domain.* New York: David McKay, 1956. A more complete discussion of the cognitive domain may be found in Unit Three of this book.

2 David R. Krathwohl, *et al. Taxonomy of Educational Objectives: Handbook II, Affective Domain.* New York: David McKay, 1964. A more complete discussion of the affective domain may be found in Chapter 4 of this book.

UNIT ONE

ADJUSTING READING MATERIALS FOR ALL STUDENTS

Introduction

Unit One consists of four chapters:

Chapter 1
Understanding How Well Students Read

Chapter 2
Judging the Difficulty of Reading Materials

Chapter 3
Finding the Appropriate Level of Materials for Each Student

Chapter 4
Assessing Student Interests in Reading Materials

Unit One has two basic purposes: *first*, to clarify how widely students differ in reading achievement, and *second*, to supply some basic techniques for the appropriate selection of reading materials in relationship to the individual student's reading achievement and interests.

Chapter 1

UNDER-STANDING HOW WELL STUDENTS READ

What is the *range* of reading achievement in a typical classroom?

How well *should* individual students read?

Why don't some students read as well as expected?

RANGE OF READING ACHIEVEMENT IN A CLASSROOM

The Facts

Let's imagine that you are teaching a typical class of tenth graders. You are meeting them for the first time and know nothing about the individuals. Let's consider their cognitive development in reading. It's important to know how well they can perform.

Let's say there are 30 teen-agers in the class. How well do you think the best reader reads, and how poorly the poorest? If you don't know, make an educated guess. Circle the grade levels that you think represent the reading achievement of the poorest and best readers in the class:

```
                                    average
  1   2   3   4   5   6   7   8   9   10   11   12   13   14   15   16   17   18          ˜
          poorest grade                        best grade
```

Did you circle 9 and 11, or 8 and 12? If so, you're way off! You're closer to the truth if you circled 6 and 14, or 6 and 15—if it's a good class. If it's a poorer class, you might have circled 5 and 13, or 5 and 14. If it's a typical class, you should have circled 5 *and 15*.

Let's try another class—this time a seventh-grade English class. Again, circle the reading-grade level of the poorest reader and that of the best reader:

```
                        average
  1   2   3   4   5   6   7   8   9   10   11   12   13   14   15   16   17   18
poorest grade                          best grade
```

What did you circle? It should have been 3 and 11.

Another? Let's take a twelfth-grade sociology class. Circle the grade score of the poorest reader and that of the best:

```
                                        average
  1   2   3   4   5   6   7   8   9   10   11   12   13   14   15   16   17   18
              poorest grade                          best grade
```

Did you circle 6 and 18? That's it.

Let's look at what we've done. In a typical seventh-grade class, the range is from third to eleventh grade:

average
1 2 ③ 4 5 6 7 8 9 10 ⑪ 12 13 14 15 16 17 18
←—7−4—→ ←—7+4—→

In a tenth-grade class, the range is from fifth to fifteenth grade:

average
1 2 3 4 ⑤ 6 7 8 9 10 11 12 13 14 ⑮ 16 17 18
←—10−5—→ ←—10+5—→

And in a twelfth-grade class, the range is from about sixth to about eighteenth grade:

average
1 2 3 4 5 ⑥ 7 8 9 10 11 12 13 14 15 16 17 ⑱
←—12−5.67—→ ←—12+5.67—→

Formula

The range of reading achievement in a typical class is two-thirds the median chronological age of the students:

$$\text{range in reading achievement} = 2/3 \,(\text{C.A.})$$

In fact, the range may be even greater.

To find the chronological age, add 5.2 *years* to the grade level, as is shown in Table 1.1. Since the chronological age of students increases from year to

Table 1.1 **Conversion of grade level to chronological age (formula: Grade + 5.2 = C.A.)**

Grade	C.A.	Grade	C.A.	Grade	C.A.	Grade	C.A.
1.0	6.2	4.0	9.2	7.0	12.2	10.0	15.2
2.0	7.2	5.0	10.2	8.0	13.2	11.0	16.2
3.0	8.2	6.0	11.2	9.0	14.2	12.0	17.2

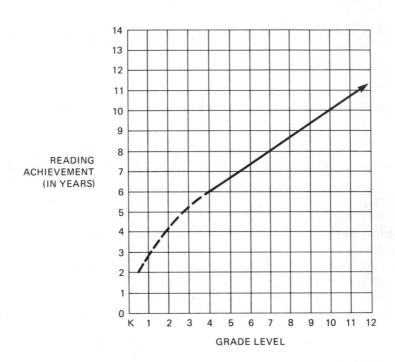

Fig. 1.1 Range of reading achievement in a typical classroom (in years).

year, the range from low to high achievement increases as the students move upward in grade level. The approximate range of reading achievement is illustrated in Fig. 1.1.

In *School, Curriculum, and the Individual,* John I. Goodlad states:

The broad spread from high to low achiever steadily increases with the upward movement of heterogeneous classes (relatively homogeneous in chronological age) through the school. In the intermediate grades, this spread is approximately the number of years designated by the number of the grade-level: that is, by the third grade, three years; by the fourth grade, four years; by the fifth grade, five years. However, since the spread in achievement accelerates slightly faster than a year-per-year of schooling, the overall range in junior high school classes is approximately two-thirds the median chronological age of the groups. In subject areas, such as reading and language arts, where children can readily proceed on their own in a variety of out-of-school situations, the spread from high to low achiever frequently is one and one-half to twice the number of the

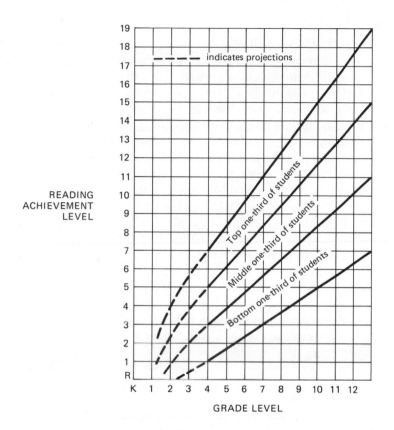

Fig. 1.2 Distribution of reading achievement levels in a typical classroom from grades 4 to 12.9.

grade level. Hence, in the fifth grade, there frequently is an eight-year spread in reading achievement between the best and the poorest readers. Differentiation in classroom group stimuli to provide for varying levels of accomplishment does not encompass this range, but the encouragement of self-selection of materials for supplementary reading at home and school facilitates highly individualized rates of progress.°

Approximately one-third of the students will read within one to two years of their current grade level. About one-third will read more poorly than this, and one-third will read better. Thus, we often find that the distribution of reading achievement levels among students in classrooms is similar to that shown in Fig. 1.2.

° Reprinted by permission of the publisher, from John I. Goodlad, *School, Curriculum, and the Individual,* © 1966 Xerox Corporation. All rights reserved.

Discussion

A teacher should not expect all students in a class to read the same book, for students are very different cognitively, as we can see from the discussion above. Affectively, they also vary greatly—perhaps more than they do cognitively.

"Requiring" everyone in a classroom to read the same book is like expecting everyone to wear the same size shoe. If the shoe is like the glass slipper of Cinderella, it would fit but one foot in a kingdom. Similarly, obliging all students to read the same text bores some and frustrates many more.

If, however, only one textbook is available to a teacher, it must be used with discretion. Provisions must be made, especially for the poorer readers, e.g., possibly, parts of the book could be taped. Often, however, the poor reader is reading as well as his mental ability allows. His problem is one of limited thinking ability (and/or limited background of information and/or limited interests). Supplying the oral counterpart for the printed symbols will not solve his problem, i.e., something other than the textbook is needed to enable him to understand the subject.

The student with a normal I.Q. who is disabled in reading,* *per se*, however, might benefit from having the book read to him—provided his disability stems from an *oral reading problem* and not from lack of comprehension skills.

Some school systems have attempted to alleviate the problem by sectioning students according to reading test scores and possibly by I.Q., too. This decreases the number of levels in a classroom, but it does not eliminate levels. Even the students in the middle group are vastly different. For example, in a tenth-grade classroom, the lowest student in the middle group might be reading at the eighth- (or 8.5) grade level, and the best at the twelfth- (or 11.5) grade level—still a wide range. Even two students who have the same total reading score may vary if we consider their relative scores on subtests within a battery. Of two students scoring at the tenth-grade level in reading, for example, one may score grade 8 in vocabulary; the other, grade 12. The first may score grade 10 in comprehension, and the second, grade 11. The first may score grade 12 in rate of reading, and the second, grade 7. They are very different in their reading profiles. They may also vary affectively.

Just as there is a strong trend today toward school integration—socially and racially—there is a trend toward integration academically. We have tried "homogeneous" grouping according to achievement and, at other times, according to I.Q. These techniques solve some problems and create others. Certainly, the poorer student misses much by being deprived of the challenge and activity commonly engendered by average and bright students in a heterogeneous class. Many people think that heterogeneous grouping is lifelike, for youngsters of

---

* A person is considered *disabled* in reading if he reads well below *his* potential level. He is *retarded* in reading if he reads below his grade-placement level.

many ability levels share common interests. There is no easy solution, but no matter how students are grouped, teachers will have to differentiate assignments within the group.

READING EXPECTANCY FOR INDIVIDUALS

At what level might we legitimately expect each student to read? Certainly not at the grade level at which he is grouped according to his chronological age, for some students far exceed that level, and others, no matter what we do, will never reach it.

The level toward which we strive depends partly on our definition of reading. If we think of reading as merely *decoding*, many children should reach the top level by the end of third grade. But if we define reading achievement in relationship to *cognition*, or intellectual development, a top level will never be reached, for our cognitive abilities continue to develop year after year.

Although far from perfect, our best measure of a person's potential cognitive *achievement* is related to his *mental age*, as determined by an I.Q. test which is selected for him in relationship to his ethnic background, reading achievement (if it is a group test), and past educational opportunities. Since such a test is often impossible to find, we compromise by selecting a test that comes close to being a good one for him, in which case the mental age is only approximate. Or, we use the same test for all students, in which case the mental age any particular student scores might be grossly inaccurate.

Let's hypothesize that we have a good I.Q. test for a student and that he scored 100 on it. Since an I.Q. of 95 to 105 is average, we would expect a student who scores 100 to be reading at grade level. A student whose I.Q. is above 105 should read above grade level. And it is likely that a student whose I.Q. is below 95 will be reading below grade level.

If we have a student's chronological age and his I.Q., it is a simple matter to compute his mental age:

$$\text{M.A.} = \frac{\text{I.Q.}}{100} \times \text{C.A.}$$

Thus, if a student's I.Q. is 110 and his C.A. is 14, his M.A. = (110/100) × 14, or 15.4 years. If his I.Q. is 90 and his C.A. is 14, his M.A. = (90/100) × 14, or 12.6 years.

There are various ways of estimating how well a student should read. Writers who feel that M.A. is all-important in estimating reading expectancy recommend the use of the formula:

$$\text{reading expectancy age} = \text{M.A.}$$

This formula gives the *age* score for reading expectancy. To find the *grade* score, subtract 5.2 years from the age score:

$$\text{reading expectancy grade} = \text{M.A.} - 5.2.$$

Albert J. Harris, in the fifth edition of *How to Increase Reading Ability*, recommends the use of the following formula to ascertain the expected reading level for students:

$$\text{reading expectancy age} = \frac{2\,\text{M.A.} + \text{C.A.}}{3}.$$

This formula "gives priority to the importance of intelligence but also recognizes the presence of other age-related characteristics in reading expectancy." [1]
   To find the expected reading-grade score, the following formula is used:

$$\text{reading expectancy grade} = \frac{2\,\text{M.A.} + \text{C.A.}}{3} - 5.2.$$

Table 1.2, composed by using this formula, gives the approximate expectancy grade-level scores for students of various chronological ages and I.Q.'s.

Table 1.2   Reading expectancy grade scores according to I.Q. and C.A., using the formula R.E. (grade) = [(2 M.A. + C.A.)/3] − 5.2

Usual grade placement	C.A.	I.Q. 80	90	100	110	120	130	140
1.0	6.2	R*	R*	1.0	1.3†	1.7†	2.2†	2.6†
2.0	7.2	1.0	1.5	2.0	2.4	2.9	3.4	3.9
3.0	8.2	1.9	2.4	3.0	3.5	4.1	4.6	5.1
4.0	9.2	2.7	3.4	4.0	4.6	5.2	5.8	6.4
5.0	10.2	3.6	4.3	5.0	5.7	6.3	7.0	7.7
6.0	11.2	4.5	5.2	6.0	6.7	7.5	8.2	8.9
7.0	12.2	5.3	6.2	7.0	7.8	8.6	9.4	10.2
8.0	13.2	6.2	7.1	8.0	8.9	9.7	10.6	11.5
9.0	14.2	7.1	8.0	9.0	10.0	10.9	11.8	12.7
10.0	15.2	7.9	9.0	10.0	11.0	12.0	13.0	14.0
11.0	16.2	8.8	9.9	11.0	12.1	13.1	14.2	15.3
12.0	17.2	9.7	10.8	12.0	13.2	14.3	15.4	16.5

* R = reading readiness
† It would be unrealistic to expect untaught children to be reading at these levels upon entering school.

Another commonly used formula is the one favored by Bond and Tinker (Table 1.3):[2]

$$\text{reading expectancy grade} = \left(\frac{\text{I.Q.}}{100} \times \text{years in school}\right) + 1.$$

Assuming that a child had never been failed at any grade level, this formula could also be charted. Remember, a child entering first grade has been in school *zero years*. The zero would cancel out the I.Q., and it is assumed that all children, no matter what their I.Q.'s, are equally ready to begin to read at age 6.2. This is a flaw of the mathematical formula, and doubtless not the philosophy of the authors. Perhaps the formula should not be used for children who have not been in school at least one year. However, the formula does assume homogeneity at age 6.2 rather than at birth, as does the former formula. Therefore, if we used the Bond and Tinker formula rather than the previous one, we would have *greater* expectancy for slower students and *lesser* expectancy for brighter ones.

Table 1.3   Reading expectancy grade scores according to I.Q. and C.A., using the formula R.E. (grade) = [(I.Q./100) × years in school] + 1

Usual grade placement	C.A.	I.Q.						
		80	90	100	110	120	130	140
1.0	6.2	1.0	1.0	1.0	1.0	1.0	1.0	1.0
2.0	7.2	1.8	1.9	2.0	2.1	2.2	2.3	2.4
3.0	8.2	2.6	2.8	3.0	3.2	3.4	3.6	3.8
4.0	9.2	3.4	3.7	4.0	4.3	4.6	4.9	5.2
5.0	10.2	4.2	4.6	5.0	5.4	5.8	6.2	6.6
6.0	11.2	5.0	5.5	6.0	6.5	7.0	7.5	8.0
7.0	12.2	5.8	6.4	7.0	7.6	8.2	8.8	9.4
8.0	13.2	6.6	7.3	8.0	8.7	9.4	10.1	10.8
9.0	14.2	7.4	8.2	9.0	9.8	10.6	11.4	12.2
10.0	15.2	8.2	9.1	10.0	10.9	11.8	12.7	13.6
11.0	16.2	9.0	10.0	11.0	12.0	13.0	14.0	15.0
12.0	17.2	9.8	10.9	12.0	13.1	14.2	15.3	16.4

Since such formulas are meant to offer only gross, or rough, estimates (since I.Q. tests are not perfect either), it might be wise to select one on a philosophical basis, or a best-fit basis, or use an average of the two. Some school systems have even devised their own formulas.[3]

There are hazards involved in using reading expectancy formulas or charts based on them after a student has reached the chronological age of about 15. The reason for this is that beyond the age of about 15, mental ability no longer grows in a linear fashion. However, these charts should prove helpful if the scores are used as approximate guidelines rather than as precise expectancy scores.

If you examine these charts carefully by reading on any one horizontal line, you will see that one of the reasons for the wide range of reading achievement in a classroom—where students are grouped by chronological age—is that there is a wide range in I.Q. Therefore, a wide range in reading achievement is inevitable—if teaching is done well. However, the actual range is often wider than the expected range, considering the I.Q.'s of the students in the class. This wider range results from the interaction of a variety of factors which are not considered in such formulas. Some of these factors are salubrious, whereas others are inhibitory.

For example, excellent teaching and the use of materials appropriate to the needs and interests of a student, as well as extraordinary interest and effort on the part of the student, might very likely result in a higher reading score than expected. Additionally, success in an experience such as reading may lead to greater success. Emotional well-being, social adjustment, and an inquiring attitude may support an atmosphere for concentration, which may help improve reading achievement.

WHY SOME STUDENTS DO NOT READ AS WELL AS EXPECTED

On the other hand, a variety of inhibitory factors might interact for the student who attains a lower score than expected. Such factors might be broadly classified as educational, psychological, sociological, and physiological.

Restraining factors of these types are frequently found "traveling together" with reading disability, i.e., several, or many, of these factors are commonly characteristic of students who read at levels lower than expected. The presence of such factors gives the teacher clues to what may have caused the reading disability.

A brief description of those restraining factors which are most important for the classroom teacher to be aware of is included here. It is recommended that those students who wish more information about this area study one or more of the sources cited at the end of this chapter.[4]

Educational Factors

Educational factors relate to the way a student has been, or is being, taught. It is extremely important for teachers and administrators to face the growing recognition that for most students, achievement depends on the kinds of materials and techniques used in the classroom and that all students do not grow optimally by using the same materials and by being taught in the same ways.

Ernest Horn in "Language and Meaning" argues:

A single textbook is commonly provided for a grade, in spite of the incontestable evidence of the wide range of knowledge and ability in that grade . . . Investigations have repeatedly pointed out that the typical textbook, even within the limits of its potential usefulness, is much too difficult for the median child in the grade for which it is designed, and it is hopelessly difficult for the children in the lowest quarter of reading ability.*

Bond and Tinker add:

Frequently, reading disability is largely due to educational factors. Any administrative policy which prevents proper individualization of instruction . . . will prevent effective progress in reading. Failure to acquire the necessary learnings or the acquisition of faulty learnings is most frequently due to ineffective teaching. One or more of the following factors may be involved in the ineffective teaching which brings about reading disability: too rapid progress in the instructional schedule, isolation of reading instruction from other school activities, inappropriate emphasis upon some technique or skill, or treating reading as a by-product of content studies. Frequently, the difficulty occurs because the instructional program has failed to maintain a proper balance in the growth of a large number of skills and abilities.†

Knowledgeable teachers are able to present ideas in a variety of ways, and if only a single textbook is available, they learn to use it as only one of the cores of instruction (see Chapters 4 and 11). They supplement it with paperbacks, pamphlets, films and filmstrips, discussions, field trips, etc. They are aware of the kinds of thought processes and reading skills necessary for understanding the content of their courses, and these are the skills they teach their students—in the ways their students can best learn them. Doing this is not a simple task. It is the purpose of this book to help teachers and prospective teachers improve in such undertakings.

Psychological Factors

Among the psychological factors which may restrict reading achievement are low intelligence, lack of interest, emotional and personal problems, and inadequate visual and auditory perception.

---

* Ernest Horn. "Language and Meaning," in *The Forty-First Yearbook of the National Society for the Study of Education Part II, The Psychology of Learning.* Chicago: University of Chicago Press, 1942, p. 390. Reprinted by permission.

† From *Reading Difficulties: Their Diagnosis and Correction,* 2d ed., p. 146. Guy L. Bond and Miles A. Tinker. Copyright © 1967. By permission of Appleton-Century-Crofts, Educational Division, Meredith Corporation.

Intelligence

George Spache states, "There is much less tendency today to attribute reading disability to low intelligence than there was a quarter century ago. . . . Two facts account for this trend: one, more adequate intelligence testing by public schools and two, the recognition that intellectually handicapped children are not disabled readers when they read about as well as their intelligence permits."[5]

Over and over, however, teachers are cautioned about the possibility of making serious errors in the interpretation of both intelligence test scores and the relationships between these scores and those on reading tests.

To do well in a group intelligence test usually requires good reading ability. The poor reader, who cannot read the questions, cannot display his intelligence. When a group intelligence test is given to a poor reader, he is labeled low in intelligence. Thus, he has a low *measured* I.Q., and we expect him to read at a low level according to our reading expectancy formulas. A vicious circle is in operation.

A poor reader should be given an individual intelligence test, such as the Stanford-Binet, the WISC (Wechsler Intelligence Scale for Children), or the WAIS (Wechsler Adult Intelligence Scale). Even such tests measure certain reading abilities and many language abilities which may be attained through reading. Also, for the culturally different child, the items in general may provide for an unfair evaluation of his potential.

I.Q. testing is fraught with hazards, especially for the poor reader and the culturally different student. Yet for the middle-class student who is an average or good reader, we have no better gauge of potential at the present time. It would be wise for teachers to be extremely cautious and avoid overreliance on I.Q. test scores.[6]

One of the better substitutes for I.Q. testing to estimate student potential in a classroom situation is explained in Chapter 3 under the heading "Standardized Reading-Listening Tests" and in the discussion of "Capacity Level" as part of the informal reading inventory.

Interests

Interest is probably as important a factor in reading achievement as is intelligence. Most people strive to do a good job of what they enjoy or are interested in. Some people put forth little effort if they do not see an immediate reward. Daniel Fader's *Hooked on Books: Program and Proof* describes this point of view.[7] G. Robert Carlsen's *Books and the Teen-Age Reader* gives many helpful ideas about the natural interests of teen-agers and ways of capitalizing on them.[8] Chapter 4 of the present book is devoted to assessing the interests of students in content-related materials.

Emotional, personality, and perceptual problems

A discussion of emotional, personality, and perceptual problems which may inhibit reading growth is beyond the scope of this book. Yet certainly the importance of such problems should not be underemphasized. Many excellent sources are available which contain brief discussions of these factors. The interested student is advised to begin by reading the references suggested in note 6 at the end of this chapter.

Sociological Factors

A student's attitudes toward ideas frequently reflect his family and community background. As explained in greater detail in Chapter 4, people tend to choose reading materials that agree with their point of view. Only the more sophisticated reader will choose to read and consider conflicting ideas.

Also, attitudes toward reading itself often reflect the student's background. Children whose parents rarely read are likely to read little themselves, and such limited reading experience leads to a limited background of experiences and information and possibly to limited aspirations.[9]

The linguistic range of a student is to a great extent dependent on both sociological and educational factors. Many culturally different children get a poor start in school because their home or community language differs from that used in the school.[10]

Physical Factors

Physical factors may also interact and/or be part of the constellation of inhibiting characteristics commonly found in disabled readers. The three physical factors considered here are vision, hearing, and lateral dominance.

Vision

At the present time, the relationship between specific eye defects and reading disability has not been established. Both good and poor readers have been found to have visual defects, although a greater proportion of poor readers often have certain types of defects.

Present research seems to suggest that visual defects alone may not cause severe reading disability, but that when certain visual defects appear along with other inhibiting factors, reading disability may be present. Possibly, a visual defect may handicap the good reader also, but he is able to compensate for it.

In light of the importance of conserving vision for all, however, care should be taken to protect the eyes of all. Teachers should watch for signs of visual discomfort: rubbing the eyes, excessive blinking, red or swollen eyes, reports of headaches or fatigue resulting from reading, etc. Vision should be checked to determine if certain types of defects appear to be present. Defects that may affect reading achievement are *hyperopia, extreme myopia, poor binocular coordination*, and poor *fusion*.[11]

A person who is *hyperopic* (far-sighted) has poor near-point acuity and therefore will find it difficult to see sharp images when reading a book. A person with *extreme myopia* (near-sightedness) may have to hold a book too close to his eyes for physical comfort, and he will have difficulty reading the board.

Normally, the two eyes are used together in reading. If the two eyes do not focus simultaneously on the same object, the image may be blurred. Also, the eye lenses must focus with precision on an object if the images seen by the two eyes are to fuse so that only one object is seen.

Unfortunately, the visual test used most frequently by schools, the Snellen Test, will screen out only those students who have myopia. Students with hyperopia normally pass the test, as do students with binocular defects.

The following tests are better for screening these other types of defects:

> Massachusetts Vision Test
>
> AO School Vision Screening Test
>
> Keystone Visual Survey Test
>
> Ortho-Rater.[12]

Hearing

Poor hearing may be a contributing factor in reading disability for several reasons. *First*, children normally learn to speak through listening; hence, both the vocabulary and sentence patterns of a person who hears poorly are likely to be inadequate. *Second*, children may be taught to read through an oral approach. Those who cannot hear well cannot auditorily perceive differences in sounds and, therefore, may not learn to read well. *Third*, students of any age who cannot hear well cannot benefit from class discussions, nor can they follow directions given orally by the teacher.

Students who are hard of hearing frequently are not aware that they hear any differently from other students, as they have no standard against which to judge. It is extremely important for students to hear well in school and, therefore, the teacher should be alert to detect any signs of hearing loss, such as inattentiveness, poor pronunciation, frequent misunderstanding of simple directions, turning one ear toward the speaker, etc.

Frequently, the results of an *audiometer* test are available to the teacher and may be found in the student's cumulative folder. According to A. J. Harris, "a hearing loss of less than 15 decibels is normal; a loss of 15 to 20 decibels is probably a handicap; a loss of over 20 decibels is almost certain to handicap a child in hearing in classroom situations and is usually accompanied by some indistinctness in speech."[13] A student who exhibits a significant hearing loss should be advised to seek professional help. In the meantime, the student should sit close to the teacher.

Lateral dominance

Most people have a dominant *eye*, a dominant *hand*, and a dominant *leg*. To find which of your eyes is dominant, for example, form a cone with an 8½" × 11" sheet of paper. Put a penny on the floor, stand up and hold the cone at arm's length, and look through the *top* of the cone at the penny. Be sure *both* of your eyes are open. First, close your right eye. Do you still see the penny through the cone? If so, you're probably *left-eyed* (for your left eye was open). Then close your left eye. Do you see the penny? If so, you're *right-eyed* (probably). I say probably, because you may go home tonight and repeat the test with the opposite results, in which case, you may have *incomplete eye dominance*, i.e., sometimes the right eye is dominant and sometimes the left.

A. J. Harris, in *The Harris Test of Lateral Dominance*, delineates other tests for eye dominance, hand dominance, and foot dominance.[14]

Many people are dominant on one side of their body. That is, their right eye is dominant, their right hand, and their right leg—or their left eye, left hand, and left leg. By *crossed dominance* we mean that the dominant hand and eye are on opposite sides. By *incomplete dominance* we mean that a person shows nearly equal use of both sides, in either hand or eye dominance.[15]

The concept of lateral dominance has intrigued some reading researchers, who see in it an explanation for *strephosymbolia* (twisted symbols—mirrored vision) or for excessive regressions. It is theorized that people who are right-sided, especially right-eyed, use the left hemisphere of their brain for memory traces for printed words. People who are left-sided, or left-eyed, by contrast, use the right hemisphere of the brain. It is thought that if a person has incomplete or mixed dominance, however, he may at times see mirror images or twisted symbols, for he may use the left side of the brain at one time and the right side at another. Alas, the theories are intriguing, but accumulated empirical evidence suggests that theories of lateral dominance explain but little in reading disability.

SUMMARY

At first glance, the *range of reading achievement* in the typical classroom seems unbelievably vast. The difference between the reading level of the poorest and the best reader in a classroom where students are grouped principally according to their chronological ages is described by the formula

$$\text{range in reading achievement} = 2/3 \, (\text{C.A.})$$

As children grow older, the range increases—if teaching is done well. Such a range indicates the need for reading materials at many levels.

Reading expectancy for an individual student is usually related to his mental ability. The brighter student is expected to read at a higher level than is the average student, and the average student is expected to read at a higher level than is a student with a low I.Q. Several formulas are currently in use for computing the reading expectancy levels of individual students. Two of these are:

$$\text{reading expectancy grade} = \frac{2 \text{ M.A.} + \text{C.A.}}{3} - 5.2$$

and

$$\text{reading expectancy grade} = \left(\frac{\text{I.Q.}}{100} \times \text{years in school}\right) + 1.$$

A major problem in using any of these formulas is getting a valid and reliable I.Q. (or M.A.) score, especially for poor readers and culturally different students. Usually, the scored I.Q.'s (or M.A.'s) of these students are vast underestimates of their true potential.

Inhibiting factors of various types are frequently found among students who fail to read as well as expected. The presence of such factors may give the teacher a lead to what may have caused the reading disability. Such factors can be broadly classified as educational, psychological, sociological, and physiological.

NOTES

1 Albert J. Harris. *How to Increase Reading Ability*, 5th ed. New York: David McKay, 1970, p. 212.

2 Guy L. Bond and Miles A. Tinker. *Reading Difficulties: Their Diagnosis and Correction*. New York: Appleton-Century-Crofts, 1957, p. 78.

3 See George D. Spache. "Estimating Reading Capacity," in *The Evaluation of Reading*, ed. Helen M. Robinson, Supplementary Educational Monographs, No. 88. Chicago: The University of Chicago Press, 1958, pp. 15–20.

4 Guy L. Bond and Miles A. Tinker, *op. cit.*, Chapters 4, 5, and 6; Albert J. Harris, *op. cit.*, Chapters 9, 10, and 11; Theodore L. Harris, Wayne Otto, and Thomas C. Barrett. "Summary and Review of Investigations Related to Reading." *Journal of Educational Research*, February or March yearly; Wayne Otto and Richard McMenemy. *Corrective and Remedial Teaching: Principles and Practices*. Boston: Houghton Mifflin, 1966, Chapters 2, 3, and 4; Wayne Otto and Karl Koenke. *Remedial Teaching: Research and Comment*. Boston: Houghton Mifflin, 1969; Helen M. Robinson. *Why Pupils Fail in Reading*. Chicago: University of Chicago Press, 1946; Leo M. Schell and Paul C. Burns. *Remedial Reading: An Anthology of Sources*. Boston: Allyn and Bacon, 1968, Parts 2 and 3; George D. Spache. *Toward Better Reading*, Champaign, Illinois: Garrard, 1963, Chapter 6; Miles V. Zintz. *Corrective Reading*. Dubuque, Iowa: Wm. C. Brown Co., 1966, Chapter 1.

5 George D. Spache. *Toward Better Reading, op. cit.*, p. 117.

6 See George D. Spache. "Estimating Reading Capacity," *op. cit.* Also in Schell and Burns, *op. cit.*, pp. 115–121.

7 Daniel Fader and Elton McNeil. *Hooked on Books: Program and Proof.* New York: Berkley, 1968.

8 G. Robert Carlsen. *Books and the Teen-Age Reader.* New York: Bantam, 1972.

9 See "Reading Problems" (Part II), in *Improving Reading Ability Around the World*, ed. D. K. Bracken and E. Malmquist. Newark, Delaware: International Reading Association, 1971.

10 See Martin Deutsch. "The Role of Social Class in Language Development and Cognition." *American Journal of Orthopsychiatry* (January 1964): 78–88; *Language Programs for the Disadvantaged.* Report of the NCTE Task Force on Teaching English to the Disadvantaged. Champaign, Illinois: National Council of Teachers of English, 1965; *Language, Reading, and the Communication Process*, ed. Carl Braun. Newark, Delaware: International Reading Association, 1971; *Language and the Higher Thought Processes*, ed. Russell Stauffer. Champaign, Illinois: National Council of Teachers of English, 1965.

11 See Helen M. Robinson and C. B. Huelsman. "Visual Efficiency and Progress in Learning to Read," in *Clinical Studies in Reading*, II, Supplementary Educational Monographs, No. 77. Chicago: University of Chicago Press, 1953, pp. 31–63.

12 Massachusetts Vision Test and AO School Screening Test, from American Optical Co., Southern, Mass. Keystone Visual Survey Test, from Keystone View Co., Meadville, Pa. Ortho-Rater, from Bausch and Lomb Optical Co., Rochester, N.Y.

13 Albert J. Harris, *op. cit.*, p. 257.

14 *Harris Tests of Lateral Dominance.* New York: Psychological Corp., 1955.

15 After Albert J. Harris, *op. cit.*, p. 232.

SUGGESTED ACTIVITIES

1. Below are listed reading-grade-level scores obtained from standardized tests given to 24 students in each of three different classes. Tell whether the range in reading achievement in each class is typical, broader, or narrower than usual.

   grade 7 scores: 7.3, 7.1, 6.5, 2.3, 5.7, 8.4, 1.9, 3.2, 9.2, 10.5, 12.3, 12.2, 11.0, 8.1, 4.8, 9.7, 6.7, 5.1, 3.4, 8.5, 11.3, 7.0, 6.6, 7.9

   grade 9 scores: 9.6, 8.5, 7.2, 11.7, 13.8, 4.0, 9.2, 9.2, 8.6, 12.4, 13.5, 6.2, 8.5, 9.6, 7.7, 5.1, 12.3, 11.1, 6.5, 7.2, 4.8, 8.9, 9.1, 9.3

   grade 12 scores: 11.5, 12.8, 9.2, 10.5, 12.1, 13.5, 10.0, 11.7, 16.5, 14.1, 15.2, 10.7, 12.2, 12.4, 11.5, 13.4, 11.1, 12.7, 9.2, 8.1, 5.9, 6.4, 11.8, 12.0

2. Using the following data, indicate the expected reading-grade level for each student according to both the A. J. Harris and the Bond and Tinker criteria.

   a) C.A. = 13.7, M.A. = 13.8   b) C.A. = 13.5, I.Q. = 120
   c) C.A. = 15.2, M.A. = 10.9   d) C.A. = 12.2, I.Q. = 90

3. Using the following information, write a brief hypothetical case study for each student, indicating factors which might have interacted to affect the reading-achievement score of each student.

   a) Alan Young, Jr.   :   C.A. = 14.2,   I.Q. = 130,   R.G. = 11.8

   b) Juan Gonzalez   :   C.A. = 15.0,   I.Q. = 100,   R.G. = 7.3

   c) Tanya K. Onassis   :   C.A. = 12.7,   M.A. = 14.2,   R.G. = 8.0

   d) Betty Kissinger   :   C.A. = 13.0,   M.A. = 14.6,   R.G. = 9.7

   e) Ray Smith   :   C.A. = 15.4,   I.Q. = 90,   R.G. = 6.1

REFERENCES FOR FURTHER READING

Bond, Guy L. and Miles A. Tinker. *Reading Difficulties: Their Diagnosis and Correction*. New York: Appleton-Century-Crofts, 1957, Chapter 4, Part 2.

Dechant, Emerald V. *Improving the Teaching of Reading*. Englewood Cliffs, N.J.: Prentice-Hall, 1970, Chapters 3 and 4.

Deutsch, Martin. "The Role of Social Class in Language Development and Cognition." *American Journal of Orthopsychiatry* (January 1964): 78–88.

Goodlad, John I. *School, Curriculum, and the Individual*. Waltham, Mass.: Blaisdell (Ginn), 1966.

Harris, Albert J. *How to Increase Reading Ability*, 5th ed. New York: David McKay, 1970, Chapters 9, 10, and 11.

Harris, Theodore L., Wayne Otto, and Thomas C. Barrett. "Summary and Review of Investigations Relating to Reading." *Journal of Educational Research*. February or March yearly.

Otto, Wayne and Richard McMenemy. *Corrective and Remedial Teaching*. Boston: Houghton Mifflin, 1966, Chapter 2.

Otto, Wayne and Richard J. Smith. *Administering the School Reading Program*. Boston: Houghton Mifflin, 1970.

Robinson, Helen M. *Why Pupils Fail in Reading*. Chicago: University of Chicago Press, 1946.

Robinson, Helen and C. B. Huelsman. "Visual Efficiency and Progress in Learning to Read," in *Clinical Studies in Reading*, II, Supplementary Educational Monographs, No. 77. Chicago: University of Chicago Press, 1953, pp. 31–63.

Schell, Leo M. and Paul C. Burns (eds). *Remedial Reading: An Anthology of Sources*. Boston: Allyn and Bacon, 1968, Parts Two and Three.

Spache, George D. *Toward Better Reading*. Champaign, Illinois: Garrard, 1963, Chapter 6.

Strang, Ruth. *The Diagnostic Teaching of Reading*. New York: McGraw-Hill, 1969. Chapters 8, 9, and 11.

Zintz, Miles V. *The Reading Process*. Dubuque, Iowa: Wm. C. Brown Co., 1970.

Chapter 2

JUDGING THE DIFFICULTY OF READING MATERIALS

What factors make printed materials easy or difficult to read?

How do we measure the difficulty of printed materials?

FACTORS THAT INFLUENCE THE DIFFICULTY OF PRINTED MATERIALS

A variety of factors, within both the reader and the printed materials, and the interaction of such factors, account for the difficulty or ease with which a reader can understand written materials. What are some of these factors?

Think of the last time you read something purely for pleasure. Did the zest with which you approached the activity help make it easy for you to understand the material? Did you read something in an area in which you are well versed? If so, your background of information about the subject helped make the printed material readable to you. On the other hand, if you chose to read something foreign to your background, chances are that it was a little harder going, for as you were reading, you came across vocabulary new to you and concepts that took time and effort to assimilate. However, your interest in the ideas helped to carry you along.

Think of other times when you have read, not because you especially wanted to, but because you had to. A basic lack of motivation may have made an assignment difficult for you to understand and remember.

Certainly, the interest that a reader brings to the material—his affective involvement—as well as his background of information as it relates to the content of the material are of vital importance in his ability to read the material. For example, an English major may be able to read difficult classical literature but be unable to read a freshman text in physics. A potential high school dropout may be fascinated by *Popular Mechanics* and may understand the contents well; yet he may be unable—or unwilling—to read a simple novel. We know that students can and will read difficult (for them) materials if they are vitally interested in them, whereas other materials objectively judged to be at the same readability level may be completely frustrating to them.

Psycholinguistic factors also affect the difficulty level of materials for specific readers. Is the reader familiar with the language patterns used by the writer, e.g., phrasing and syntax, semantics, and the paragraph, chapter, and book organization?

Linguistic factors related to syntax which seem important in readability are sentence patterns and intonation clues. Normal subject-to-predicate patterns (Hortense arrived late) are probably easier to read than are transformations of these patterns (Late arrived Hortense). Sentences in which the oral intonation patterns are clear are easier to read and understand than are those in which the intonation patterns are ambiguous: (*Bob* didn't catch the fish. Bob *didn't* catch the fish. Bob didn't *catch* the fish. Bob didn't catch *the* fish. Bob didn't catch the *fish*.)

Semantics, or word meanings, also needs consideration. What makes a word easy or difficult to read and understand? Is word length a factor? Are multiple or remote meanings a factor? Are denotations easier to understand than connotations?

How are paragraphs organized? What types of headings does the author use? (Has the reader formed the habit of studying headings?) What kinds of illustrations, if any, are used? Do they add to, or subtract from, the intended meanings? (Does the reader notice illustrations?) What kind and size print is used? (Is it appropriate to the reader?) Is the paper slick or dull? Is the book hardcover or paperback? (Which does the reader prefer?)

All of these factors affect the difficulty of printed materials. In most cases, there is a definite interaction between factors found in written materials and factors found within the person who is reading.

But how do we objectively judge the difficulty of written materials? The final section of this chapter deals with techniques that are often used to do this. Such techniques can be used on materials when prospective readers are not available. These techniques are frequently used by publishers, by book-selection committees, and by teachers who want an objective, though restricted, measurement of the difficulty of certain materials. (Chapter 3 deals with techniques that can be used in classrooms to evaluate the difficulty of materials in relationship to the students in the class.)

MEASURING THE DIFFICULTY LEVEL OF PRINTED MATERIALS

Let's imagine that you have been asked to select one or more textbooks for your students and that you have found four books that seem to be satisfactory in content. Two of these books seem somewhat difficult; the other two seem easier. How can you estimate their *readability levels*; that is, how can you find their levels of difficulty?

There are several readability formulas that you can use to find the approximate grade-level score of written materials, or more accurately, to compare the *relative difficulty* of materials. When using any of these formulas, you will consider two characteristics of printed materials:

1. word difficulty (the greater the number of long or unusual words the selection contains, the harder the selection is likely to be); and

2. sentence length (the longer and more complex the sentences are, the more difficult the selection is likely to be).

It is possible to use two or more formulas on the same passage and get different readability levels. This occurs because *word difficulty* is defined differently in various formulas. Even *sentence length* at times is defined differently.

Is this strange? Not at all! Ask yourself how you would decide whether a word is difficult or easy. You might say that if you know a word well, it is easy; if not, it is hard. You might say that if three-quarters of your students know a word, it is easy for them; otherwise, it is hard. Or, you might say that if a word is short, it is easy; if it's long, it's hard. What other techniques might you use? Would you consider any of them scientific?

Similarly, how would you decide how long the average sentence is in a passage of, say, 100 words? Oh, that's simple, you say. You just count the number of periods, question marks, etc., and divide that number into 100. Not so simple, really!

Consider this brief item: "If the user is good enough, slalom skis are ideal for recreation, for they handle well in every type of snow condition, except powder, and are the best style on any type of ice." One sentence? Now consider this: "If the user is good enough, slalom skis are ideal for recreation, for they handle well in every type of snow condition, except powder. And they are the best style on any type of ice." Two sentences? Finally: "If the user is good enough, slalom skis are ideal for recreation; for they handle well in every type of snow condition, except powder, and are the best style on any type of ice." One or two sentences?

All answers are correct. The first example is one sentence, the second is two sentences, and the third is one sentence according to some formulas and two sentences according to others.

Rudolf Flesch "Reading Ease" Formula

Let us look at how we might use one formula to evaluate the difficulty level of a short passage. The formula that we will use is the Rudolf Flesch "Reading Ease" formula. This formula can be used on materials at the fifth-grade level and above.[1]

Word difficulty

According to Flesch, a word is difficult or easy according to the number of syllables it contains: the more syllables, the harder it is. Flesch recognizes that there are exceptions to this generalization, but he feels that the number of syllables a word contains is usually a good index to its difficulty.

To use the Flesch formula, you count the number of syllables in each 100-word passage you are sampling. You simply count the syllables by saying the words orally and keeping tab.

You might try doing this on the following selection:

> Southwesterners who love sunshine and still want the pleasures of wintertime sports in the snow enjoy an ideal situation in the El Paso area, with Cloudcroft less than two hours away. Ski Cloudcroft has become the perfect snow setting for skiers and outdoor enthusiasts who want all their ski pleasures close at hand.
>
> Ski Cloudcroft is found in the nearby Sacramento Mountains of southern New Mexico; it towers to a height of 9,000 feet above sea

level, just three short miles from the neighboring town of Cloudcroft.
The ski area boasts three lifts and perfectly groomed slopes to

(100 words)

accommodate all skiers, from beginners who / have never skied

(106 words)

before to experts./

Let's check to see if you did it properly:

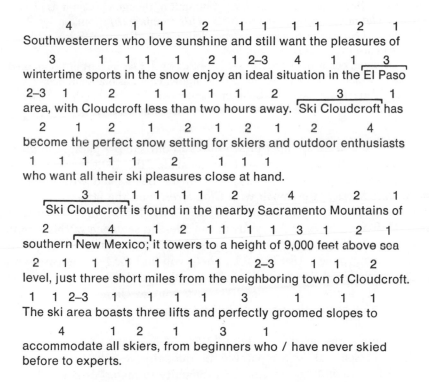

In this 100-word passage, there are about 155–159 syllables.

Now select a 100-word passage in a content area textbook you have chosen to work with. Count the number of syllables in this passage, and write this figure on a piece of paper.

Average sentence length

Flesch instructs:

In counting sentences, count as a sentence each unit of thought that is grammatically independent of another sentence or clause, if its end is marked by a period, question mark, exclamation point, semicolon, or colon. Incomplete sentences or sentence fragments are also to be counted as sentences. For example, count as two sentences: *What did the minister talk about? Sin.* Count as two sentences: *The Lord is my shepherd; I shall not want.* Count as three sentences: *There are two arguments against this plan: (1) It is too expensive. (2) It is impractical.* Count as two sentences: *Result: Nobody came.* But count as one sentence only: *He registered, but he did not vote.* (Two independent clauses, combined into a compound sentence with only a comma.) Count as one sentence: *There were three people present: Mary, Robert, and John.* (The words after the colon are not a separate unit of thought.) Count as one sentence: *The project is supposed to: (a) provide training; (b) stimulate suggestions.* (No part of this is an independent clause. Count such material as one sentence even if it is paragraphed.)

In dialogue, count the words *he said* or other such tags as part of the quoted sentence to which they are attached. For example, count as one sentence: *He said: "I have to go."* Count also as one sentence: *"That's all very well," he replied, showing clearly that he didn't believe a word of what we said.**

Let us now count the number of sentences in our sample paragraph on pp. 28–29. Counting to the end of the sentence in which the 100th word is found, we have *five* sentences. The first ends with *away*, the second with *hand*, the third with *New Mexico*, the fourth with *Cloudcroft*, and the fifth with *experts*. We have *five* sentences and 106 words (*experts* is the 106th word). Therefore, we have 106 divided by 5, or 21 words in the average sentence in this sample.

Now compute the number of words per sentence in your passage. Write its number on your paper. Use Fig. 2.1 to help you find the reading-ease score. Simply draw a diagonal line from the index number in the *words-per-sentence* column (here 21) to the *syllables-per-100 words* column (here 155–159) in Fig. 2.1. Read the number at the point of intersection in the "reading-ease score" column.

For our sample, the number is about 52–54. This is fairly difficult material according to Flesch. It is comparable in difficulty to magazines such as *Harper's* and the *Atlantic* and is similar in difficulty to materials normally considered to be at grade levels 10 to 12.9 (high school). Table 2.1 gives an interpretation of various reading ease scores. Now follow the same procedure in finding the difficulty level of the passage you have selected.

Caution: Remember, you have sampled only a 100-word passage from your book, and, therefore, you have found the difficulty level of this passage only— not of the complete book. In difficulty, this passage may be typical of the whole book, or it might be quite unusual.

---

* Rudolf Flesch. *How to Test Readability*. New York: Harper & Row, 1951, p. 3. Reprinted by permission.

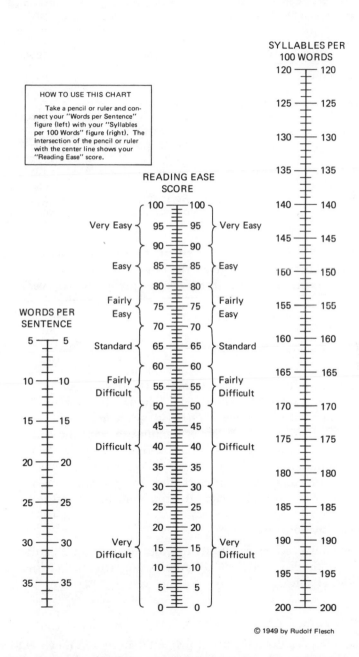

Fig. 2.1 How easy? (Reprinted by permission from *The Art of Readable Writing* by Rudolf Flesch, New York: Harper & Row, 1949, p. 5.)

Table 2.1   Interpretation of reading ease scores. (Adapted by permission from Rudolf Flesch, *How to Test Readability*, New York: Harper & Row, 1951, pp. 6, 43.)

Reading-ease score	Description of style	Typical magazine	Grade
90 to 100	Very easy	Comics	5
80 to 90	Easy	Pulp fiction	6
70 to 80	Fairly easy	Slick fiction	7
60 to 70	Standard	Digests, *Time*, Mass nonfiction	8 and 9
50 to 60	Fairly difficult	*Harper's, Atlantic*	10–12 (high school)
30 to 50	Difficult	Academic, scholarly	13–16 (college)
0 to 30	Very difficult	Scientific, professional	College graduate

To find the difficulty level of the complete book, you should take 25 to 30 samples at equal intervals throughout the book. You should take these samples *at random*; for example, start with the second paragraph on every tenth page. The mean average score of these samples will indicate the difficulty level of the book according to the Flesch criteria.

Factors Within the Material—Affective

Just as Flesch has a "Reading Ease" formula, he also has a "Human Interest" formula, suggesting that he, at least, thinks it is possible to judge the intrinsic interest factor in a piece of writing. His "Human Interest" score is found by counting the percent of *personal words* (all pronouns other than neuter pronouns, all words that have masculine or feminine gender, and names of people). Also counted are "personal sentences" (spoken sentences, questions, commands, requests, exclamations, and grammatically incomplete sentences). According to Flesch, these factors add to interest; the lack of them causes dullness. By using his scale, one can rank materials from dull to interesting to dramatic.[2]

Other Readability Formulas

There are, of course, other readability formulas which might be used, including the Dale-Chall, the Fry, and SMOG formulas. A partial list of these is given at the end of this chapter.

SUMMARY

Factors that influence the difficulty of printed materials as they relate to readers of such materials were discussed. Such factors include the reader's interest in the content of the materials and his background of information as it relates to this content. Also important is his familiarity with the kind of language which is used—in terms of syntax, semantics, and organizational patterns. If utilized by the reader, section and paragraph headings and illustrations might add to ease of reading. Additionally, the type and size of print, the kind of paper used, and the type of cover might influence the readability of the material.

The use of one readability formula, the Flesch "Reading Ease" formula, was explained. By using this formula, one can compute the approximate level of difficulty of written materials.

NOTES

1 Rudolf Flesch. *How to Test Readability*. New York: Harper and Brothers, 1951. Another widely used formula, usable on materials at the fourth-grade level and above, is the Dale-Chall formula. Refer to Appendix A for a brief explanation of its use.

Two other formulas are widely used for secondary level materials: the Fry readability formula (Edward Fry. "A Readability Formula that Saves Time." *Journal of Reading*, 11, 1968, pp. 513–516+) and the SMOG formula (Harry G. McLaughlin. "SMOG Grading—A New Readability Formula." *Journal of Reading*, 12, 1969, pp. 639–646). These formulas are considered by many to be simpler to use than the Flesch and Dale-Chall, but many do not consider them as accurate. A major reason for not including the Fry or SMOG formulas here is that they are readily available in recent journals.

2 Rudolf Flesch, *op. cit.*

SUGGESTED ACTIVITIES

1. Compute the readability level of a 100-word passage in a content area book by using the Flesch formula. Listed below are the steps to follow:

    a) Make a copy of a passage at least 100 words long from a content area textbook at the fifth-grade level or above.

    b) Count off 100 words. Draw a slash after the 100th word, and write 100 above it.

    c) Write the number of syllables above each word in the 100-word passage.

    d) Count the total number of syllables in the 100-word passage. Write the number on the worksheet.

    e) Count the number of words to the end of the sentence in which the 100th word occurs. Write the number above the punctuation mark that ends the sentence.

    f) Count the number of words to the end of the sentence in which the 100th word occurs. Indicate the end of each sentence by putting an asterisk above the punctuation mark.

    g) Divide the number of sentences into the total number of words to get average sentence length. Write the number on your worksheet.

h) Use the Flesch "How Easy?" chart to get the "reading-ease score." Write the score on your sheet.

i) Write the interpretation of the score on your sheet—in terms of "description of style" and "typical magazine" and "grade level."

2. Compute the readability level of the same passage by using another formula, possibly one suggested in this chapter.

3. Compare the results of the two formulas. Are they similar or quite different in terms of grade-level scores? If they are different, what factors within the formulas caused the scores to differ? Which formula do you prefer for use with your book? Why?

4. You have computed the readability level of only one short passage within your book. Design a reasonable strategy for computing the readability level of the whole book.

5. Explain why factors other than word difficulty and sentence length have not been included in most readability formulas. Using your content area book, explain what additional characteristics of the book might make the book readable. Which characteristics of the same book might make it less readable than the formula score indicates?

6. Comment on the following statement: "Jane and George both received the same score on the standardized reading test recently given at school. Yet George finds my textbook, *Biological Science*, easy to read, but Jane has a constant struggle with it." (Assume that the standardized test score for each is valid.)

REFERENCES FOR FURTHER READING

Dale, Edgar and Jeanne Chall. "A Formula for Predicting Readability," *Educational Research Bulletin* (January 21, 1948): 11–20, 28.

Dale, Edgar and Barbara Seels. *Readability and Reading: An Annotated Bibliography*. Newark, Delaware: International Reading Association, 1966.

Flesch, Rudolf. *How to Test Readability*. New York: Harper and Brothers, 1951.

Fry, Edward. "A Readability Formula That Saves Time," *Journal of Reading*, 11 (1968): 513–516.

Goodman, Kenneth S., *et al. Choosing Materials to Teach Reading*. Detroit: Wayne State University Press, 1966.

Harris, Theodore L. "Making Reading an Effective Instrument of Learning in the Content Fields," *Forty-seventh Yearbook, Part II: Reading in the High School and College*. Chicago: National Society for the Study of Education, 1948, p. 129.

Klare, George R. *The Measurement of Readability*. Ames, Iowa: Iowa State University Press, 1963.

Koenke, Karl. "Another Practical Note on Readability Formulas," *Journal of Reading*, **15** (December 1971): 203–208.

Lorge, Irving. *The Lorge Formula for Estimating Difficulty of Reading Materials.* New York: Bureau of Publications, Teachers College, Columbia University, 1959.

McLaughlin, G. Harry. "SMOG Grading—A New Readability Formula." *Journal of Reading*, **12** (1969): 639–646.

Chapter 3

FINDING THE APPROPRIATE LEVEL OF MATERIALS FOR EACH STUDENT

What level of materials can a student read independently?

What level of materials can a student read when he has the help of a teacher?

What level of materials frustrate the student?

INTRODUCTION

This chapter deals with some techniques that can be used to assess the cognitive reading achievement of students. Our purpose is to explore a variety of procedures that will give us an intelligent estimate of the level of materials which individual students can read successfully.

Cognitive reading achievement can be measured by using both standardized tests and informal (nonstandardized) instruments or techniques. Standardized tests are especially valuable in helping us compare our students' reading achievement with that of students in a national norming group. Informal reading tests are especially helpful in determining which of our available materials are best suited to the needs and achievement of individual students in our classes. By using informal tests, we can determine which of our available materials are on a student's frustrational reading level, which are on his instructional reading level, and which are on his independent reading level.

Materials that are on a student's *frustrational reading level* are normally too difficult for him to read, even with the help of a teacher. Materials that are on his *instructional reading level* are suitable for him to read if he has guidance from a teacher. Materials on his *independent reading level* are easy enough for him to read on his own.

Ideally, textbooks and other materials read by students under the guidance of a teacher should be selected at each student's instructional level. Other materials, such as supplementary materials which the student reads with little or no guidance from the teacher, should be at his independent reading level. Only rarely, and only when the student is strongly motivated, should a student read materials at his frustrational reading level.

Unfortunately, many teachers do not have at their disposal multilevel materials. If such is the case, it is still of value to know:

1. for which students the available material is well suited
2. for which students the material is too difficult for them to succeed with—even with the help of the teacher
3. for which students the material is quite easy—perhaps too easy and unchallenging.

The proper use of an informal reading inventory will give the teacher such information.

Both standardized tests and informal reading inventories can also be used in another way. It will be explained in this chapter how they can be used, under certain circumstances, as a valid substitute for an I.Q. test in determining the potential, or capacity (reading expectancy), level for a student.

First, let us look at standardized reading tests.

STANDARDIZED READING TESTS

Let's say that you are a classroom teacher in the tenth grade. You know that in a typical tenth-grade classroom, you will expect to find a range in reading achievement of about ten years ($\frac{2}{3}$ of $15 = 10$). The poorest reader may be reading at the fifth-grade level; the best, as well as an average university junior.

If you have I.Q. scores for your students, you know approximately how well each student should be reading:

$$\text{reading expectancy grade} = \frac{2\,\text{M.A.} + \text{C.A.}}{3} - 5.2$$

or

$$\text{reading expectancy grade} = \left(\frac{\text{I.Q.}}{100} \times \text{years in school}\right) + 1.$$

But you don't know the *actual reading-grade level* of each student. How will you find it?

Probably the best way of finding the reading-grade level of a student is by administering a standardized reading test and using the grade score supplied by the publisher. This seems like a very simple task. However, the more you examine the many standardized reading tests available for your use, as well as the interpretation of grade scores supplied by publishers, the more complex your decisions become.

Different reading tests do not measure the same reading abilities. There are two *broad* categories for classifying reading tests: oral and silent. Some very reputable oral reading tests measure *only* oral reading—no comprehension questions are asked. Obviously, different types of reading ability are being measured when a student takes such a test and when he takes a silent reading test in which he is asked to indicate synonyms or antonyms for words as well as to respond to study skill and comprehension questions.

To get the maximum amount of usable information from a reading test, a wise choice of tests must be made. As a teacher, you must ask yourself what you most want to know in relationship to a student's reading achievement.

Oral Reading Tests

Do you want to know how well your students compare with students nationally in oral reading? If so, give a good oral reading test. (Some of these tests are listed at the end of the chapter.)

If you have been trained in giving an oral reading test, you may also be able to derive valuable *diagnostic information* from it. By observing a student's error patterns, you can set up a program for correcting his oral errors. Thus, you might look at such behavioral characteristics as:

1. mispronunciations—are there patterns to his mispronunciations, e.g., syl-labication errors, certain types of vowel errors, errors principally in word endings, etc.?
2. substitutions—does he misread words, usually putting in a synonym for the word given by the author?
3. omissions—does he skip words?
4. insertions—does he include words that are not in the passage?
5. regressions—does he repeat words or phrases?
6. hesitations—does he pause for long periods of time?
7. punctuation errors—does he ignore punctuation?

By observing the *types of errors* a student makes in oral reading, a reading teacher is able to set up a program for the correction of these errors.

Some teachers may wonder about the value of oral reading tests—espe-cially for junior and senior high school students. Theoretically, the value lies in an assumption that the kinds of errors a student makes when he reads orally serve as a clue to the kinds of errors he makes when he reads silently. The assumption is that if he ignores punctuation when he reads orally, he also does so when he reads silently. If he mispronounces words when he reads orally, he really doesn't know the meanings of these words when he reads silently, etc.

Such assumptions may or may not be true. Many students who read rapidly when they are reading silently find it difficult to shift gears. When they read orally, therefore, they often skip words and may also appear to be ignoring punctuation. Also, they may know meanings of words they cannot pronounce.

Oral reading tests may serve as valuable diagnostic tools for some students —especially elementary school students and secondary students who are having serious reading problems. For all students, such tests may give us *clues* for designing programs for reading improvement, especially if used in conjunction with silent reading passages used to evaluate comprehension.

Silent Reading Tests

As a content area teacher, you are probably more interested in knowing how well a student comprehends when he reads silently. Since silent reading tests vary among themselves, you should select the test that requires the student to do the kind of reading you are interested in assessing. Not every test will give you this information.

You may wish to refer to the end of this chapter, where there is an anno-tated list of available tests. From this list, you may wish to select a few tests to order for further examination. Most tests used in schools have been critiqued in Buros' *Mental Measurements Yearbook*. If you wish to be somewhat sophisticated in selecting a test, you should refer to these reviews, which are written by experts in the field of the test.

Precautions

When an oral reading test is administered by a well-trained person, *diagnostic information* which could be used in setting up a corrective reading program might be obtained. However, silent reading tests are rarely diagnostic because too few items of any one type are given in any one test. Standardized silent-reading tests are usually *survey tests*, i.e., they yield a grade score or a percentile score.* But despite what some manuals say, they do not give reliable information, though they may give clues, for designing a reading program for an individual student.

Also, most silent reading tests, especially those used above the primary level, *inflate* the grade-level scores. The grade score usually indicates the *frustrational* level for the student. That is, the grade score a student gets on a silent reading test tells you that *material at that level is too difficult for him*. You must drop back a year or more to find the student's *instructional level*, the level at which he can successfully learn—*with your help*. You must drop back even further to find his *independent level*, the level at which he can read material without outside help.

Standardized Reading-Listening Tests

At the present time there are two standardized reading-listening test batteries on the market. These are the Durrell Reading-Listening Test and the Brown-Carlsen Reading-Listening Test. Each of these tests contains parallel subtests, one of which is read *by* the student and one of which is read *to* the student.

Usually, the student will score the same on both subtests. However, some students receive a higher score on the test read to them than they receive on the test that they themselves must read. If the listening test score is significantly higher than the reading test score, it is assumed that the student has an undeveloped capacity for reading. That is, it is assumed that he has greater mental capacity than he is using in the reading situation. It is also assumed that he is disabled in reading and that he needs help principally in oral reading, possibly including phrasing.

---

* A percentile score indicates the percentage of students who score at a lower level than the person receiving that score. A percentile score of 60 means that 60% of the norming group scored more poorly than the person receiving that score. A score of 30 means that 30% scored at a lower level.

INFORMAL (NONSTANDARDIZED) TECHNIQUES

Although standardized tests may give us information about a student's—or a class's—reading-grade or percentile levels, such tests fall short of providing all of the information we need in assuring ourselves that the student is able or unable to read the materials that are available to him in our classroom. Major values of standardized silent reading tests are: (1) they allow us to compare our students' reading achievement with national norms or other norming groups, and (2) they provide us with an easy way to grossly rank our own students from strongest to weakest.

However, results of standardized reading tests can rarely be used to indicate whether or not a particular book is at the *frustrational, instructional,* or *independent* reading level for a particular student. The problem is compounded because readability formulas used by various publishers differ, and no one formula is equally valid on all types of materials. Thus, for example, if there are two books of equal difficulty, one publisher might say his is at the tenth-grade level, and the other might grade his at the eighth-grade level.

What techniques can *you* use to give you reasonable assurance that your students are placed at their optimal levels in reading materials in your class? This question is particularly important in relationship to the textbook they are expected to read, since the textbook normally is used regularly throughout a semester or year, and so much of a student's course work is dependent on success with the textbook.

Using a type of informal reading inventory is probably the answer. Two types are explained here: a modification of the standard IRI and John Bormuth's Cloze readability technique.

A Modification of the Informal Reading Inventory

The standard informal reading inventory, widely discussed in the literature, consists of two parts—one oral and the other silent. Since the value of an oral reading test given to students who read above the sixth- or seventh-grade level is widely questioned and since giving an oral reading test is extremely time-consuming and impractical for a classroom teacher, it is not recommended that the oral part of an informal reading inventory be given to most secondary school students. For these reasons, only the silent reading part of the inventory is described here. The oral part of the test is explained briefly in Appendix B.

Procedure

Ideally, the teacher will have at his disposal several books at various levels of readability. For each of these books, the teacher prepares a test which covers the following kinds of items: using parts of a book, vocabulary, comprehension, and rate. The test might also include items on reading maps, graphs, and charts and on skimming.

The first part of the test is designed to see if students know how to use important parts of the book. The students are asked to use their books in answering these questions. The questions in the example below are based on a science book. The parenthetical comments do not appear on the student's test.

Book: *Science Today*
1. What is the name of the unit in which the chapter titled "Why Is Clean Air Important?" found?

    _____
    (Use of Table of Contents)

2. According to the author, what does the word "perception" mean?

    _____
    (Use of Glossary)

3. On what pages will you find information about the "dandelion problem"?

    _____
    (Use of Index)

4. When was this book copyrighted?

    _____
    (Use of publication information)

5. Give the name of one book the author suggests you might read about "radiation."

    _____
    (Use of Table of Contents and Selected References at the end of one chapter)

Next, the students are directed to read a six- to eight-page selection from which the remainder of the items are drawn. This section should be close to the beginning of the book.

The teacher briefly introduces the selection by relating it to the background experiences of the students. In addition, the teacher directs the students to think along certain lines by stating purposes for reading. The purposes should relate to the kinds of questions asked. (Various kinds of comprehension questions are explained in Chapters 7, 8, 9.) This is an important part of this reading inventory because we are trying to find the students' instructional levels. When students use materials in the classroom at their instructional level, it is hoped that the teacher will both relate the ideas to their experiences and also state purposes for reading before the students actually read the passage.

Students are timed while they read this section. Usually, the teacher has a stop watch and writes the time on the board at quarter-minute (15-second) intervals. The student writes down the last time recorded when he finishes reading the passage. *Later*, the words-per-minute score is computed by dividing the time into the total number of words in the passage. For example, if the passage is 2007 words long and the student read it in 9½ minutes, he would divide 9.5 into 2007 to get 211 words per minute.

The student closes the book when he finishes reading. He then answers the questions, which might look like the following:

Time:_____

Number of words: _____2007_____ $(time) \overline{)2007}$ = words per minute

Vocabulary

6. Define the word *techniques* as used by the author in the following sentence: ". . . all too often we learn more about the results achieved than about the *techniques* used."

7. Your *hypothesis* is:
    a) a statement you are sure about
    b) the side opposite the right angle of a triangle
    c) your best guess
    d) your religion

8. The word *attack*, as in "a carefully designed *attack* on the question," means:
    a) force used against answering the question
    b) procedure to follow to get results
    c) initial harmful act in solving the question
    d) assault

9. The word *ingredient*, as used in the following question, "How do you know that it was moisture itself and not an *ingredient* of the water added that produced the difference?" means:
    a) element, part
    b) color, shade
    c) odor, scent
    d) temperature

10. What is a *controlled experiment?*_____

_____

_____

Noting details (Circle True or False)

11. True–False:

    To test a hypothesis on molding bread, you would need two pieces of bread from the same loaf.

12. True–False:

    The author suggests that you should examine each piece of bread every second day.

13. True–False:

    The author suggests that one of the best ways to organize your materials for experiments in this course is to store results in stacks and put them in the same box.

14. True–False:

    You should date and enter in a ledger (book) every observation at the time it is made.

15. True–False:

    Later in this course you will be asked to refer to data collected early in the course.

Main ideas and sequence

16. Where or how does an experiment begin?

17. Put the following steps of a controlled experiment in the order in which they occur: attack, results, hypothesis, question.

    1._____

    2._____

    3._____

    4._____

18. Can a single experiment answer the question, "What causes bread to mold?" *yes-no.* If "no," why not? If "yes," which experiment?

19. Give—in order—the four steps the author suggests you follow to find out if moisture produces molding in bread.

    1._____

    2._____

    3._____

    4._____

20. Why does an entire experiment depend on the nature of the hypothesis?

Interpretation of results

For those students who score between 70%–90% correct, this part of the book, at least, is said to be on their *instructional reading level,* the correct level for them to use with teacher guidance. For those who score 90%–100% correct, it is said to be on their *independent reading level.* For those who score 60% or below, it is on their *frustrational reading level.* These are the same comprehension scores used on the standard IRI.

If an additional book is available on an easier level, those students who scored on the frustrational level should be similarly tested with it. If they score 70%–90% correct on this second book, it is on their instructional level and is the book they should use—with teacher guidance.

If an additional book is available on a higher level, those students who scored on the independent level should be similarly tested with it. If they score 70%–90% correct on it, it is on their instructional level.

Thus, it is suggested that if multilevel materials are available, the initial test be given on the materials of middle level in difficulty. Those who score below 70% on this test should be given a test on easier materials. Those who score 90% or better should be given a test on the more difficult materials.

Capacity level can also be determined if the teacher reads a passage and the questions to the student or to a group of students. If a student scores 70%–80% correct using such a procedure, the material is said to be on his capacity (reading expectancy) level. If the teacher wishes to use this technique, he normally reads passages from a book that was found to be at a student's frustrational reading level. A student whose instructional level is found to be considerably below his capacity level should be referred to a remedial reading teacher for further diagnosis and help.

Besides looking at the total percentage score, it is often interesting to look at patterns of both errors and correct responses, but this can be done only if there is a sufficient number of questions of the types analyzed. A student might be considered deficient in a skill if he misses two or more out of five items in a category. He might be considered strong in a skill if he scores 100 percent in a category. From such an analysis, a teacher might get *clues* as to what types of items need emphasis among certain groups of students.

The teacher might compose a chart for either the entire class or the group of students who are using a particular book. Table 3.1 shows hypothetical charts for a science classroom in which three books are being used.

Other comprehension skills, such as interpretive and critical-creative reading skills, could be added to these charts a little later—after the students have used the books and the teacher has had an opportunity to observe each student's strengths and weaknesses in these areas of reading achievement. In addition, the teacher might at regular intervals time students when they read passages from the book. These rate scores could also be recorded on the master sheet.

Table 3.1 (a)   *Science Today*—readability level: grades 7–8

Instructional level for	Initial rate	Parts of the book	Vocab-ulary	Details	Main idea, sequence	Add other skills later
Armstrong, Henry	150	o	*			o
Bardet, Marie	104		*	o		
Dorsey, George	75	o	o		*	*
Klein, Baron	200	*			*	o

Table 3.1 (b)   *The Modern Scientific World*—readability level: grades 9–10

Anderson, John	257	o		*	*	
Jones, Carolyn	140	*	o			
Martinez, Maria	210		o	*		
Rollins, James	95	o	*			o

Table 3.1 (c)   *Earth Science*—readability level: grades 11–12

Calabresa, Betty	250	*		*	o	
Fignewton, Jeremy	400	*	o	*		
Hodges, Mary	275	o	*	o	*	
Jahnke, Eleanor	200	o	o	*		

Comprehension: * = strength; o = weakness

Bormuth Cloze Readability Technique

The Bormuth Cloze readability technique may be used as a substitute, or partial substitute, for the previously explained informal reading inventory.[1] The Cloze technique is elegant in its simplicity. Once a passage is selected that is representative of the book upon which the student is to be tested, the procedure is simple to use. However, selection of the passage is more complex. This will be explained last.

Let us say that we have the representative passage. It will be 250 words of continuous writing, and *every fifth word* will be "CLOZED." That is, every fifth word will be omitted, and in its place will be an underscoring. Each underscoring must be of uniform length (about 12 typewriter spaces). All students in a class can be given the same passage at the same time. They are asked to write in the *exact* word that has been omitted. There is no time limit.

In a 250-word passage, there are 50 clozures since every fifth word is deleted. Each correct response counts for two percentage points. To be correct, the student must supply the author's *exact* word, though it might be misspelled. That is the way the procedure has been standardized, and that is the way the passage must be scored. Credit is *not* given for synonyms—what one person may consider a synonym, another may not.

The percentage score a student receives is used to determine his reading level for the passage:

58%–100% correct—independent level

44%– 57% correct—instructional level

0%– 43% correct—frustrational level.

For the logic behind the "CLOZE" procedure, see Bormuth's article. This procedure is becoming increasingly popular with reading experts, for hidden in the correct response is an understanding of the author's style and technique as well as a revelation of the background of information and syntax of the student being tested.

Selection of a passage that is representative of the book

Obviously, the passage which is selected is of utmost importance. It must come very close to being representative of the book of which it is a part. Bormuth instructs that originally *12* passages should be selected from a book. If the book appears to be of uniform difficulty throughout, the passages are selected at equal page intervals throughout, e.g., every 50 pages. If the book becomes progressively more difficult, the 12 passages are selected from the beginning of the book, again at equal intervals, perhaps every eighth page.

Each passage is 250 words long and need not end with the last word of a sentence. The passage is the first 250-word passage of continuous writing that is found on or after the designated page number. Each *fifth* word is clozed to the end of the sentence in which the 250th word occurs. Only the first 50 clozures are scored.

The passage is typed on a single sheet of paper and should look something like the following:

Learning all we can _____ all that we observe
_____ surely an important phase _____
science and, consequently, a _____ of the scientist.
Think, _____, of the vast amount _____
information we could assemble _____ of how difficult
it _____ become to find a _____ item of this
information _____ we did not group _____ in
some convenient manner. _____ how much simpler our
_____ will be if we _____ the objects we
are _____ into classes or kinds _____ we begin
to gather _____ data. By doing this _____
may generalize about many _____ of the group after

_____ careful study of only _____ few
members. In effect, _____ did this in our _____
on the single sugar _____ when we grouped our
_____. We said that in _____ trials a spot
appeared _____ 34 and no spot _____ 66.
This classification made _____ simpler to describe what
_____ had observed and easier _____ us to
evaluate our _____ in order to draw _____
about what could not _____ observed directly. This
grouping, _____ sorting, activity is the _____
of classification; it is _____ taxonomy.
     Classification is a _____ operation and can be
_____ according to many different _____.
The plan we use _____ on our purpose. The
_____ of sorting also varies _____ the
situation. Your grocer _____ certain kinds of food
_____ in the store for _____ shopping
convenience and for _____ convenience in restocking
supplies. _____ cans of food you _____ at
                        (250 words)
home may be _____/ in the cabinet with _____,
vegetables, and soups on _____ shelves, or at different
_____ on a single shelf.

The clozed passage is reproduced so that each student has his own copy, and the student fills in the blanks. Numbers and answer sheets cannot be used, for this would invalidate the results. (Each blank filled in serves as a clue to another blank. An answer sheet would make these clues more difficult to recognize.) Each of the 12 passages is given to at least 30 students. If six classes of 30 students each were being used, each student would be given only two passages.

To ensure a random distribution of passages, the teacher should refer to the alphabetical listing of students in his grade book. He divides the list into six equal parts, or counts off students: 1, 2, 3, 4, 5, 6 / 1, 2, 3, 4, 5, 6, etc., and designates the groups as 1, 2, 3, 4, 5, 6. Each of the 12 passages is also numbered. The chart that follows can be used for the distribution of passages to students:

Student groups	Passages
1	4 and 7
2	3 and 12
3	6 and 11
4	1 and 8
5	5 and 10
6	2 and 9

After each passage has been scored, the mean average (arithmetic average) for the passage is computed by adding all of the percentage scores and dividing by the number of students who were tested on the passage. Thus, we might have the following average scores for the passage:

Passage	Mean average
1	40
2	26
3	70
4	36
5	52
6	58
7	40
8	65
9	43
10	48
11	36
12	54

Next, the mean of the means is computed. For these passages it would be:

$$\frac{40+26+70+36+52+58+40+65+43+48+36+54}{12} = \frac{568}{12} = 47.3.$$

The passage whose mean is closest to the mean of the mean is selected as representative of the book. In this case it would be *passage 10*, whose mean is 48.

Now, all students (except those in group 5, who have already had it) are given this passage. Also, whenever testing is done on this book in the future, this passage should be used. Therefore, the "selection of passage" procedure is no longer necessary for this book.

Comment

All of the percentages given for use with the modification of the IRI and the Bormuth technique are meant as *guidelines* only. They are *not meant to serve as rigid cutting-off points*. The teacher must carefully observe his students in other ways to be certain that the books they are using are appropriate.

Students vary greatly in their ability and desire to cope with easy and/or difficult materials. A student with a great deal of interest in a subject may not mind being frustrated a bit. Another who lacks interest may find material which is considered to be on his instructional level too difficult to be worth the effort. Indeed, the affective dimensions of reading must also be considered.

SUMMARY

Standardized and informal techniques are commonly used in order to assess students' cognitive level of reading achievement. Usually, *standardized reading tests* provide us with information that (1) allows us to compare our group of students with a national norming group, and also (2) allows us to roughly rank order our students. If we know how to administer a *standardized oral reading test*, and if we are working with children who read at about the sixth-grade level or below, we may get valuable information that will help us design a partial reading program for children to whom we have given the test. Few, if any, *standardized silent reading tests* give us enough diagnostic information for preparing a program of study in needed comprehension and study skills. *Standardized listening-reading tests* help us to locate students who may be disabled in reading.

It is difficult to know the exact meaning of the grade-level scores supplied by test publishers. Frequently, a student's grade score on a standardized oral-reading test suggests his *instructional level*, i.e., the level at which he can succeed with the help of a teacher. The grade score a student gets on a standardized silent reading test frequently suggests his *frustrational level*, the lowest level at which he cannot succeed, even with the teacher's help. His instructional level is usually one or two years below this. The scores a student receives on a standardized listening-reading test are meant only for comparing the level of the two skills; if the listening score is sufficiently higher than the reading score, the student may need corrective or remedial help in reading.

In order to determine which reading materials at our disposal are at the correct level for individual students, *informal techniques* are the most useful. Among these techniques are (1) a modification of the Informal Reading Inventory, especially appropriate for use in the content areas, and (2) the Bormuth CLOZE Readability Technique. Each of these techniques enables us to intelligently estimate the student's *independent, instructional,* and *frustrational reading levels* in relationship to the materials used in testing. The IRI also enables us to estimate his capacity level. Only one of these techniques need be used by a content area teacher.

NOTE

1 John Bormuth. "The Cloze Readability Procedure," *Elementary English,* **XLV** (April 1968): 429–436.

SUGGESTED ACTIVITIES

1. Design an Informal Reading Inventory for use with your content area text-book, following the model explained in the section of this chapter titled "A Modification of the Informal Reading Inventory."

2. Plan a microteach session to last for about three minutes, demonstrating exactly how you would introduce the timed section of your I.R.I. to your class. In this session briefly relate the ideas of the passage to the students' past experiences, and lay the foundation for your students to anticipate ideas which will be covered in the reading material. Tell them what you want them to think about while they are reading.

3. Explain the value of giving an I.R.I. if you have multilevel materials available in your classroom. What is its value if you have only one set of materials?

4. Using your context area textbook, tell from which pages you would select the 12 passages to be used initially with the Bormuth Cloze Readability Technique. Give the 12 page numbers and the first four words of each passage. Remember to begin each passage at the beginning of a paragraph.

5. Set up the first passage, clozing every fifth word.

6. Compare the I.R.I. and the Bormuth Cloze Readability techniques. Which is easier to set up initially? Which is easier to administer? Which gives you more diagnostic information? Which do you think you would prefer to use?

REFERENCES FOR FURTHER READING

Bond, Guy L. and Miles Tinker. *Reading Difficulties: Their Diagnosis and Correction.* New York: Appleton-Century-Crofts, 1967, Section 3.

Bormuth, John. "The Cloze Readability Procedure," *Elementary English,* **XLV** (April 1968): 429–436.

Buros, Oscar (ed.). *Mental Measurements Yearbook.* Highland Park, N.J.: Gryphon Press.

Farr, Roger (ed.). *Measurement and Evaluation of Reading.* New York: Harcourt, Brace and World, 1970.

Hafner, Lawrence E. (ed.). *Improving Reading in Secondary Schools, Selected Readings.* New York: Macmillan, 1967, pp. 172–174, 192–228.

Harris, Albert J. *How to Increase Reading Ability.* New York: David McKay, 1970, Chapters 7 and 8.

Johnson, Marjorie Seddon and Roy Kress. *Informal Reading Inventories.* Newark, Delaware: International Reading Association, 1965.

Karlin, Robert (ed.). *Teaching Reading in High School—Selected Articles.* Indianapolis: Bobbs-Merrill, 1969, Chapter 4.

Leibert, Robert E. (ed.). *Diagnostic Viewpoints in Reading.* Newark, Delaware: International Reading Association, 1971.

Olson, Arthur V. and Wilber S. Ames (eds.). *Teaching Reading Skills in Secondary Schools.* Scranton, Pa.: International Textbook, 1970, Section 4.

Strang, Ruth. *The Diagnostic Teaching of Reading*. New York: McGraw-Hill, 1969, Chapters 2–7 and 10.

Viox, Ruth G. *Evaluating Reading and Study Skills in the Secondary Classroom*. Newark, Delaware: International Reading Association, 1968.

Zintz, Miles V. *The Reading Process*. Dubuque, Iowa: Wm. C. Brown Co., 1970, Chapter 3.

SILENT READING TESTS (STANDARDIZED)

California Reading Test, 1957 edition with 1963 norms. Grades 4–6, 7–9, 9–14. Three scores: vocabulary, comprehension, total. California Test Bureau, Del Monte Research Park, Monterey, California 93940.

Davis Reading Test, 1962. Grades 8–11, 11–13. Two scores: level of comprehension and speed of comprehension. Psychological Corporation, 304 East 45th St., New York, New York 10017.

Gates-MacGinite Reading Tests, 1965. Grades 4–6, 7–9. Three scores: speed and accuracy, vocabulary, comprehension. Teachers College Press, Teachers College, Columbia University, New York, New York 10027.

Kelley-Greene Reading Comprehension Test, 1955. Grades 9–13. Five scores: paragraph comprehension, directed reading, retention of details, reading rate, total. Harcourt, Brace and World, Inc., 757 Third Ave., New York, New York 10017.

Nelson-Denny Reading Test: Vocabulary—Comprehension—Rate, 1960. Grades 9–16. Four scores: vocabulary, comprehension, total, rate. Houghton Mifflin Co., 2 Park Street, Boston, Mass. 02107.

Reading Comprehension: Cooperative English Tests, 1960. Grades 9–12, 13–14. Four scores: vocabulary, level of comprehension, speed of comprehension, total. Cooperative Test Division, Educational Testing Service, Princeton, N.J. 08540.

SRA Achievement Series: Reading, 1967. Grades 4–9 (multilevel). Three scores: comprehension, vocabulary, total. Science Research Associates, Inc., 259 East Erie St., Chicago, Ill. 60611.

Sequential Tests of Educational Progress: Reading, 1963. Grades 4–6, 7–9, 10–12, 13–14. Cooperative Test Division, Educational Testing Service, Princeton, N.J. 08540.

Stanford Achievement Test: High School Reading Test, 1966. Grades 9–12. Harcourt, Brace and World, Inc., 757 Third Ave., New York, New York 10017.

Tests of Reading: Cooperative Inter-American Tests, 1963. Grades 1–3, 2–3, 4–7, 8–13, 10–13. A series of parallel tests in English and Spanish. Three or four scores depending upon level: vocabulary, comprehension, total; or level of comprehension, speed of comprehension, vocabulary, total. Guidance Testing Associates, 6516 Shirley Ave., Austin, Texas 78752.

ORAL READING TESTS (STANDARDIZED)

Diagnostic Reading Scales, by George Spache, 1963. Grades 1–8 and retarded readers in grades 9–12. California Test Bureau, Del Monte Research Park, Monterey, Calif. 93940.

Durrell Analysis of Reading Difficulty, New Edition, by Donald Durrell, 1955. Grades 1–6. Harcourt, Brace and World, Inc., 757 Third Ave., New York, New York 10017.

Gates-McKillop Reading Diagnostic Tests, by Arthur Gates and Anne S. McKillop, 1962. Grades 2–6. Teachers College Press, Teachers College, Columbia University, New York, New York 10027.

Gilmore Oral Reading Test, by John Gilmore. Grades 1–8. Harcourt, Brace and World, Inc., 757 Third Ave., New York, New York 10017.

Gray Oral Reading Test, by Wm. S. Gray and Helen Robinson, Grades 1–Adult. Bobbs-Merrill Co., Inc., 4300 West 62nd Street, Indianapolis, Indiana 46206.

Chapter 4

ASSESSING STUDENT INTERESTS IN READING MATERIALS

Why do people choose to read?

What do students choose to read?

How can we measure a student's intensity of involvement in a school subject?

INTRODUCTION

Teachers have always been concerned with the degree of interest students display in their school subjects. Most teachers can immediately tell an inquirer which students seek extra tasks, which always do the prescribed assignments well, which do as little as possible, and which do almost nothing in or out of class.

To measure the degree of involvement a student has in a course is perhaps not as difficult as to explain why one student is interested and another is not. Some students have *limited aspirations* in life and have little desire to continue an academic education. Others are interested in only specific areas of the curriculum. Still others are vitally concerned with many courses, and for them interest is easily sparked.

Some students are inflexible in their rate of reading. Some relatively rapid readers do well in literature and history classes but cannot slow down enough to seek out the details of mathematics and science and to plot courses of action that solving a mathematics problem and following a science experiment require. Still others read everything slowly. These students may find the preciseness of mathematics and science well suited to their reading habits, but they find that reading a novel is a tedious job.

Over several years' time, those students whose reading habits lead them to success in mathematics and science and to less than success in history and literature will undoubtedly find that their backgrounds of experience are rich in some areas and deficient in others. Further, their reading skills are unevenly developed; they may find that courses in which literal comprehension skills are stressed are to their liking (because they do well in these). But they may find that courses in which discussions center on higher level cognitive skills—such as deciding on motives of characters or real people or judging the worth of a novel or biography—are dull. Similarly, the opposite type of reader exists.

So, accumulated experiences in a variety of courses may in itself channel students. Yet, in most classes, a wise teacher can somewhat circumvent an otherwise almost certain poor showing for some students—and can build achievement in areas where students are weak and capitalize on areas of strength—by allowing students, at least sometimes, to pick their favorite genre (novel, biography, essay, poetry, newspaper or magazine article, documents, etc.) and also their area of interest, probably within prescribed boundaries.

The remainder of this chapter will help you understand: (1) why people choose to read; (2) techniques to use to find out what *specific students* are interested in and/or choose to read; and (3) a taxonomy of affective involvement, which enables us to judge the intensity of interest a student has in a subject. It is hoped that these explanations will help you to better meet the interests of your students.

REASONS FOR READING

Understanding what *motivates* students to read may help us to make willing readers of them. That is, if we know their basic drives and can satisfy these drives, we will get students involved.

Given time, why do people *choose* to read? Waples, in his book *What Reading Does to People*, gives us five reasons.[1] He says that people read for: (1) the instrumental effect, (2) prestige, (3) reinforcement of an attitude, (4) vicarious aesthetic experiences, and (5) respite. Let us look at each of these reasons in a little detail. You may wish to refer to Waples' book for more complete explanations.

Instrumental Effect

According to Waples, people read for the instrumental effect when they have a problem to solve, a test to pass, a speech to give, a cake to bake, a model airplane to build, etc. They seek printed materials that are lucid and to the point. If one set of materials—such as a textbook, a magazine or newspaper article, a set of directions, a biography, etc.—is not complete, they seek supplementary materials. Usually, they are looking for books or articles that help them to work efficiently.

After they have read the materials and used their ideas to solve the problem, pass the test, give the speech, etc., they have obtained the instrumental effect. Given another problem, another test, another speech, they're back at it again—seeking and reading lucid materials that will help them to achieve another goal.

Prestige Effect

People also choose to read for prestige—especially to improve their own self-image. Some adults read all of the books on the "best seller" lists to enhance their own egos. Others read the sports pages regularly, or the society pages, or certain magazines or journals—so that they are not caught short when asked a question.

Students frequently read, or pretend to read, the classics, not because they enjoy or appreciate them, but because such reading impresses the teacher. Encouraging students to read for such a reason is unwise. Such reading does *not* build a permanent interest in reading. We are rapidly developing a nation of people who can read but will not!

However, another facet of this category may lead to worthwhile goals, although it may also lead to self-deception. The deception enters if the stories chosen are pat, slick, stereotyped, and biased. If the stories have substance and truth, such reading can be therapeutic and inspiring. Choice of materials is therefore all-important.

The idea here is that people often choose to read the kind of story that glamorizes their real-life situation. A boy chooses a sports story in which the leading character is like him—a football hero but a poor student. This reader may resolve his anxieties about his poor scholarship by seeing his hero in the book succeed despite poor grades in school. More easily done in a book than in real life? The reader, especially if he concentrates on such books, may be in for a shock later on.

Similarly, a poor girl may read romantic stories about other poor girls who grew up to marry wealthy prince charmings. All well and good if such reading leads the reader to self-improvement, but even so, she may be in for a letdown, for there may not be enough prince charmings to go around.

But what of the budding scientist who reads authentic biographies of scientists? Through such reading, he may begin to understand how the scientific mind works—how a scientist got his start and how he continued to grow in creative ability. Or, a young home economist might read about Julia Child or the *Cordon Bleu* and thereby become involved. The lives of Einstein, Schweitzer, Frank Lloyd Wright, Florence Nightingale, Lincoln, Benjamin Franklin, Madam Curie, Thoreau, Cousteau, Helen Keller, and hundreds of others could inspire our young to travel a creative route if they see something in the lives of these people with which they can empathize.

Reinforcement of an Attitude

People sometimes choose to read in order to reinforce their opinions or feelings. They "know" they believe in something—their political party, their religion, their styles, or even their superiority—but they may not know exactly why, or they may not have all the latest arguments at their fingertips. They read to reinforce their attitude, possibly even to give them ideas for their next verbal encounter.

This is fine—perhaps. Certainly we can all learn more about many things we honestly believe in. But, and this may not surprise you, people tend to choose to read only those books and articles which *reinforce* their beliefs. If, for example, each of two local newspapers leans toward a different political party, it is likely that readers will choose to read the one that backs their favorite party, for they would find it distressing to read the other paper. Only the very sophisticated reader chooses to look at the other side of an issue.

Many people by nature build and strengthen one point of view and are unaware of any logical arguments on the other side. They even "tune off" people who speak on the other side, frequently becoming so emotional that they are unable to listen.

The duty of our schools is to present multiple points of view—to help students see that there may be other ideas worth considering. Students should learn to weigh, to compare, to evaluate. Of course, conversion may occur if a student considers another point of view.

Schools, themselves, are guilty of presenting biased points of view. If only a single textbook is available, for example, students get a one-sided argument. Textbooks differ in what they include. Even mathematics and science textbooks differ. What the author and publisher consider to be important is included, and that's all. History texts, for instance, are summary statements of the author's ideas. The statements often are broad, and the details included are those the author wished to include. Compare a textbook written by a Southerner about the Civil War and one written by a Northerner. Certainly, multiple reading materials are needed to help students see many points of view. Fiction, biography, essays, and poetry are necessary to enable the student to empathize with course content.

Frequently, literature anthologies include the same selections edition after edition. (Note the "staying power" of *Silas Marner* in tenth-grade texts, etc.) Also, the very *organization* of anthologies channels thought, e.g., consider the different kinds of thinking and relating that are likely to occur when one studies a chronological presentation, a genre presentation, or a thematic presentation.

Vicarious Aesthetic Experience

People may choose to read for vicarious aesthetic experiences. An author can state ideas more clearly, more forcefully, more beautifully than most readers can. Through the words of a writer, people can see clearly what another age was like or what another country is like.

Classical writers have uncommon insights, and they have the ability to portray these visions through words. We grow in depth and breadth by reading Shakespeare and Cervantes, Chaucer, Molière, Byron, Keats, and others. We learn about human nature—about what motivates people. By reading, we can live in all ages—past, present, and future. And we can live in all places— on earth, on the moon, in a harem, under the sea, atop mountains, in a palace, in a ghetto, in a submarine, in a chemistry laboratory with the Curies, as an observer, or even as a member of the President's cabinet. We can live vicariously as almost anyone—anywhere. We can learn to understand a variety of personalities. We can experience the full range of human emotions. Unfortunate is the man who does not read, for his life is lived within restricted boundaries—of places, ages, and people.

Respite

We also read for respite—for temporary relief from pain or sorrow, or for escape. We must all escape sometimes, and reading is a ready avenue of escape. The further removed reading matter is from our actual experience, the greater the respite is likely to be.

It is well known that English professors and college presidents love to read mysteries. They enjoy books they can read just for pleasure and then forget. By doing such reading, they get a short vacation. Why deny such pleasure to our students?

Surely, teachers in all content areas can find books for their students to read that are pure pleasure. *They should be allowed to read them in class sometimes.* Science fiction, sea stories, historical mysteries, delightful biographies, historical fiction, and mathematical puzzles are some appropriate categories.

As teachers, we needn't feel guilty if we set aside class time—even one hour a week—for such "free" reading. We may be giving some students the therapy they need, and we may be lighting flames in many. Students may even begin to *enjoy* our classes—and why not? Surely *we* enjoy them.

Comment

If one of our goals is to have students *enjoy* reading (so that they will become readers), we must avoid asking them too many questions. Sometimes just a simple inquiry, "Did you like it?" is enough. And an answer of yes is enough from them. Perhaps you can see that they enjoyed a book just by watching them while they were reading it. What do we think we—or they—are gaining by having them answer so many questions?

Many students will *wish* to share what they have learned or experienced through reading. There are many ways in which they might do this: telling about it, reading a passage to the class, pantomiming, being in a skit or a member of a panel, drawing a mural, etc.

WHAT STUDENTS CHOOSE TO READ

In addition to knowing what motivates students to read, it is helpful to know what kinds of things they like to read. Of course, students' reading interests are as diverse as are the students themselves. Some like to read one kind of book and others, another. Yet it is possible to describe types of books that appeal to a large number of students at various chronological age levels.

It is important to note that chronological age, rather than mental age (or I.Q.), is a major factor in determining a student's reading interests. Bright students tend to enjoy the same types of stories as do average students of the same chronological age. Youthful adolescents, no matter how bright, do not seek out adult fiction. In general, they like stories about young people—their age mates. Yet, surely, no one can generalize about individual students.

Numerous studies have been conducted about the reading interests of students. One of the most complete and readable guides is *Books and the Teen-Age Reader* by G. Robert Carlsen.[2] Carlsen carefully describes the "stages of reading development" which students frequently progress through —from early adolescence (grades 5–9), to middle adolescence (grades 9–11), to late adolescence (grades 11–college). He also discusses numerous books that appeal to teenagers. You would do well to study this and other similar sources carefully.

Yet, knowing the interests of teenagers in general is not the same as knowing the interests of specific teenagers—your classes of students—or of a specific teenager. How can you discover what a specific student likes?

Self-Selection

One of the best ways known to find out what book a specific student will like is to use a very simple technique. Lay before him a banquet table, and see what he selects. Bring to your classroom a wide variety of books, and see which ones he takes. Like the good boy who would prefer the chocolate cake but takes spinach because his mother is watching, a student or two or three may select a book for the prestige effect. Be alert to this!

Be sure that the atmosphere is free. And be sure that you *don't* compliment a student for having made a wise (or good or any other kind of a) choice.[3] Anything goes in a self-selection situation as long as the student is happy. Remember, you're trying to find out what *he* is interested in, not whether he will read a book you want him to read. You can, of course, control some factors, for you may bring to class only certain kinds of materials, but be *as broad as possible* in your choices and include a variety of genre (biography, essays, poetry, fiction, newspaper and magazine articles, documents, etc.), a variety of themes, when possible, and a wide range in level of difficulty.

Some students may pile selected materials high on their desks, whereas others may find nothing they like. You may wish to take some students to the school library, where there may be a greater range of materials.

To add variety, you may from time to time give "book talks," introducing something by reading it to the class or to a group of students. Then set it aside and see who takes it. Students, too, may wish to give "book talks" or to use some other technique to interest their classmates in a particularly interesting book or article.

Such activities should go on in *all* content area courses, not just in English class. And they should occur frequently.

Questionnaire Technique

If you wish to survey the reading interests and/or favorite activities of a group of students, you might use one, or several, questionnaire techniques. A simple technique to use is an open-ended questionnaire.

QUESTIONNAIRE

Name _____

1. Do you read a newspaper regularly? _____

2. Which parts of a paper are your favorites:

   _____ news stories   _____ funnies

   _____ sports pages   _____ crossword puzzles

   _____ editorials   _____ astrology

   _____ fashions   _____ inspirational articles

   _____ society pages   _____ art, theater, movie critiques

   _____ ads for _____   _____ other: _____

3. Do you read any magazines regularly? _____ If so, name them: _____

   _____

4. Do you enjoy reading comic books? _____ Which are your favorites?

   _____

   _____

5. Name some of the favorite books you have read:

   _____   _____

   _____   _____

   _____   _____

6. If you could read about *anything*, what would you read about? _____

   _____

7. Number in order of preference your favorite kinds of reading materials and put a zero before those you dislike:

   _____ short stories

   _____ novels

   _____ biographies or autobiographies

   _____ poetry

   _____ newspaper article— news

   _____ newspaper article— sports

_____ newspaper article—
society

_____ essays

_____ plays

_____ science fiction

_____ mysteries

_____ comic books

_____ "how to do it"
materials

_____ religious articles
or books

_____ other: (name)

_____ other: (name)

8. Name any T.V. programs you watch regularly:

_____   _____

_____   _____

_____   _____

9. Do you watch any news program regularly? _____

10. Did you watch telecasts of our astronauts' trips to the moon? _____

11. What are your favorite hobbies or sports?

_____   _____

_____   _____

_____   _____

12. How do you most enjoy spending your free time?

_____   _____

_____   _____

Content area teachers might wish to gear questions toward specific chapters or units of study included in their courses. For example, a unit of study on the Second World War might include the following questions. (See Chapter 11 for a discussion of reference aids useful for selecting materials related to a specific topic or theme.)

QUESTIONNAIRE—WORLD WAR II (HISTORY)

Name _____

Would you like to read a book or article about (circle Yes or No):

1. Yes–No: Norwegian children who helped smuggle millions of dollars
            out of Norway to America to keep it from their German captors?
            (*Snow Treasure*)

2. Yes–No: a Jewish girl who spent several years in an attic room in
            Amsterdam to escape the Nazis? (Anne Frank: *Diary of a
            Young Girl*)

3. Yes–No: a hunchback who sailed the British Channel to rescue stranded
            soldiers in Dunkirk who were being forced into the sea by
            the Nazis? (*Snow Goose*)

4. Yes–No: five men who lived through the atomic attack on Hiroshima
            and tell their story? (*Hiroshima*)

5. Yes–No: a Japanese girl who saw her mother die in the atomic attack
            on Hiroshima and later fell in love with an American
            soldier—her dilemma? (*Flowers of Hiroshima*)
   •
   •
   •

40. Yes–No: a possibly true account of attempted surrender by the
             Japanese before the dropping of the atom bomb? ("Was It
             the Deadliest Error of Our Time?")

Such a technique is similar to the "self-selection" technique, except that it's possibly more efficient and also includes brief descriptions of reading materials. A classroom teacher may wish to vary the technique, alternating the types used.

MEASURING INTENSITY OF INTEREST

David Krathwohl is the senior author of the book *Taxonomy of Educational Objectives: Handbook II, Affective Domain*.[4] An article titled "Evaluating the Affective Dimension of Reading," by David W. Darling, delineates this domain

```
                        R
                  RECEIVING
                        S
                        P
                        O
                        N  O
                        D  R
                  VALUING
                        N  A
                        G  N
                           I
               CHARACTERIZING
                           I
                           N
                           G
```

and gives excellent suggestions of ways to develop interests of students through the use of printed materials.[5]

The taxonomy gives us a "hierarchical continuum" of the affective domain. By using this taxonomy and observing student behavior, we can recognize the affective level of each student as it relates to our classroom activities. Such recognition may, when necessary, encourage us to provide more appealing materials and ideas. Thus, we may raise the level of involvement of some students. According to Krathwohl *et al.*, there are five major levels of affective involvement, and these form the basis of the present author's elaboration in the sections that follow.

Receiving

If a student is not receiving information or ideas, he is not affectively involved, even at the lowest level. One can spot such a student easily: he may be reticent, daydreaming, or highly aggressive. To know the reason for his non-involvement, however, may be more difficult. He may display several of these characteristics: he may be hard of hearing; his vision might be inadequate; he may read English poorly; he may already know the ideas being imparted or may lack the background to understand them; his friends or his family may discourage him from learning; or his family may push him too much. Some of these factors can be remedied more easily than others. Frequently, the help of a specialist is required.

The student who is at the lowest end of the affective continuum—in the *receiving* category—will be seen to listen and observe, but not to respond. His eyes and ears follow the teacher and the class discussion, but he is only mildly involved. He may be merely *aware* of what is going on; or better, he may be *willing to receive* ideas; or better still, he may exhibit *controlled attention*. It is sometimes difficult to know the degree of a student's reception or even his sincerity.

Some students appear to be receiving when they are not, for they have developed a facial set which gets them through many—to them —dull or frustrating experiences. Other students are timid and shy and observe intensely, but with a sort of hidden interest. A good number of students—especially teenage boys—*pretend a lack of interest* by squirming and wiggling, and may display what at first appears to be dislike for a subject or book. But on second glance, a teacher can see that their souls are alive. When they're alone with the teacher, they may not be able to keep up the pretense, and the teacher may find that they are really *committed!*

When I first began teaching reading in high school, I was fooled a few times by such boys. Later, I saw a pattern, and instead of being disturbed by such overt behavior, I appreciated it and even hoped for it. Such boys in my class usually had records of juvenile delinquency and/or were often in the vice-principal's office for discipline. Somehow, they all got to take reading (they were disabled readers, of course). Like the boys in *Hooked on Books*, they usually *could* read, but would not.

Well, they read in my classes, where they were given free choice from an extensive classroom library. These boys (like Lester in *Hooked on Books*, who read *The Scarlet Letter*) read—amazingly— books like *Cry, the Beloved Country, To Kill a Mockingbird, Old Man and the Sea*, etc. They might, however, hide such a book in a school notebook so their classmates would not catch on to them. But they would come to my reading center, even if I had a class, during their study halls and read more of such books. They knew immediately that I was on to them, though I never told them or asked them questions. I just gave them passes to come and had enough books I knew would interest them.

Such boys only *appeared to be merely at the receiving level.* Many teachers, thinking these students were basically lacking in interest or were hostile, easily provoked their hostility. I did, too, when I first started teaching—until I found that hidden under that toughness was a rarely awakened sensitivity and interest.

Responding

However, when a stimulus is given, we usually look for more than simple receiving. We hope for some type of response. In fact, the stimulus-response theory of learning is widely respected. Students who progress beyond the receiving category can be further classified by the type of responding behavior they display—those who *acquiesce in responding*, those who are *willing to respond*, and those who display *satisfaction in responding*, replying, or reacting.

It is simple to observe which students must be strongly encouraged to openly react in class. They must always be called upon, and their answers are usually brief and half-hearted. Some may, however, be interested but insecure, and this may account for their *acquiescence* in responding.

Other students know they should respond in class, so they do—but with little satisfaction. Their hands are up because they want a better grade or because they want to fill in a time gap, not because they feel they have a fascinating idea or because they love to share their thoughts with others. These students are *willing* to respond.

Others, however, are enthusiastic about a book they read or an idea that just flashed through their mind—or they may find that they learn by sharing ideas. They volunteer and are *satisfied* by responding.

Valuing

A level above responding is valuing. A student may value the act of reading, and thus he will be a reader (provided that satisfactory materials are available), and/or a student may value subject matter (perhaps in a specific area) enough to pursue this interest. In other words, he may be devoted to reading, *per se*, or he may be devoted to specific ideas he gets through reading.

Again, there are three sublevels in this category of behavior. The lowest level is *acceptance of a value*—the student approves of reading or of what he learns through reading. A higher level is *preference for a value*—when given a choice of alternatives, he chooses to read or to read certain things. An even higher level is *commitment to a value*. To evaluate commitment by observing external behavioral characteristics, "the teacher should look for (a) constant reading, (b) depth reading in special areas, and (c) a dependence on reading as a means of recreation as well as a means of becoming informed." [6]

Students can be helped to recognize their own value system if the teacher asks them such questions as: " 'What books [or activities] did you reject before settling on this one?' Or, 'Why did you decide to major in English rather than math, science, or history?' (*preference level*). Or, 'Are you willing to recommend that author [or book, idea] to the class?' (*commitment level*)." [7]

Retrospective-introspective questions might be utilized to help the student recognize his degree of valuing. Such questions as the following might help him recognize his own value system.

Retrospective

1. How long have you enjoyed mathematics (science, history, literature, music, manual arts, home economics, art, etc.)?
2. During your study periods, when your homework is finished, have you frequently thought of your mathematics (etc.) problems—and perhaps of ways of using your math (etc.) out of school?
3. Have you used what you have learned *in mathematics*, for example, in building a cabinet or other piece of furniture; *in literature* in

figuring out why someone acted as he did; *in social studies* in analyzing propaganda; *in history* in seeing similarities between what has happened in the past and what is happening now; *in science* in seeing how a plant in your yard grows; in *home economics* in cooking at home?

4. Have you ever found yourself dreaming about mathematics (science, literature, writing, history, music, etc.) and thinking of unique problems or ways of using it?

Introspective

1. Why do you enjoy mathematics (science, history, literature, etc.)?
2. Under what conditions do you think you will continue to enjoy it?
3. Have you noticed that you find time to read about and/or study mathematics (science, history, literature, etc.) when there are other things you might be doing? Is this desirable or is it inconsistent with your present and/or future needs?

When such retrospective and introspective questions are suitably answered by the student, he may move into the *organizing* level, the level at which he displays a conscious awareness of his value system and sees a value as part of his life structure.

Organizing

If a student has a well-organized value system, he is aware of what he values, and there is a degree of consistency in his value system. The two areas within the organizing category, thus, are *conceptualization of a value* and *organization of a value system*.

Retrospective and introspective questions help him become aware of, and thereby *conceptualize*, his values. Questions that will lead the student to analyze whether this value is consistent with his philosophy of life and with his immediate and future goals are important here. For example, the student might be asked how long he has felt the way he does about reading (or the content). If the content is science, for example, he might be asked if he feels he has the ability and means to become a scientist—if he thinks of science as a vocation or avocation, if he is especially interested in a specific area of science. He might be asked if he thinks his interest is temporary or permanent.

Characterization by a Value or a Value Complex

A person who reaches the very highest level—characterization—is completely devoted to a value or group of values. He embodies the value in an internally consistent way. Actors and actresses sometimes temporarily *become* the person they are portraying. Students sometimes become scientists, mathematicians, poets, or lovers of poetry. These people have reached the highest level of affective involvement. Unfortunately, sometimes youngsters *become* delinquents or dropouts because they have not learned to love anything the school offers and, therefore, they must look elsewhere.

Discussion

We may feel that the content we think we must teach is more important than the interests of our students. We may feel that we must cover the syllabus or the textbook—whether the students like it or not. If we feel this way, we may "cover the material" even though our students are not listening. If students are not "plugged in" and willing to receive—willing and, perhaps, anxious to respond and react—willing to pursue and value what they are learning, we are failing. In most cases it is *we* who are doing something wrong and thereby failing both them and society. If they do not receive, they should be elsewhere. If they do not react, they are robots. If they do not value, they do not enjoy, they do not continue to grow and prosper, they do not love: they are devoted to nothing.

SUMMARY

If we wish to encourage students to read, it is helpful to know why they might choose to read. Waples explains that people read: (1) for the *instrumental effect*, (2) for the *prestige effect*, (3) to *reinforce an attitude*, (4) for *vicarious aesthetic experience*, and (5) for *respite*. Frequently, such motives are in harmony with the goals of a content area classroom, and a wise teacher can capitalize on them. The kind of student reporting, if any, done after such reading should be related to the purpose.

To find out what types of materials individual students choose to read, one need only observe what they select when given a wide choice and when no value judgments are made by an authoritarian figure such as a teacher or parent. Questionnaire techniques, possibly of a general nature, or perhaps geared to specific materials related to course work, might also be used.

An affective taxonomy was explained to help the teacher more fully develop his ability to observe the intensity of interest which students display toward course work. Typical student behavior at each level ranges from *receiving* to *responding* to *valuing* to *organizing* to *characterizing*.

NOTES

1 Douglas Waples. *What Reading Does to People.* Chicago: University of Chicago Press, 1967.

2 G. Robert Carlsen. *Books and the Teen-Age Reader.* A Bantam Book, H3468, 1972.

3 See David Darling. "Evaluating the Affective Dimensions of Reading," in *The Evaluation of Children's Reading Achievement*, ed. Thomas C. Barrett. Newark, Delaware: International Reading Association, 1967, pp. 127–141.

4 David Krathwohl. *Taxonomy of Educational Objectives: Handbook II, Affective Domain*. New York: David McKay, 1964.

5 David Darling, *op. cit.*

6 *Ibid.*

7 *Ibid.*, p. 138.

SUGGESTED ACTIVITIES

1. Waples gave us five reasons why people choose to read. In terms of your content area subject and the amount of class time available, evaluate the relative worth of each reason as deserving of class time. That is, which do you feel is most deserving of class time? Least deserving? Why?

2. Describe four interest centers you would like to have in your classroom when you are teaching a specific concept or set of concepts. What specific printed materials would you hope to have in each center? What other materials would you like to have? When would your students use these centers?

3. Design an interest inventory in which you include brief descriptions of 40 books, pamphlets, or articles which relate to a theme or genre you might teach in your content area. Use a format similar to the "Questionnaire— World War II (History)" model given in this chapter. Use the reference aids explained in Chapter 11.

4. Describe the behaviors—in class and out—that you feel would characterize one of your students who is at the lowest end of the *receiving* category of the affective domain. What behaviors would a student display if he were at the preference level in your course (valuing level: preference for a value)? How does the latter's behavior differ from the behavior of a student who has reached the *characterization* level?

5. Explain what you would do if you found that one or more students in your class were at the lowest level of the affective domain. Would you change your teaching methods? Materials? What would you do if many students reached the responding level but apparently were not going to move any higher?

REFERENCES FOR FURTHER READING

Andresen, Oliver. "Evaluating the Author's Theme in Literature," in *Corrective Reading in the High School Classroom*, ed. H. Alan Robinson and Sidney J. Rauch. Newark, Delaware: International Reading Association, 1966, pp. 64–74.

Burton, Dwight L. *Literature Study in the High Schools*, 3rd ed. New York: Holt, Rinehart and Winston, 1970.

Carlsen, G. Robert. *Books and the Teen-Age Reader*. New York: Bantam, H3468, 1972.

Crosby, Muriel (ed.). *Reading Ladders for Human Relations*. Washington, D.C.: American Council on Education, 1963.

Darling, David. "Evaluating the Affective Dimension of Reading," in *The Evaluation of Children's Reading Achievement*, ed. Thomas C. Barrett. Newark, Delaware: International Reading Association, 1967, pp. 127–141.

Fader, Daniel. *Hooked on Books*. New York: Berkeley Publications, 1968.

Hafner, Lawrence E. (ed.). *Improving Reading in Secondary Schools, Selected Readings*. New York: Macmillan, 1967, Section 11.

Huus, Helen. *Children's Books to Enrich the Social Studies for the Elementary Grades*. Washington, D.C.: National Council for the Social Studies, 1966.

Jennings, Frank. *This Is Reading*. New York: Bureau of Publications, Teachers College, Columbia University, 1965.

Krathwohl, David R., *et al. Taxonomy of Educational Objectives: Handbook II, Affective Domain*. New York: David McKay, 1964.

Massialas, Byron, and Jack Zevin. *Creative Encounters in the Classroom: Teaching and Learning Through Discovery*. New York: John Wiley, 1967.

Torrance, E. Paul and R. E. Myers. *Creative Learning and Teaching*. New York: Dodd, Mead, 1970.

Waples, Douglas. *What Reading Does to People*. Chicago: University of Chicago Press, 1967.

the small society   by Brickman

Reprinted by permission of The Washington Star Syndicate, Inc.

INTEREST INVENTORIES

Austin, Mary C., C. L. Bush, and M. H. Huebner. *Reading Evaluation*. New York: The Ronald Press, 1961.

Harris, A. J. *How to Increase Reading Ability*, 5th ed. New York: David McKay, 1970, pp. 462–466.

Karlin, Robert. *Teaching Reading in High School.* Indianapolis: Bobbs-Merrill, 1964, pp. 212–215.

Strang, Ruth. *The Diagnostic Teaching of Reading*, 2d ed. New York: McGraw-Hill, 1969, pp. 110–117.

Witty, Paul. *Reading in Modern Education.* Boston: D. C. Heath, 1949.

UNIT TWO

DEVELOPING CLASSROOM STRATEGIES FOR READING IN CONTENT FIELDS

Introduction

Chapter 5
Selecting Teaching Strategies for Reading Development

Chapter 5 focuses on:

(1) the teacher's responsibility in presenting a reading assignment and in providing for post-reading activities. Skills needed for reading, and purposes for reading, in four content areas —science, mathematics, social studies, and English—are listed, with cross-references to chapters, or sections within chapters, of this book where more complete explanations and techniques for teaching are given.

(2) a technique designed for independent study of expository material, including two variations of the technique, one for use in reading science materials, and the other for use with mathematical problems.

(3) classroom management in terms of grouping procedures, including whole class instruction, personalized instruction, and small group instruction.

Chapter 5

TEACHING STRATEGIES FOR CLASSROOM USE

What is the teacher's responsibility in presenting a reading lesson to a group of students?

What guidelines, or models, can be used in presenting a lesson?

What can a teacher do to provide for, and encourage, individualized and/or group reading following a required assignment?

What are some grouping procedures commonly used in content area classrooms?

INTRODUCTION

The focus of this chapter is on the teacher's responsibility in presenting a reading assignment, his role in the discussion which follows the reading assignment, and his role in helping students extend their interests. Also included is a discussion of some grouping procedures commonly used in content area classrooms.

The *directed reading activity*, a five-step plan, is explained first. This plan includes pre- and post-reading activities. It is these activities, which the teacher should plan well for, that allow a student to successfully read on his *instructional level*, a higher level than his independent level.

SQ3R, also a five-step plan, is designed especially for mature students, although many of its provisions are also useful for other students. Teacher guidance in the use of SQ3R will aid many students attain independence in the skillful study of expository materials.

Whenever students read assigned lessons, it is hoped that they will wish to pursue interests which have grown in this reading. To help this occur, teachers should follow certain procedures. Among them are helping students clarify their interests, helping students locate varied materials, providing class time for the pursuit of such interests, and providing opportunities for making full use of what is learned.

There will be times when students and teachers will recognize the need for further skill development. Opportunities for this should also be provided. Such activities may find nourishment in class-wide sharing, but at other times individualization, or personalization, of instruction will be desirable. Also, there are many times when group activities are most useful.

The final section of this chapter deals with classroom management as it relates to class-wide, individual, and group procedures.

DIRECTED READING ACTIVITY

The directed reading activity (DRA) is a five-step lesson plan especially designed to help those students who are reading materials that are on their *instructional*, rather than *independent*, reading level. It is designed to be used in a group or class-wide situation, for this plan is too lengthy to be used with individuals.

Step 1

Explore students' backgrounds in regard to *information* related to the reading assignment and *skills* the students will need in order to understand the assignment. *Build students' backgrounds* when it is apparent that they have insufficient *information* to be able to understand the assignment and/or insufficient *skills.* Relate the assignment to their previous learning. Part of this step and the next is to *motivate* students so that they will wish to read the assignment.

The following kinds of activities might be useful in accomplishing Step 1:

1. Review a previous chapter and/or related readings or experiences.

2. Review, or teach for the first time, a necessary word attack skill such as a syllabication generalization, a type of context clue, the meaning of morphemes that relate to the assignment, etc. (See Chapter 6 of this book.)

3. Possibly list new vocabulary words on the board. *If desirable,* explain their meanings, if possible by using illustrations or models. (See "Dimensions of Vocabulary" in Chapter 6. You may wish to use one of the teaching techniques suggested in Chapter 6, e.g., see pp. 108–115.) Such techniques can be used before the content area chapter is read by the students. Some of the other techniques might legitimately be used after the chapter has been read by the students.*

4. Review, or teach for the first time, a comprehension skill such as outlining (see Chaper 7: "Sequence"), which is necessary for understanding the assignment.

5. Review, or teach for the first time, a critical-creative skill, such as an area of semantics (connotations, etc.) or propaganda analysis, fallacies of reasoning, syllogistic reasoning, etc., synthesis activities, or evaluation. The skill that should be reviewed or taught is the one that is necessary for the understanding of the assignment to be read. (See Chapter 6: "Connotations" and Chapter 9: "Analyzing, Synthesizing, and Evaluating Ideas Through Reading.")

6. Show a film or filmstrip to build the students' background of experience so that they can better understand the assignment and/or so that they gain interest in it.

7. Show the class a picture or real object—especially in science or mathematics—so that they can better visualize what is being discussed in the assignment.

8. Have someone who is knowledgeable about the subject or a related subject —a student, another teacher, a parent, a member of the community, etc.— talk to the class.

---

* According to George G. Mallinson, "The lists of key words . . . should not be studied *before* the materials in the chapter are covered. Otherwise, the student will acquire a number of atomistic definitions that are out of context. These lists may well be studied for post-testing, but hardly for pre-study." From "Methods and Materials for Teaching Reading in Science," in *Sequential Development of Reading Abilities,* ed. H. M. Robinson. Supplementary Educational Monographs, No. 90. Chicago: University of Chicago Press, 1960, pp. 145–149.

Step 2

The second step includes: (1) *previewing* the assignment, (2) *clarifying purposes* for reading the assignment, and (3) possibly making a statement about the *rate of reading* that is appropriate for the assignment. The purpose of this is to give definite guidance to learning. Purposes should be stated clearly and should be suited to the content of the materials and to affective goals of instruction. First, *preview* the assignment by using a survey technique. (See "S" in SQ3R in this chapter and "Skimming" in Chapter 10.)

Second, *state purposes for reading* the assignment, or better still, *have students state purposes.*

1. Purposes might include the acquisition of literal information, for example, getting meanings of specific words from context, getting main ideas, sequence, theme, following directions, etc., and translation activities. (See Chapters 6 and 7.)

2. Purposes might also include a specific question about interpretation (e.g., What will happen if what the author recommends does occur? etc.) (See Chapter 8.)

3. Purposes might also include eliciting critical-creative reactions. (Are any fallacies of reasoning used? Is there card stacking? Is there one idea that you find useful? By what standards would you evaluate the ideas included in this chapter? etc.) (See Chapter 9.)

4. Purposes might also include affective responses or reactions: How do you feel about . . . ? Would you like to have been there? Which character, or real person, would you most like to be? When would you most like to have been the protagonist? Least? Does the resolution of the problem seem fair to you? Which topic was most interesting to you? Why? Would you like further information about any topic? (See Chapters 4 and 11.)

Third, if desirable, make a statement about an appropriate *rate of reading* to use for the assignment. (See Chapter 10.)

Step 3

Students read silently. (This might be homework.)

Step 4

Students *discuss* the assignment or in some other way respond to it (by writing about it, by doing what is suggested in it, by drawing a picture or other illustration about it, etc.). They carry through and/or are helped in carrying through the activities whose foundations were laid and whose purposes were stated in Steps 1 and 2, respectively, of the DRA. At this time, students might read aloud brief statements from the assignment to prove an answer they have given to a question. Additional useful activities might emerge from student thought and discussion during or after the reading of the assignment.

This fourth step is extremely important. The teacher must decide just how this sharing activity is going to be carried on. He has at his disposal many possibilities. Among them are:

1. *a teacher-directed discussion or quiz:* This might be best when certain kinds of learnings are to be achieved by the student, and the teacher is interested in assuring himself that such is the case. This is particularly useful when convergent thinking is desired. Normally, questions are asked by the teacher, and students respond to them— orally, in writing, or by performing an activity.

2. *a nondirective, or inquiry-centered, discourse:* This is best when the teacher does not pose as an authority figure. Students are free to respond to, and question each other about, the assignment.

    The teacher's job might be one of prodding students to explore and test alternatives, to encourage students to defend any statements they make, to ask for the clarification of points made by students, to raise additional questions at a time of impasse, to legitimize creative expression, to perform certain managerial tasks such as recognizing students, planning many of the topics that will be explored, spacing and sequencing topics, locating materials, introducing materials and topics, serving as a springboard for inquiry and discussion, and summarizing discussions.[1]

Step 5

Extend the activity. This might mean going on to the next chapter or having students do related reading or other activities.

The original assignment might lead to reading related exposition, including newspaper and magazine articles and pamphlets, biography, poetry, fiction, etc. (See "The Unit Plan" in this chapter and "Using Library Resources" in Chapter 11.)

It might lead to an interview with another person, or seeing a play, a movie, or a T.V. show. It might lead to writing an original communication or work of art, such as a skit, which might be performed for the class. (See Chapter 9: "Synthesis.") It might lead to the setting up of an experiment and performing it.

Assignment: Keep the steps of the DRA clearly in mind as you read the next five chapters of this book. After you finish these chapters, you will be asked to write your own DRA for a chapter in your content area book.

Skills Needed for Reading in Specific Content Areas

The most commonly needed skills for reading in specific content areas are described in the following pages.

Science

Vocabulary

1. learning and recognizing terms that are unique to science, e.g., photosynthesis, phylum, stromata, multicellular (see Chapter 6: "Denotations of words, meanings of new words" and "Morphology" and "Phonic Syllabication");

2. learning scientific meanings of common words, e.g., culture, power, belt (see Chapter 6: "Denotations of words, multiple meanings of simple words");

3. learning scientific and mathematical symbols and abbreviations, e.g., H_2O, Fe, $<$, $>$, Σ (see Chapter 6: "Symbols and Abbreviations");

4. understanding how new words enter our language or are coined, e.g., television, astronaut, sputnik (see Chapter 6: "Diachronic Linguistics");

5. consider also: over-heavy vocabulary load (see Chapter 2: "Judging the Difficulty of Reading Materials" and Chapter 3: "Finding the Appropriate Level of Materials for Each Student").

Comprehension

1. selecting significant details, recognizing main ideas, classifying convergently, following directions, getting sequence, recording information in outline, graph, map, and chart form, and reading outlines, graphs, maps, and charts (see Chapter 7 and "Skimming" in Chapter 10);

2. formulating main ideas from evidence, classifying, seeing likenesses and differences, assuming cause-effect relationships, retrospecting and anticipating, applying ideas to new situations (see Chapter 8);

3. dissecting, analyzing information, establishing validity of source of information, determining author's purpose, establishing cause-effect relationships, syllogistic reasoning, synthesizing ideas, divergent production, evaluating (see Chapter 9).

Comprehension and appreciation

4. developing the habit of extensive and intensive reading in science—for greater cognition and appreciation (see Chapters 4 and 11).

Speed of comprehension

1. developing the ability to adjust speed according to the purpose for reading and the difficulty of materials (see Chapter 10).

Mathematics

Vocabulary

1. learning and recognizing terms that are unique to mathematics, e.g., perpendicular, quadrilateral, congruent, numerator (see Chapter 6: "Denotations of Words, meanings of new words" and "Morphology" and "Phonic Syllabication");
2. learning mathematical meanings of common words, e.g., square root, improper fraction, reduce (see Chapter 6: "Denotations of Words, multiple meanings of simple words);
3. learning mathematical symbols and abbreviations, e.g., bu, pk, ÷, √ (see Chapter 6: "Symbols and Abbreviations");
4. consider also: over-heavy vocabulary load (see Chapter 2: "Judging the Difficulty of Reading Materials" and Chapter 3: "Finding the Appropriate Level of Materials for Each Student").

Comprehension

1. selecting significant details, classifying convergently, following directions, recognizing main ideas, recognizing sequence, recording information in graph and chart form, and reading graphs and charts (see Chapter 7);
2. seeing likenesses and differences, anticipating approximate answers, applying ideas to a new situation, formulating main ideas (see Chapter 8);
3. analyzing information, establishing validity of a source of information, syllogistic reasoning, synthesizing ideas, evaluating (see Chapter 9).

Comprehension and appreciation

4. developing the habit of extensive and intensive reading in mathematics— for greater cognition and appreciation (see Chapters 4 and 11).

Speed of comprehension

1. developing the ability to adjust speed according to the purposes for reading and the difficulty of materials (see Chapter 10).

Social Studies

Vocabulary

1. learning and recognizing terms that are unique to social studies, e.g., communism, democracy, imperialism, centralization (see Chapter 6: "Denotations of Words, meanings of new words" and "Morphology" and "Phonic Syllabication");

2. learning social studies meanings of common words, e.g., race, bill, cabinet, left and right (see Chapter 6: "Denotations of Words, multiple meanings of simple words");

3. learning word connotations, understanding figurative language and allusions, e.g., liberal, hot potato, money talks, modern David (see Chapter 6: "Word Connotations and Figurative Language");

4. understanding that words change in meaning, e.g., propaganda, melting pot, unique (see Chapter 6: "Diachronic Linguistics");

5. understanding how new words are coined or how they enter our language, e.g., smog, UNESCO, NATO, SALT, zapped (see Chapter 6: "Diachronic Linguistics");

6. consider also: over-heavy vocabulary load (see Chapter 2: "Judging the Difficulty of Reading Materials" and Chapter 3: "Finding the Appropriate Level of Materials for Each Student").

Comprehension

1. selecting significant details, classifying convergently, following directions, selecting main ideas, recognizing sequence, recording information in outline, graph, map, chart form, and reading outlines, graphs, maps, charts (see Chapter 7 and "Skimming" in Chapter 10);

2. formulating main ideas from evidence, classifying, anticipating and retrospecting, assuming cause-effect relationships, inferring time and place, determining motives of real people, applying information to new situations (see Chapter 8);

3. analyzing information, establishing authenticity of sources of information, analyzing propaganda, recognizing fallacies of reasoning, synthesizing ideas, evaluating (see Chapter 9).

Comprehension and appreciation

4. developing the habit of extensive and intensive reading in social studies materials—for greater cognition and appreciation (see Chapters 4 and 11).

Speed of comprehension

1. developing the ability to adjust speed according to the purpose for reading and the difficulty of materials (see Chapter 10).

English

Vocabulary

1. learning and recognizing terms that are unique to English, e.g., adjective, apostrophe, ballad, antihero (see Chapter 6: "Denotations of Words, meanings of new words" and "Morphology" and "Phonic Syllabication");
2. learning English (literary or grammatical) meanings for common words, e.g., romantic, comedy, subject, feet, act (see Chapter 6: "Denotations of Words, multiple meanings of simple words");
3. learning word connotations and understanding figurative language and allusions, e.g., lemon, two peas in a pod, Narcissus, Pygmalion (see Chapter 6: "Word Connotations and Figurative Language");
4. understanding that words change in meaning and pronunciation, e.g., "lewd and nice," criticism, perfect, poem, family (see Chapter 6: "Diachronic Linguistics");
5. understanding how new words are coined or how they enter our language, e.g., motel, SNAFU, morpheme, antsville (see Chapter 6: "Diachronic Linguistics");
6. consider also: over-heavy vocabulary load (see Chapter 2: "Judging the Difficulty of Reading Materials" and Chapter 3: "Finding the Appropriate Level of Materials for Each Student").

Comprehension

1. selecting significant details, classifying convergently, following directions, selecting main ideas, recognizing sequence, recording information in outline, graph, map, chart form, and reading outlines, graphs, maps, charts (see Chapter 7 and "Skimming" in Chapter 10);
2. formulating main ideas from evidence, classifying, anticipating and retrospecting, making comparisons, inferring time, place, mood, and motives of characters, responding to imagery, empathizing, applying ideas to new situations (see Chapter 8);
3. recognizing semantic devices, making judgments about the authenticity of sources of information, distinguishing between fact and opinion, analyzing propaganda, detecting fallacies of reasoning, synthesizing, writing unique communications, evaluating (see Chapter 9).

Comprehension and appreciation

4. developing the habit of extensive and intensive reading in language arts materials and literature—for greater cognition and appreciation (see Chapters 4 and 11).

Speed of comprehension

1. developing the ability to adjust speed according to the purpose for reading and the difficulty of materials (see Chapter 10).

SQ3R

SQ3R can serve as a substitute for a directed reading activity when students are working on the *independent reading level*.[2] It can also serve as an alternative DRA, to be used as a teacher guided activity in a group or class-wide situation to achieve certain purposes.

It is especially helpful as a *teacher directed activity* in introducing and reviewing a textbook. And it is especially helpful as a *student directed activity* for mature readers who are reading expository material without the aid of a teacher's guidance in the form of a DRA. Parts of it can even be built into a DRA, but it provides for less guidance by the teacher than does the DRA. That is why it is best to use SQ3R when the student is working on his independent reading level, whereas the DRA is best when the student is working on his instructional reading level.

The five steps of SQ3R are as follows.

S = Survey[3]

Read the title of the book. Read the author's name. What are his credentials? Is he likely to be biased? Does he represent a particular school of thought? Are there other schools of thought to be compared with his?

Study the Table of Contents. From it you can get an outline of the whole book. Is there card stacking? Are any important major ideas not included? (Of course, no book can include everything on a topic.) Must I consult other sources to get a complete view?

Read the Introduction and/or Preface. What is the author's point of view? For whom is the book written?

Survey each of the chapters in the following way: read the title, the introductory statement, and all main headings in order. Study illustrations, and read the concluding statement or summary. Try to recall the outline of the chapter before going on to survey the next chapter.

Glance through the Glossary and Appendixes to see what additional information is given.

Finally, when you begin to read the book chapter by chapter, survey each chapter again before reading it. Try to construct an outline in your mind—or on paper—before studying the chapter. Also ask questions, e.g., Is anything important omitted?

Q = Question

Look at the first main heading. Ask yourself what it means. Ask yourself questions that you think might be answered in the section. For example, if the heading is "Formal English," ask yourself questions such as: What is formal English? Do I ever use formal English? When should I use it? Are there times when I shouldn't use it? What other levels of English are there?

R_1 = Read

Read to find the answers to your questions. If the answers are not there, you may wish to find them somewhere else. These are good questions to ask in class or to go to find the answers to in the library.

R_2 = Recite

Recite the answers to yourself to help you remember them. Ask yourself if the answers given by the author make sense. Ask yourself if you have a new idea which you can use—perhaps in a written assignment or in conversation or in performing a task, etc.

Q, R_1 R_2 = Go to the next heading and repeat: Question, Read, Recite. Then go to the next heading and repeat, etc., until you have finished the chapter.

R_3 = Review or Reconstruct

Review the whole chapter in a "survey" fashion, but with the details filled in. Then reconstruct the outline in your mind or on a piece of paper. Try to recall important ideas the author has discussed. Ask yourself some interpretive level or critical-creative-evaluative level questions. Also try to think of applications of the ideas learned.

At this point you may wish to *extend* your reading to find additional sources which give you information in greater depth or give you another point of view. Even reading of a tangential nature may be interesting.

Variations of SQ3R

Variations of the SQ3R technique have been suggested in the literature. One is for science; the other, for mathematics.

Science

For science, George Spache suggests the use of the PQRST technique.[4]

Preview: rapidly skim the total selection

Question: raise questions to guide the careful reading to follow, in terms of the study purposes

Read: read the selection, keeping the questions in mind

Summarize: organize and summarize the information gained

Test: check your summary against the selection

Mathematics

For problem reading in mathematics, Leo Fay recommends the use of the SQRQCQ technique.[5]

Survey: read the problem rapidly to determine its nature

Question: decide what is being asked, what the problem is

Read: read for details and interrelationships

Question: decide what processes should be used

Compute: carry out the computation[6]

Question: ask if the answer seems correct, check the computation against the problem facts and the basic arithmetic facts.

EXTENSION ACTIVITIES

Whenever reading is done in any one source or in a limited number of sources, there is the distinct possibility that it may be desirable to read and study other materials. The original source may be so interesting that it will lead to in-depth related readings. Or, the source may be incomplete, and other materials are needed so that more answers can be found. It is possible that the original source is biased, and other points of view may be needed to round out the discussion. Whatever the reason, and that reason may vary from person to person, additional sources are often needed or desired.

The wise teacher provides for such additional reading or research. Such activities fan out into group work, individual study, or possibly to whole class activities. The activities are usually *student-inspired*, although the teacher may provide guidelines.

Guidelines

The teacher may follow certain guidelines in providing for extension-type activities. Among them are:

1. *The teacher helps students clarify and extend interests.* Students may wish to study additional materials, but may have hazy ideas about focusing on a topic. Without teacher help, they may waste a great deal of time because of their naivity in self-direction. The teacher should provide guidance to those who need it, helping them explore possibilities for extended activities and possibly helping them in formulating an outline of how to proceed.

2. *The teacher helps students locate varied materials,* or at least assures himself that the students are knowledgeable about using resource aids and materials. The teacher may have varied materials available in the classroom. Even some of these, such as dictionaries, almanacs, *Who's Who,* atlases, encyclopedias, etc., require the student to have reference techniques for their proper use. The card catalog, Dewey decimal system, *Reader's Guide to Periodical Literature,* and such other indexes as the *Agricultural Index, Art Index, Industrial Arts Index,* etc., are useful tools each student should know about. The teacher's job is to ensure that students know how to use these tools and/or to teach their effective use. (See Chapter 11 for further information about library use and reference aids.)

3. *The teacher provides class time for group or individual work.* At more advanced levels, he may provide "homework time" for such activities. During this time the students might go to the library, to an experimental room, to small seminar rooms or special areas of the classroom for discussions, or use the classroom library. Individual students might just read their books in class or perform some creative activity.

4. *The teacher provides opportunities for making full use of what is being learned or experienced.*[7] The teacher allows students to share—informally or otherwise—what they have learned. He may provide help in organizing the information, in relating it to other ideas they have, in critically responding to it, and in creating with it. Also, the teacher helps students in assessing their growth through these extended activities. The teacher may also provide help in further extending in-depth or wide-reading activities.

CLASSROOM MANAGEMENT—GROUPING PROCEDURES

The following types of grouping plans within the classroom are useful at various times.

Whole Class Instruction

There are many occasions when everyone in a classroom will benefit from the same instruction or activity. When new ideas or skills are being introduced, the whole class could be oriented together. Often, the whole class will read the same chapter in a book. A film or filmstrip might be shown or a recording or possibly a speaker listened to. There might be classroom discussions, panel discussions, debates, choral reading, etc.

Even teenage "show and tell" activities could be very rewarding: a student might bring an important newspaper article or editorial to any class—or a recipe in home economics, a floor plan in manual arts or arts and crafts class, a political cartoon in social studies, etc. Or, objects might be brought by travelers or just by those who carefully observe the neighborhood in science class.

There are many occasions when it would be mutually profitable for students to share with the whole class what they have learned individually or in small groups. Such sharing may happen spontaneously, or it may be carefully planned for, as when a unit of study is being completed. There is no need for such sharing to be stiff, stilted, or stereotyped. There are numerous creative ways for students to share ideas with one another.

Some students might prepare bulletin boards. Some might highlight an interesting story. Others might write news items for a class paper—in any class. Some might work on mathematical models or puzzles—or prepare cross-word puzzles for their classmates. Such possibilities are infinite. Many students themselves will pleasantly surprise the class with unique ideas.

Let's look at a model for whole class instruction. The *English* or *history* teacher might lead a discussion about men and women who have displayed *courage* in order to get the students ready to read individual or group selections related to the theme of courage (in English class) or a particular period, e.g., the Revolutionary War period, in history. Students might contribute examples of courageous acts they have observed, read about, or even seen on television. Some students might even tell about their own most courageous acts.

Following this, the class might engage in the choral reading of a poem depicting a relevant courageous act. Parts might be assigned for a short play, which could be read orally to the class. Even a film might be shown and perhaps a recording played, for example, Churchill's "blood, sweat, and tears" speech. Hypothetical cases might be advanced: "What would you do if . . . ?" Also, cases that relate to available reading materials might be stated: "What would you do if . . . ?" And after students answered, they read to find out what really (real or fictional) happened.

When a whole class does read the same selection—a chapter in a textbook, a poem, a pamphlet, an article—a discussion usually precedes the reading.

This discussion usually takes the form of a directed reading activity, discussed earlier in this chapter.

Many examples have been given for class-wide activities. In all classrooms, there ought also be frequent opportunities for individual work.

Individualized and Personalized Instruction

Often, it is advantageous for students to work individually. If we call this *individualized instruction*, we mean that the student *seeks* his own area of interest, *selects* his own reading materials, and *paces* himself, i.e., he does as much reading as he himself wishes to do. "Seeking, self-selection, and pacing" are key words advanced by Olson to describe modern, individualized reading programs.[8]

In such programs, the student is given free rein (although there are frequent pupil-teacher conferences). Such freedom of choice in interest areas is usually not possible in content area subjects, where the range of topics is limited. Individualized instruction, such as Olson describes, might be found in reading class and in English or language arts classes at times, but only rarely in other classes.

In content area classrooms, however, *complete freedom* of choice in interest areas may not be possible. But within a certain range—within a particular theme or genre or skill—students (at least sometimes) should be given a choice. When there are limitations placed on the "seeking, self-selection, and pacing," we term the kind of reading that occurs *personalized reading*, rather than individualized reading.

Students might contract to do certain units, but within the units, different students might read different things (self-selection and pacing principles). *Work centers* might be organized around the classroom, each featuring a different area of interest or a different skill and each containing a *variety of materials*. Students could choose the materials they wish to work with within the unit. They might freely choose their units (if they are interest units) or possibly be assigned to them (if they are skill units).

At other times, personalized reading in a content area classroom might be freer. In a mathematics classroom, for example, students may freely *choose* to read almost anything that relates to the course work. Some may choose biographies of mathematicians, or of architects or scientists, or even artists or musicians who are known to have used related mathematical principles. Still others may look for immediate practical applications of the mathematical principles—in a purchasing situation, or in building a cabinet, designing a room divider, or multiplying or dividing a recipe. Still others may look for relationships in nature—for balance and structure in sea shells, trees, flowers, and so on.

In history class, if the Civil War period is being studied, some students might also wish to read biographies of Lincoln, Lee, Grant, or Mrs. Lincoln, etc. Some may wish to read *Uncle Tom's Cabin, Gone with the Wind, Red Badge of Courage, Spoon River Anthology*, etc. Still others may wish to study documents, to read poetry of the period, essays, or even newspaper accounts. A variety of materials should be available from which students may choose. Even filmstrips could be viewed and music listened to.

Surely, there is no dearth of materials available for use in a science class. If the class is studying animal or plant life, magazines such as *National Wild-life* and *National Geographic* are available. Biographies and science fiction are also available. Many library books suggest experiments some students might wish to try.

There is much excellent material available for the English teacher. Among the best sources are *Books and the Teen-Age Reader* by G. Robert Carlsen, *Literature Study in the High Schools* (third edition) by Dwight L. Burton, *Reading Ladders to Human Relations* by Muriel Crosby, *Good Reading for Poor Readers* by George Spache, and *Hooked on Books* by Daniel Fader. Prepared collections of paperbacks—for personalized and/or unit reading— are also available. In addition, "club memberships" are available for the purchase of paperbacks by students.

Most of the discussion in this section has revolved around the development and extension of *interests* by using a personalized approach. A *skills* approach is also possible, and often necessary. Usually, however, the teacher must know which skills the individual student is in need of improving: is it rate, flexibility of rate, word attack, vocabulary, main idea and sequence, critical reading, study skills—or what? The student should work on the skills appropriate to *his needs*. He usually does not know what his are, and, therefore, he needs guidance from the teacher to channel him to the correct area of skill development.

Practical suggestions for improving reading and study skills will be given in later chapters. All teachers should give aid to students in the development of such skills—as a means of helping them to understand the content area subject.

Small Group Instruction

When students have common *reading achievement* levels, common *skill needs*, or common *interests*, they can be grouped together. Frequently, such grouping is fluid: groups are formed, students work together for a short period of time, and when a goal is reached, the groups disband. Then, other groups are formed and soon disbanded, etc.

Achievement grouping

For example, several textbooks or trade books may be available on a variety of *levels*—one set quite difficult, another easier, and another quite simple.

Students might be grouped together to read the materials they are capable of reading, as revealed by the informal reading inventory they were given. Thus, students might be grouped homogeneously according to their level of reading achievement.

Sometimes, it might be useful to group students heterogeneously according to reading achievement, as, for example, in pupil-team teaching, where one student may read to the other. Or, cross-grade grouping may be used, where a poor reader in a higher grade may be unashamed of reading "easy books" to a younger student, and both may learn.

Skill grouping

But some students in each achievement group may need help in a particular *skill*, such as how to use a microscope, how to use the *Reader's Guide to Periodical Literature* or the *Art Index*, how to divide words into syllables, etc. When this skill is being taught, the teacher could group these students together for instructional purposes. As soon as the skill is learned, there is no need for this group, so its members will scatter and need not meet together again. Then, other skills will have to be taught, and new groups will be formed, only to disband when the skill is learned.

Interest grouping

A group of students may share similar *interests*. They may or may not wish to, or be able to, read the same materials, but they may desire to share their learnings with one another. Thus, temporary interest groups may be formed for sharing ideas of interest to all, but possibly not of interest to the whole class. For example, several students might be interested in reading war stories; others may wish to read plays. Some may wish to study weather maps (in science), or products of a particular region, etc. Or, students might be grouped together because they have *diverse interests*. For example, a Republican and a Democrat might be paired off to discuss an imminent election, etc.

Social grouping

In some classrooms *social grouping* can be used. A social studies teacher might group together students who have similar social backgrounds, so that they can work together, for example, in planning a budget. Or, students who are socially diverse might be grouped together to help them understand one another better. They might discuss ways holidays are celebrated, their favorite foods, or their feeling about how well or how poorly they are accepted by other groups of people.

Discussion

We have just discussed four basic criteria by which students might be grouped in classes: achievement, skill, interest, and social factors. We have briefly discussed both *homogeneous grouping* and *heterogeneous grouping* according to each criteria.

Try now to fill in the cells in Table 5.1, showing the pros and cons of homogeneous grouping and the pros and cons of heterogeneous grouping according to each criterion. Each cell should be completed.

Constellation Grouping—The Unit Plan

Constellation grouping provides for the logical and meaningful combination of all of the previously mentioned forms of grouping. For example, whole-class activities may lead to small group activities and/or personalized activities. These, in turn, may lead back to whole class activities, and the cycle may begin again. This is what happens if we use the *unit approach.*

A unit may be developed around a *theme,* i.e., a particular idea, such as ecology, the next election, drug addiction, men who survived against great odds, careers, a weekly menu, foods around the globe, building home furniture, tennis, golf, sportsmanship, weather prediction, controlling harmful pests in the garden, the Revolutionary War period, the Vietnam war, mathematical principles in music and art, one aspect of solid geometry, etc. Or, a unit may be developed around a *genre,* i.e., a literary form, such as biography and autobiography, the essay, poetry, novels, short stories, newspaper articles, etc. In addition, a unit might be developed around a needed *skill,* such as how to use various machines in the woodwork shop, how to develop vocabulary and word power, how to punctuate, how to get the main idea and sequence of a selection, how to use various instruments in science class, how to multiply using various number systems, how to use the library, etc.

A unit usually consists of four phases:

Phase 1—class-wide activities orienting the student to the unit.

Phase 2—small group activities built around interests, skill needs, social factors, or achievement which flow from the class-wide activities and reinforce and more fully develop the unit according to group needs or interests.

Phase 3—personalized activities which flow from the small group activities, but which pinpoint individual needs or interests more accurately than can group work.

Phase 4—sharing of interests and/or learnings with the groups of Phase 2 and/or the whole class.

Table 5.1 Pros and cons of homogeneous and heterogeneous grouping according to various criteria

| Criteria for grouping | Grouping | | | |
| | Homogeneous | | Heterogeneous | |
	Pros	Cons	Pros	Cons
Achievement				
Skill				
Interest				
Social				

Keep the following principles in mind when planning and working on a unit.

I. Planning the unit
   A. Determine the reading levels and abilities of students.
   B. Identify suitable materials for reading.
      1. Select materials in harmony with unit objectives.
      2. Use a systematic method of estimating the difficulty of materials.
      3. Furnish a variety of materials, including reference and supplementary materials of different levels of difficulty.
   C. Provide a suitable environment for reading.
      1. Plan both socialized and individualized reading experiences.
      2. Plan suitable physical conditions for reading.

II. Producing the unit
   A. State concretely the purposes for reading and for preparatory activities to reading, relate the purposes to student experience, and help students formulate their own purposes for reading.
   B. Explore and clarify the experience background of students through class discussions, pretests, autobiographies, conferences, special reports, etc.
   C. Extend and enrich the background of students through the judicious use of instructional aids such as illustrative flat pictures, projected still pictures, motion pictures, phonograph records, the radio, oral reading, objects, field trips, excursions, etc.
   D. Discuss with students the location of materials and the use of reference aids to guide wide reading activities.
   E. Suggest the use of appropriate general methods of reading, text signals, and other more specific aids to reading in the content field.

III. Developing the unit
   A. Aid students in actually locating materials and using library aids effectively.
   B. Assist students in adjusting their method of reading to varying purposes, materials, and abilities.
   C. Help students practice organizing, remembering, and applying what they read through the use of such techniques as intent to remember, self-recitation, outlining, making summaries and précis, and the use of the whole-part-whole approach to reading.
   D. Continue those activities suggested in introducing the unit as they are needed.

IV. Concluding the unit

    A. Provide for both student and teacher evaluation of the effectiveness of the learning activities.

    B. Encourage students to apply the results of their learning to new problems, activities, and situations.*

SUMMARY

The teacher has definite responsibilities in presenting a reading assignment in any content area. When the whole class or a group of students is being instructed, a plan that has proved highly effective might be used. It is called the directed reading activity (DRA).

There are five steps in the DRA. Step 1 involves *exploring the backgrounds* of students as they relate to the reading material—in terms of both ideas and skills, and it involves pointing out relationships between what they know and what they are about to learn. It also includes *building the background*, when necessary, and motivating the students to learn. Step 2 involves *setting up purposes* for reading to direct the students to focus on points of major importance. Step 3 involves *silent reading* of the assignment, and might be done as a homework assignment. Step 4 deals with *follow-up activities*, which might be *teacher-directed* or *inquiry-centered*. Step 5 relates to *extending the activity*.

Skills commonly needed for reading in four different content areas were listed, with cross references to chapters, or sections within chapters, where theory and techniques for teaching them are explained in greater detail.

SQ3R was also explained. S stands for *survey*; Q stands for *question*; R_1 represents *reading*, R_2 means *reciting*, and R_3 means *review*, or reconstruct. It is hoped that mature students will learn to use this study skill independently. Variations of this technique, known as PQRST in science, and SQRQCQ, in mathematics, were also noted.

In addition to providing for whole class learning, the teacher's job includes encouraging and providing for extended (often individual or group) learnings. To help students go beyond the assigned lesson, the teacher should help students clarify individual or group interests as they relate to the assignment and help them locate materials which warrant further perusal or study. The teacher should provide class time for such pursuits and opportunities for sharing and using what has been learned.

---

* Theodore L. Harris. "Making Reading an Effective Instrument of Learning in the Content Fields," in *Reading in High School and College*, N.S.S.E. 47th Yearbook, Part II. Chicago: University of Chicago Press, 1949, pp. 133–134. Reprinted by permission.

In order to capitalize on the diverse abilities and interests of students, and to help develop students as individuals, it is necessary to use a variety of class-room organizational plans. Groups formed in the classroom should be *fluid* rather than fixed. Students gather together and disburse as their needs and interests develop and change.

Whole class instruction and sharing can and should be used frequently. There are numerous occasions when all students can learn together. This may happen when the group is being oriented to new ideas and skills. It may occur when a film is being shown, a recording listened to, a story or chapter read. It may take the form of choral reading, of a game or activity, of the spontaneous sharing of an idea by someone. There may be panel discussions, skits, bulletin board displays, even "show-and-tell."

But there are also times for *personalized instruction*, when individuals want to, or need to, "do their own thing." This may be true for skill development and/or interest development. Olson's principles of "seeking, self-selection, and pacing" are well worth considering for "letting things happen" in a prepared way.

Frequently, students might form *small groups*—either homogeneously or heterogeneously—in the classroom. They may group according to *interests* (similar or diverse), *skill needs* (similar or pupil-team), *social characteristics* (similar or different), or *achievement* (similar or pupil-team).

Constellation grouping is especially useful in content area subjects, where the unifying force may be supplied by a *theme* (or a chapter in a textbook), a *genre,* or a *skill.* All students are oriented together (Phase 1); they then select or are assigned to a group that takes off from the whole (Phase 2); next, individuals orbit around their groups (Phase 3) in personalized activities; finally, they return home (Phase 4) to share their discoveries. Although such flexible grouping may seem difficult, it is really easier—and more profitable—for all (including the teacher) than continual whole class work.

NOTES

1 Byron G. Massialas and Jack Zevin. *Creative Encounters in the Classroom—Teaching and Learning through Discovery.* New York: John Wiley, 1967, pp. 25–26. This excellent book contains classroom examples of this technique in action in most content areas.

2 For the rationale of this technique see Francis P. Robinson. "Study Skills for Superior Students in Secondary School." *The Reading Teacher,* **25** (September 1961): 29–33+.

3 Also see David Ausubel and his discussion of the "advanced organizer," in *The Psychology of Meaningful Verbal Learning.* New York: Grume & Stratton, 1963, pp. 85–87.

4 George Spache. *Toward Better Reading.* Champaign, Illinois: Garrard, 1963, p. 94.

5 After Leo Fay. "Reading Study Skills: Math and Science," in *Reading and Inquiry*, ed. J. Allen Figurel. Newark, Delaware: International Reading Association, 1965, p. 93.

6 In this book it is recommended that an estimate be made before the actual computing is done (see Chapter 8: "Anticipation").

7 These four points are taken from "Individualized Reading: More than New Forms and Formulas," by Alexander Frazier. *Elementary English*, **XXXIX** (December 1962): 809–814.

8 Willard Olson. "Seeking, Self-Selection, and Pacing in the Use of Books by Children," in *The Packet*. Boston: D. C. Heath, Spring 1952, pp. 3–10.

SUGGESTED ACTIVITIES

1. Design a 10- to 15-minute microteach session in which you do the pre-reading activities of a Directed Reading Activity designed to introduce a specific chapter or section of your content area book.

2. Compare the conditions under which you feel a teacher directed discussion or quiz is a highly appropriate follow-up activity to a reading assignment with those conditions under which you feel that a nondirective, or inquiry-centered, discourse is preferable in your content area.

3. Review the section in this chapter that relates to the skills needed for reading in your content area. React to the following questions: Is the list complete? Are there some irrelevant items? Do you see the teaching of such skills as a means of implementing the understanding of content in your subject? Why or why not?

4. Do you use the SQ3R technique when you study? If not, try it for a month. Begin by surveying a complete textbook. Then SQ3R each chapter as you study it. After doing this for one month, evaluate the strengths and/or weaknesses of the approach.

5. Evaluate the strengths and weaknesses of the unit approach. In setting up the criteria against which you will evaluate the unit approach, consider the range of reading achievement in a typical classroom, the range of interests, and any other factors you feel are important. Then consider the possibilities within the unit approach for satisfying these criteria. Would you like to use the unit approach in your teaching? If so, when?

REFERENCES FOR FURTHER READING

Amidon, Edmund and John Hough. (eds.). *Interaction Analysis: Theory, Research, and Application*. Reading, Mass.: Addison-Wesley, 1967.

Ausubel, David. "Learning by Discovery: Rationale and Mystique," *Bulletin of the National Association of Secondary School Principals*, 1961, pp. 18–58.

Ausubel, David. *The Psychology of Meaningful Verbal Learning*. New York: Grune and Stratton, 1963.

Bruner, Jerome. *The Process of Education*. New York: Vintage Books (Random House), 1960.

Fay, Leo. "Reading Study Skills: Math and Science." *Reading and Inquiry*, ed. J. Allen Figurel. Newark, Delaware: International Reading Association, 1965.

Harris, Theodore L. "Making Reading an Effective Instrument of Learning in the Content Fields," in *Reading in High School and College*, N.S.S.E. 47th yearbook, Part II. Chicago, University of Chicago Press, 1949, Chapter 7.

Herber, Harold (ed.). *Developing Study Skills in Secondary Schools*. (Perspectives in Reading #2). Newark, Delaware: International Reading Association, 1965, Chapters 3 and 4.

Herber, Harold. *Teaching Reading in Content Areas*. Englewood Cliffs, N.J.: Prentice-Hall, 1970, Chapters 3 and 4.

Howes, Virgil M. (ed.). *Individualizing Instruction in Reading and Social Studies*. New York: Macmillan, 1970.

Karlin, Robert. *Teaching Reading in High School—Selected Articles*. Indianapolis: Bobbs-Merrill, 1969, Chapter 13.

Marksheffel, Ned D. *Better Reading in Secondary School*. New York: The Ronald Press, 1966, Chapters 2 and 10.

Massialas, Byron and Jack Zevin. *Creative Encounters in the Classroom*. New York: John Wiley, 1967.

Olson, Arthur V. and Wilber S. Ames. (eds.). *Teaching Reading Skills in Secondary Schools*. Scranton, Pa.: International Textbook Co., 1970, Sections 6 and 7.

Robinson, Francis P. "Study Skills for Superior Students in Secondary School." *The Reading Teacher*, **25** (September 1961): 29–33+.

Smith, James A. *Creative Teaching of Reading and Literature in the Elementary School*. Boston: Allyn and Bacon, 1967.

UNIT THREE

IMPROVING LEARNING THROUGH READING DEVELOPMENT IN CONTENT FIELDS

Unit Three focuses on the skills necessary for understanding reading materials in all content areas of the curriculum. Explanations of major skills are given, usually followed by examples of techniques which might be used to teach each skill. Examples are drawn from the following content areas: science, mathematics, social studies, and English.

Chapter 6

TEACHING CONCEPTS THROUGH VOCABULARY BUILDING

How large are the vocabularies of students?

How can we teach denotations and multiple denotations of words?

Which morphemes are important in your content area? How can they be taught?

How can we teach connotations and literary uses of words?

How can we teach students about the fluidity of English, i.e., its ever-changing quality?

What are our three phonic syllabication generalizations? How can they be taught?

INTRODUCTION

Vocabulary power is an extremely important facet of reading power, and vocabulary study for many is intriguing. To help our students develop a strong vocabulary, a variety of techniques can be used.

The content area teacher, of course, is most interested in building vocabulary strength and diversity in his field. Indeed, this is one of his responsibilities. In order to succeed in his duty, the content area teacher should choose the words and techniques best suited to promoting growth in the understanding of the materials students explore and read for his classroom. An understanding of diverse ways of doing this will help him make the wisest choice.

In this chapter several facets of word power are examined. An attempt is made to answer the question, "How large are the vocabularies of children and young people?" Thereafter, the discussion proceeds from the examination of denotations (literal meanings) of words, to connotations (interpretive meanings) of words and figurative language, to diachronic linguistics (changes in language), to a brief consideration of phonic syllabication generalizations, which might help students pronounce multisyllabic words.

VOCABULARY SIZE

How large is your vocabulary? That seems like a simple question, doesn't it? Ask a few friends—or the students in one of your classes. Chances are that after a short deliberation, they will give you a few answers—like 5000 words or 15,000 words, perhaps 20,000 words, or even 80,000 words. Then you will probably be asked which of these estimates is closest to being correct.

The question about vocabulary size is deceptively simple. It is not as difficult a question to answer as "What is truth?" But it possibly has not been answered satisfactorily as yet.

Multiple Denotations

But why not? Ask yourself just what it means to "know" a word or even to "know the meaning of" a word. For example, what does the word *run* mean? To move rapidly? Surely not in these sentences:

> Charles will *run* for class president.
>
> There's a *run* on the bank.
>
> These towels *run* long.
>
> Try not to *run* up a bill.
>
> Jack made a home*run*.

There are at least 130 different definitions of the word *run* in most collegiate dictionaries. How many of these meanings must you know before you can say that you know what the word *run* means? One—or the majority—or all? And so on for other words with multiple denotations.

Multiple Connotations

You know what a *plum* is, don't you? Of course, you had one for breakfast yesterday. But what is "a *plum* of a job?" If you do not know the figurative meaning of *plum*, do you really know the word?

Two Types of Vocabulary

We all have two types of vocabularies—*receptive* and *expressive*. Our receptive vocabulary is composed of the words we recognize through reading and listening. This vocabulary is usually several times larger than our expressive vocabulary, which is made up of the words we use when we speak and write. Our total vocabulary is composed of the words we recognize and/or use in receptive and expressive ways.

Basic and Total Vocabularies

Let me ask you another question: "What is a word?" Simple, you say. It's made up of a letter or letters (when it's written, that is) and has space on both sides of it. Does someone say it's a free morpheme? Or a bound and a free morpheme? Wait, you're ahead of the game.

Let me ask the question this way: Is *sing* a word? Of course! But is *sang* another word? And what about *sung* and *sings* and *singer* and *singing*? Do we have one word or six words? And what about *air*? Is that a word? And *port*—another word? Then what about *airport*? Is that a third word? If we are going to estimate the size of someone's vocabulary, we must define a word. We might talk about the size of our *basic vocabulary*—or the size of our *total vocabulary*, including derivatives and compounds. Obviously, if we talk about the basic vocabulary, the word count will be much smaller than if we talk of the total vocabulary.

Size of Basic Vocabulary

Perhaps an analogy will help you understand what is meant by "knowing" a word in research studies. If I should ask you if you know a certain person, say Marie Ashworth, and you reply yes, I would expect you at least to be able to point her out to me if she were in a small group of people. You might, of course, know her well and be able to tell me many things about her—but this is not necessary when you just say that you know her.

When a researcher says that someone "knows" the meaning of a word, he usually means that the person can select, from several choices, a correct meaning of the word. In-depth meaning is rarely tested. Another technique used is to count the number of different words people say and/or write. Table 6.1 shows the average size of the *basic vocabulary* of children and young people estimated by various researchers.

Table 6.1   Estimates of the average size of children's and young people's basic vocabulary

	Dale *	Smith †	Seegers and Seashore ‡
Grade 1	2,500–3,000	17,000	
Grade 6	8,000	32,000	
Grade 12	14,000–15,000	47,000	
College	18,000		58,000

* Edgar Dale. "Vocabulary Measurement: Techniques and Major Findings," *Elementary English* (December 1965): 895–901, 948.

† M. K. Smith. "Measurement of the Size of General English Vocabulary through the Elementary Grades and High School, *Genetic Psychology Monographs*, **24** (1941): 313–345.

‡ J. C. Seegers and R. H. Seashore. "How Large are Children's Vocabularies?" *Elementary English* (April 1949): 181–194.

You can see that there is a wide variation in the estimates of vocabulary size. Dale's study suggests that school children learn about 1000 *new words* per year, or about three new words per day (365 days of the year). Smith's and Seashore's studies suggest that children learn approximately 3000 *new words* per year, or about eight new words per day. Which seems more realistic to you?

Whichever you choose, what is of extreme importance to you as a teacher is that you be committed to improving the word power of your students—*in your content area.* Your approach must be varied to maintain interest. Let us look at some aspects of vocabulary and some ways of enriching our students' vocabularies.

DENOTATIONS OF WORDS

When we talk about the denotation of a word, we are talking about the literal meaning of the word. If the word has a physical referent, that object represents the denotation. The denotation of the word *cat*, for example, is a four-legged animal, usually with a tail. The denotation of the word *lemon* is a small, yellow citrus fruit. The denotation of *green* is the color we call green.

Denotations are very different from connotations, for connotations of words are interpretive meanings—poetic, emotional, colored. Consider the meaning of the word *cat* in the following sentence: Mrs. Glowgruber is a *cat*. What does *lemon* mean in: This T.V. is a *lemon*. And what is the meaning of *green* in:

Leslie turned *green* when she heard Joanna had won. Can you think of other ways of using these same three words *connotatively?*

One of the most fascinating tales is one that can be told only because a certain word is ambiguous. It may be the horror story of all time. First reported in *Harper's Magazine*, March 1953, the account is by William J. Caughlin and is titled "The Great Mokusatsu Mistake—Was This the Deadliest Error of our Time?"

Mokusatsu is a Japanese word that has no direct English counterpart. In English it can mean "refrain from comment" or "ignore." According to the story, Premier Suzuki, when questioned about the Japanese cabinet's response to the Potsdam Declaration, said that his cabinet "was holding to an attitude of *mokusatsu.*" Mistranslated, news flashed to the Western world that the Japanese chose to "ignore" the ultimatum. Thus were triggered the first two atomic attacks the world has ever known, for "to ignore" is quite different diplomatically from "to refrain from comment."

Certainly of lesser impact on the world is the fact that most words have more than one denotation. A serious vocabulary problem in content area subjects grows from words that have restricted and specific meanings peculiar to a particular subject matter field.

Because a student can pronounce a word, and because he knows a meaning or two for that word, he may think he knows the word every time he sees or hears it. Imagine his confusion when he comes across the word *root* (which to him means the part of a plant that is underground) in the following sentences:

Find the square *root* of 9.

What is the *root* of the word unhappy?

We must find the *root* of his problem.

The love of money is the *root* of all evil.

Imagine his confusion if he knows the following italicized simple words as they are used in the given sentences, but does not know their content area meanings.

Term in mathematics	*But he knows the word as used in:*
1. difference	What *difference* does it make?
2. division	Dad was in the 32nd Army *Division.*
3. product	Many artistic *products* come from Mexico.
4. sign	A cloudy sky is a *sign* of possible rain to come.
5. times	These are sad *times.*

6. reduce	John's mother promised to *reduce*.
7. pound	Don't *pound* too hard on the nail.
8. foot	I cut my *foot*.
9. rod	The curtain *rod* broke.
10. yard	Jack cleaned the *yard*.
11. peck	The bird *peck*ed on the orange.
12. figure	How do you *figure*?
13. base	Jim is at the air *base*.
14. center	The youth *center* closed.
15. point	It's not polite to *point*.
16. side	Whose *side* are you on?
17. power	America is a world *power*.
18. mean	John didn't *mean* that!
19. mode	What *mode* of clothing do you prefer?
20. root	The *root* of the plant was dry.

Term in science	*But he knows the word as used in:*
1. culture	The *culture* of the Southwest is unique.
2. root	Find the square *root*.
3. seal	*Seal* the envelope.
4. iron	Mother will *iron* tomorrow.
5. soil	Please don't *soil* your clothes.
6. mine	That book is *mine*.
7. belt	My *belt* was tight.
8. pole	The boys were playing *pole*-vault.
9. mouth	Sue has a small *mouth*.
10. port	The sailors were on *port* side.
11. rapid	Bob is a *rapid* reader.
12. sound	What does it *sound* like to you?
13. spring	She has a *spring* in her walk.
14. cape	The lawyer's *cape* had to be shortened.
15. plain	Speak *plain*ly.
16. power	Raise six to the eighth *power*.
17. graft	There is much *graft* in the government.

18. cell	The prisoner returned to his *cell*.
19. matter	That doesn't *matter*.
20. boil	Henry was *boil*ing mad.
21. base	The *base* of the triangle was three inches.
22. colon	A *colon* indicates that something is to follow.

Term in social studies	*But he knows the word as used in:*
1. race	Who won the *race*?
2. cabinet	Our kitchen *cabinet* needs a new door.
3. state	Please *state* your question again.
4. union	His *union* suit was torn.
5. act	I wish Sue would *act* logically.
6. bill	Don't forget to pay the *bill*.
7. article	The magazine *article* was interesting.
8. motion	John made a jerky *motion*.
9. duty	You must pay *duty* on that article.
10. power	The telescope is *power*ful.
11. civil	Try to be *civil*.
12. ticket	Did you get a parking *ticket*?
13. trust	I *trust* that you enjoyed the movie.
14. class	The *class* met on Monday and Wednesday.
15. right	Your answer is *right*.
16. left	He *left* before she came.
17. graft	Will the skin *graft* take?
18. period	Put a *period* at the end of a sentence.
19. stable (gov't)	The horse *stable* burned.
20. movement	We observed the *movement* of the stars.
21. draft	There was a *draft* in the room.

Term in English	*But he knows the word as used in:*
1. draft	He was *draft*ed when he became twenty.
2. period	What do you think is the most interesting historical *period*?
3. root	The love of money is said to be the *root* of all evil.

 4. appendix   Her *appendix* gave her trouble.
 5. feet, foot   A *foot* is 12 inches long.
 6. act   It would take an *act* of Congress to change that.
 7. romance   Girls like books about *romance*.
 8. novel   What a *novel* idea!
 9. article   What is that *article* of clothing called?
10. dash   *Dash* to the store.
11. subject   What is your favorite school *subject*?
12. sentence   The judge announced the *sentence*.
13. future tense   The *future* looks *tense*; the past, imperfect.
14. first person   Jack was the *first person* in line.
15. second person   Who was the *second person* in line?
16. critic   You're always *critic*al!
17. style   The flower's *style* was broken.
18. case   Where is your suit*case*?
19. stem   The rose's *stem* was long.
20. scene   What a *scene* she made!

Multiple Meanings of Simple Words

Teaching Strategies

Multiple meanings of words can be taught in a variety of ways.

1. Use the word in a sentence. Have the student select the correct definition from a dictionary:

    Jack Snowden is a *left*-winger, whereas his brother leans to the *right*.

    left—definition number _____
    right—definition number _____

    left (left):   1. of or designating that side toward the east when one faces south.   2. a liberal or radical position or political party.   3. past participle of *leave*.

    right (rīt):   1. straight.   2. in accordance with law.   3. correct.   4. suitable. 5. a conservative or reactionary political position or party.

2. List four sentences, each containing the word being taught. Two of the sentences should use the word in the same way, and this should be the definition that is being taught. Have the student indicate the two sentences that use the word in the same way.

Rod

a) Jim lost his fishing *rod*.

b) A *rod* is a measure of length equal to 5½ yards.

c) The thieves beat their victim with an iron *rod*.

d) Translate the length of a football field from yards to *rods*.

(b, d)

Compact

a) A bilateral *compact* was signed by England and France.

b) Ann took out her *compact* to powder her face.

c) Parking a *compact* is simpler than parking a large car.

d) The *compact* was broken by the four nations concerned.

(a, d)

3. Use illustrations or real objects. Have students draw lines from the sentence to their correct Illustrations.

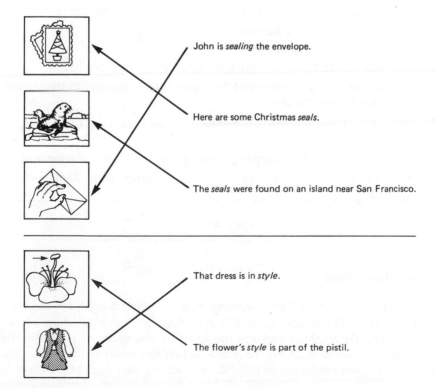

John is *sealing* the envelope.

Here are some Christmas *seals*.

The *seals* were found on an island near San Francisco.

That dress is in *style*.

The flower's *style* is part of the pistil.

4. Have the class play a game.

   a) First, ask each student to write as many sentences as he can using the word *run* (or another word of your choice) with a different meaning each time. Give them between three and five minutes to do this.

   b) Next, randomly divide the class into six groups by having the students count off: 1 - 2 - 3 - 4 - 5 - 6; 1 - 2 - 3 - 4 - 5 - 6; etc. Group all one's together, all two's together, etc.

   c) Each group in turn contributes one sentence using *run* in a way it has not been used before by another group. The first time around, each group giving a correct response gets one point. The second time around, each group gets two points for a correct response; the third time around, three points, etc. Students police this, not the teacher. So students must listen carefully to all group responses.

   d) The group having the highest score wins.

5. A similar game can be played with *overused words*, e.g., *said.* Students supply words that could be used instead of *said*, e.g., replied, responded, retorted, questioned, hissed, commented, shouted, etc. You might expect 150–200 different words to be suggested, so allow enough time.

6. Use a nonsense word to substitute for a new word being taught. Familiar uses of the word must be given in the other sentences. For example:

   a) Mom bought a new electric *flam.*

   b) The forest *flammer* sighted a fire.

   c) There was a wide *flam* in the price of motorcycles from city to city.

   d) The *flam* in reading achievement in a classroom is two-thirds the chronological age of the children.

   e) The mountain *flam* was 200 miles long.

   flam = _____

   The new use of the familiar word is given in *sentence d.* In which sentence is the word used in the same way? _____ What does flam mean in *sentence d*? _____

   _____

   _____

Meanings of New Words

Often, of course, it is not multiple meanings that are being taught, for the word is completely new. The teacher should be sure that the students can pronounce each new word. He might pronounce the word for the class, or have the students use their phonics skills on the word—when the word is phonetic. The following techniques might prove helpful for teaching meanings of new words.

Teaching Strategies

1. Supply a picture of the object the new word represents.

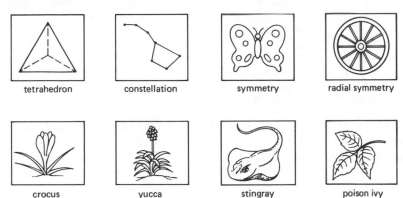

| tetrahedron | constellation | symmetry | radial symmetry |

| crocus | yucca | stingray | poison ivy |

2. Better still, display the real object, a three-dimensional model of it, or take the students on a field trip, or show a film.

3. If context clues are clear in the passage to be read, list on a dittoed sheet the new words, followed by multiple-choice items from which the student makes a selection of the answers he thinks are correct *before* he reads the passage. Then, while he is reading, or after he has finished, he makes corrections. The more corrections, the better, for he is learning that context can serve as a clue to understanding new words.

    Since this is a teaching rather than a testing technique, it is helpful to make the correct multiple-choice item fairly obvious, i.e., obvious after the reading has been done. All choices should grammatically suit the syntax of the sentence, but only one of the choices should make sense semantically.

epitomize: vocalize   typify   gratify   harmonize
vintners: villains   expungers   wine merchants   miners
esquires: administrators   strong men   questioners   horseback riders
envoy: escorter of ships   artery   diplomat   refugee
lyrics   musical patterns   words of poetry   ballads   songs of nature

Passage

Chaucer's life and career seem to epitomize the history of the later Middle Ages. His name, being French for *shoemaker* (the French *chausseur* means "cobbler"), suggests that his family had followed that trade, but for as far back as his ancestors can be traced on English soil, they had been vintners. As the son of a well-to-do wine merchant living in London, and later as a customs official, Chaucer was a member of the rising middle class.

Most of his life Chaucer was associated in one way or another with the royal household. Through his father's court connections, he probably was given his first position as page in the service of Elizabeth, Countess of Ulster, daughter-in-law of

Edward III. While still in her service, he went as a soldier to France in the division of Prince Lionel, Elizabeth's husband and third son of the King. Here, he had the misfortune to be captured by the French, but he was soon ransomed by King Edward. Later Chaucer became one of the King's esquires, which in those days meant that he worked in the administrative department of the King's government. One of his duties was to act as a government envoy on foreign diplomatic missions, carrying on such work as that performed by embassies of our day. His diplomatic missions took him first to France and later to Italy. While in France Chaucer came in contact with French literature, and from his very earliest writings through 1370 a French influence is noticeable. To the French period can be assigned many of his lyrics, which follow models laid down by earlier and contemporary French poets.*

4. A more detailed study of sentence patterns might help students understand how many authors use context clues.[1] Sentence-pattern context clues are usually of the following types: (a) definition or explanation, (b) restatement, (c) examples, (d) contrast. Examples are given below.

A. Definition or explanation

   1. N_1 Lv N_2: Noun$_1$ = word being taught (here in italics)
               Lv   = linking verb (here circled)
               Noun$_2$ = the known, i.e., the definition, etc. (here under-lined)

     a) Remember ≠ (is read) "is not equal to."

     b) The term *set* (means) a group or collection.

     c) A *hybrid plant* (is) the offspring of two parent plants which have opposite or different characteristics.

   2. N_2 Lv N_1

     a) Fish that feed on the bottom of the ocean (are known as) *ground fish.*

     b) The stockholder's share of the company's profits (is called) a *dividend.*

     c) Persons who ridicule each other good-naturedly (are known as) *banterers.*

B. Restatement of meaning in other words

   1. Unknown word in basic sentence, appositive introduced by using the word *or,* or an article—*a, an,* or *the,* or *other signal words* (here circled).

     a) The problem of *farm surpluses,* (or) having more food than is needed, is one of the major agricultural problems of the U.S.

° From *England in Literature* by Robert C. Pooley, *et al.* Copyright © 1968 by Scott, Foresman and Company. Reprinted by permission of the publisher.

b) Many mackerel are caught by *seining*, or snaring with nets.

c) There the Indians had built their homes on *piles*, or long timbers, above the water near the shores of the lake.

d) Such an airship is called a *dirigible*, a word that means steerable.

e) We will begin our discussion of the parts of a cell with the *nucleus*, the control center of all cell activity.

f) *Barbados*, an eastern island of the Lesser Antilles, is one of the most crowded lands on earth.

g) *Sieve tubes* are the most prominent, appearing as rows of rather large living cells that have thin walls and protoplasm but no nucleus.

h) A current of this kind is part of a *convection current*, that is, a current that carries heat.

i) The guards were ordered to be *neutral*, that is, they were not to take sides in the fight.

2. Unknown word given in the appositive

a) Each section, or *stage*, is a rocket with its own fuel and burning chamber.

b) Inside the cortex lies the innermost layer of bark, the *phloem*.

c) There are six different arrangements, or *permutations*, of the letters x, y, and z.

C. Examples help clarify a family name (here underlined)

1. Family name given first, followed by examples

a) *Ground fish*, including cod, hake, haddock, and halibut, are caught along the Atlantic coast.

b) *Condiments*, such as cinnamon, nutmeg, and paprika, were once too expensive for most people.

c) Eyesight is well developed in the *primates*—gorillas, chimpanzees, orangutans, gibbons, monkeys, marmosets, and lemurs.

2. Examples given first, followed by the family name

a) Rats and mice are among the most common *rodents*.

b) The <u>cow, ox, bison, sheep, goat, antelope, camel, llama, giraffe, deer, elk caribou, and moose</u> are all *ruminants*. These animals have four-chambered stomachs.

c) <u>3 + □ = 7 and 10 − □ = 6</u>. This sentence is neither true nor false because *both clauses are open. (open clause)*

D. Contrast—tells what the word does not mean, not necessarily what it does mean

1. Contrasting phrase introduced by the word *not* (here circled)

a) This is a *survey*, (not) a diagnostic, test.

b) This is a *nebulous*, (not) a clear, statement.

c) Mr. Jones was noted for his *caustic*, (not) gentle, remarks.

2. Compound sentences—contrasting independent clause introduced by the word *but* (here circled)

a) The older folk were <u>eager</u> to go home, (but) the children were *reluctant* to leave the beach.

b) Much of the land in the Maracaibo Basin is <u>swampy</u>, (but) the *cultivable* land is fertile.

c) The mountain goat looks <u>clumsy</u>, (but) he is remarkably *nimble*.

5. Students might keep files of *flash cards* for learning and reviewing words. Three-by-five cards might be cut into four or five pieces. On one side of the card, the student could write the new word and also use it in a sentence. On the other side of the card, the meaning should be given. For example:

amphibious The amphibious craft was seen on the shoreline.	compunction Roseanne felt no compunction after telling the lie.
↕	↕
amphibious (ăm-fĭb ĭ-ŭs): able to live or navigate both on land and in water	compunction (kŏm-pŭngk shŭn): regret, a sense of guilt

Such cards can be flexibly used. One a day might be taped to a bathroom mirror, or the student might clip a different one on a notebook each day—or until he learns it. The cards could be kept in several files—one file for words he thinks he knows well. These might be reviewed monthly. Another file could be composed of words he is not sure of, to be reviewed weekly. New words could be in another file—to be studied daily. Rubber bands or paper clips around each file should be sufficient to keep the cards together. Things should be kept simple so the cards can be stuck into a pocket or purse. At times, students might pair off, or work in larger groups, quizzing each other on their words.

6. Cards of formerly known and new words could be filed according to some classification system. This technique is known as *card sorting* and is a useful technique for *concept development* and for laying the foundation for *breaking the stereotype*, an area of critical thinking.

    For example, in how many *different* ways could the following words (ideas) be grouped? (Note that each different way of grouping results from stressing different aspects, or facets, of the words (ideas). Unusual classifications result from creative thinking, i.e., synthesis level of the cognitive domain—divergent production. Common classifications result from convergent thinking.)

7. In a content area classroom, there could be a *card bank*, a container with a hole large enough for a hand to go through. Each student could insert one or more cards per week with content area words he knows. Periodically—or at the end of the hour when time permits—a "worddown" could be held. One student would draw the words and write them on the chalkboard. The student whose turn it is must pronounce the word correctly, use it in a sentence, and define it—or else sit down and let the chance go to the other team. (When the word is picturable, the student might sketch it on the board, possibly in lieu of defining it.)

Morphology

Morphology is an area of descriptive linguistics. *Morpheme* is a useful new word for a very useful old idea. A *morpheme* (often called a *morph*, for short) is the smallest unit (eme) of meaning (morph) in our language. The word *cat* is a morpheme, as are the words *dog, fish, octopus, rhinoceros,* and *blotch*. The following are also morphemes: *un-, re-, super-, trans-, -ful, -less*.

It can be seen from these examples that there are two kinds of morphemes —*free* morphemes and *bound* morphemes. Free English morphemes are uninflected English words (cat, dog, rhinoceros, etc.). Put two together and you have a compound word: airport, oatmeal, housewife, scarecrow.

A bound morpheme (formerly known as a prefix or suffix, or possibly a root), on the other hand, must be attached to another morpheme—*either free or bound*—to form a word.* Examples of a bound morpheme combined with a

---

* Some linguists do not consider all suffixes to be morphemes. Some suffixes such as *-ing, -ed, -ly, -er,* and *-est* are still referred to as inflections, having little or no meaning, serving principally to alter the part of speech. Other suffixes, such as *-less* and *-ful,* which function principally to change meaning, are considered morphemes. At the present time it appears to this writer a waste of time to split hairs over this terminology—except for linguistic researchers who are formulating our base for reorganized thinking in linguistic terms.

free morpheme to compose a word are: *un*kind, *re*make, thought*ful*. Examples of two bound morphemes combined to form a word are: *geography*, *philosophy*, and *inert*. The simplest such formations for children to understand are combinations of a bound morpheme with a free English morpheme.

Teaching Strategies

Sequence in teaching morphology might progress from:

1. *First*—teaching simple compounds, such as:

milkman	postman	mailman	fireman
boxcar	oatmeal	airport	windmill
sandbox	baseball	toothbrush	flagpole
houseboat	birthday	horseshoe	classmate

It should be pointed out to children that these words are divided into syllables between the two morphemes (words).

2. *Second*—teaching simple bound morphemes attached to *free* English morphemes, such as:

unwrap	unfair	unpaid	unhappy
unknown	unlike	unlock	unbroken
dislike	disloyal	disagree	dishonest
disappear	disown	distrust	displease
refill	return	rewrite	recount
reopen	repay	rename	recall
indoors	incorrect	inland	inhuman
infield	informal	inborn	inlaid
powerful	thoughtful	helpful	graceful
powerless	thoughtless	helpless	graceless

Students should be taught that (a) the words are syllabicated between the two morphemes, and (b) the morphemes have *meaning*. An exercise such as the following might be helpful.

Prefixes

1. anti—against
2. ante—before
3. pro—forth, for
4. trans—across
5. dis—not
6. ex—out of, from
7. sub—under
8. auto—self

9. hyper—above, more than
10. tele—far, distant
11. non—not
12. re—again
13. circum—around
14. pseudo—false
15. contra—against
16. a—not, without
17. uni—one
18. mono—one
19. bi—two
20. tri—three
21. poly—many
22. omni—all
23. pan—all
24. semi—half
25. hemi—half
26. inter—between
27. intro—into
28. in—not
29. in—into, within
30. post—after
31. pre—before
32. homo—same

Word	Prefix	Prefix meaning	Word meaning
1. antisocial	anti	against	against society
2. anteroom			
3. proceed			
4. transport			
5. dislike			
6. extract			
7. submarine			
8. automobile			
9. hyperactive			
10. telegraph			
11. nonconformist			
12. return			
13. circumference			
14. pseudonym			
15. contradict			
16. atypical			
17. unicycle			
18. monocle			
19. bigamy			
20. trilateral			
21. polytheism			
22. omnipotent			
23. pan-American			
24. semicircle			
25. hemisphere			
26. international			
27. introspect			
28. indecisive			

29. inside
30. postgraduate
31. prefix
32. homogeneous

3. *Third*—Morphemic combinations important to content area subjects should be taught in meaningful ways. See the chart in Appendix C for some morphemes important in understanding various content area concepts and reading materials. You can easily add to this chart by becoming aware of the morphemes that are commonly used in reading materials in your field.

4. When a widely used morpheme occurs in a reading assignment or in a class discussion, take time to write it on the board. Ask students if they know the meaning. Next, ask them if they can suggest any other words that use the same morpheme. Write these on the board, and then, if possible, branch off as illustrated below. The teacher should be able to fill in when necessary.

For example: The morpheme is *-nym*, as in the word synonym.

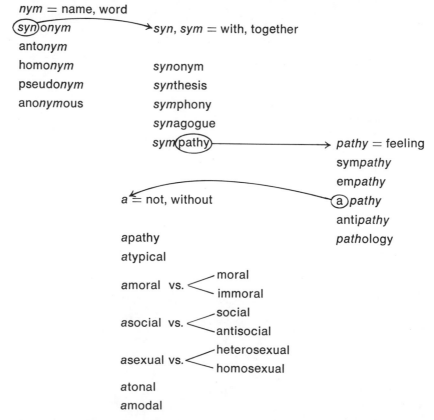

And that's enough for one day.

5. Morpheme discs can be designed easily by the students or the teacher. Pick morphemes that are frequently used in your subject. For example:

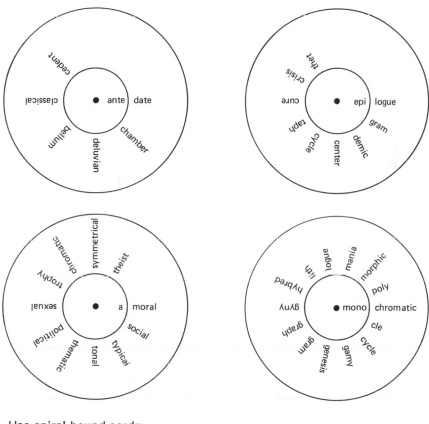

6. Use spiral-bound cards:

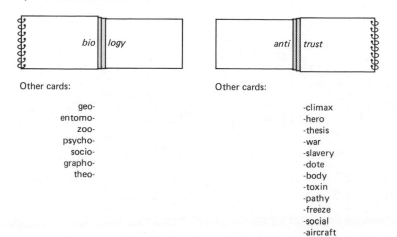

Other cards:

geo-
entomo-
zoo-
psycho-
socio-
grapho-
theo-

Other cards:

-climax
-hero
-thesis
-war
-slavery
-dote
-body
-toxin
-pathy
-freeze
-social
-aircraft

7. Use fold-ins:

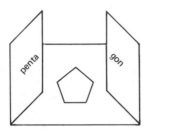
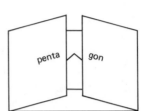

8. Use crossword puzzles. They're easy to make. Keep a supply of graph paper and use only infrequent crossovers. For example, if you wish to use the words telegram, telephone, teletype, telescope, phonograph, stenography, photograph, geography, cablegram, autograph, fill them in on your graph paper, thus:

				G					T								
				E		T			E								
				O		E	T	E	L	E	S	C	O	P	E		
				G		L			E								
			C	R		E			P	P							
			A	A	U	T	O	G	R	A	P	H	H				
			B	P		R			O	O							
			L	H		A			N	N							
T	E	L	E	T	Y	P	E		M		S	T	E	N	O	G	R	A	P	H	Y
			G										G				
			R					P	H	O	T	O	G	R	A	P	H	
			A										A				
			M										P				
													H				

Next, clip this sheet over a ditto stencil and use a ruler to draw in the needed boxes. Take off the graph paper and number the boxes. Write the key on the bottom of the page, thus:

Across:
4. instrument for "seeing from far"
7. the writing of one's own name
8. typing from far
9. writing in shorthand
10. picture writing, "light writing"

Down:
1. "earth writing," study or writing about the earth
2. "sound from far"
3. "writing from far"
5. message sent through an underwater tube
6. "sound writing"

9. For fun, have students make up new words by combining morphemes. Have them either define the new word or illustrate it. Remind them that there are many newly coined words: astronaut, cosmonaut, aquanaut, television, etc.

Busalogue

Three new words were recently minted by the Army in a single written order: *embus*, *debus* and *reembus*, meaning, respectively, to get on, to get off and to get back on a motor bus. Splendid! If the Army doesn't mind, we'd like to play too. How about *suprabus*, meaning to ride on top? Or *subbus*, to travel hanging on to the crankcase like a hobo under a coal car? A platoon that has reached its destination in a single vehicle might be said to *monobus*; but if the platoon had to transfer, it would *bibus*. (The driver from whom the soldiers obtained their transfers was obviously a *bus-agogue*.) If the weather was pleasant, the scenery beautiful and the bus not over-crowded, the platoon *eubussized* the trip; if contrary conditions prevailed, and there was a blowout in the left hind *busotrope*, the trip would probably be *dysbustic* for one and all. A soldier who turned bus-happy and rode on them to excess would *hyperbus*, while a soldier who hated buses and didn't use them enough for his own good would *hypobus*. Soldiers arriving at a new post by bus would be *imbusogrants*; any rookie who *misbussed* would be sure to get good and chewed by his sergeant. To *heterobus* clearly means to get on a bus containing members of the opposite sex; after the GIs met up with the Wacs, the vehicle would be a *zoobus*, a bus filled with life. Any love affairs that resulted would be *busogenic* in origin; any crackups, *busomatic*. What the Army needs is a less inhibited *busicographer*.*

Can you make a list of words that match the several parts of this development? How logical are the words presented here? Can you add further *bus*-words, such as *busophile* (or *-phobe*)?

Symbols and Abbreviations

Symbols and abbreviations have a unique place in vocabulary-concept development. Symbols are not an alphabetic, or phonic, counterpart for the oral word or words they represent. Abbreviations may or may not be shortened alphabetic counterparts for their words. An abbreviation is a higher level abstraction than is the printed word because it is a shortened way of representing the word. A symbol is an alternative way of expressing an idea; a symbol does not necessarily signal the word, but may, in fact, bypass the word to signal the idea.

Symbols

Many of the "words" of mathematics are symbols, i.e., the symbols represent an idea, possibly a process. They may or may not represent (in the reader's mind) their *oral* counterpart. Thus, for some students, the symbol is easier to read than are the words it represents. For other students—those who go from symbol to oral counterpart—it is more difficult.

For example, when a student sees

$$6 + 2 = ?,$$

does he automatically respond 8, or does he say to himself "6 plus 2 equals" 8? When he sees

$$5 - 3 = ?,$$

does he automatically respond 2, or does he say to himself "5 minus 3 equals" 2?

In other words, does he go from symbol to concept, or does he go from symbol to word to concept? The symbol is not an alphabetical representation of the oral word; however, most printed words are. So, the student in mathematics

---

* From *Life*, December 1, 1952. Copyright, 1952, by Time, Incorporated. Reprinted by permission.

needs a type of paired-associate skill that those who read in other fields do not need.

When a student of mathematics sees

+, he must think *plus* (i.e., the word and/or the concept)

−, he must think *minus*

=, he must think *equals*

≠, he must think *does not equal*.

If he has not memorized these symbols, he is unable to supply the oral counterpart. Phonics cannot be used. Yet some students find that reading the symbols is easier than reading the words. The important point here is that the task is different.

How many of the following commonly used mathematics symbols do those of you who are not in mathematics remember:

$$+ \quad - \quad = \quad \neq \quad < \quad > \quad \sim \quad \cong \quad \Sigma \quad \div \quad \% \quad @ \quad '' \quad ' \quad \times$$

$$\pm \quad \sqrt{} \quad \pi \quad // \quad \triangle \quad \perp \quad \odot \quad \square \quad \square \quad \angle \quad \llcorner \quad \therefore$$

Abbreviations

Certain abbreviations commonly used in some content area subjects may cause problems among students. Some examples follow.

in mathematics   bu, doz, ft, gal, hr, in., lb, min, oz, pk, pt, qt, sq, wk, yd, yr

in English: e.g., i.e., *ibid.*, *op. cit.*, *viz.*, A.S., Fr., Sp., etc.

in chemistry: Ag, Al, As, B, Ba, Bi, Br, C, Ca, etc.

WORD CONNOTATIONS AND FIGURATIVE LANGUAGE

When we talk about denotations of words, we are referring to the literal, or scientific, meanings of words. But when we talk about *connotations* of words, we are referring to the interpretive meanings of these words—the poetic and emotional meanings.

Most science and mathematics books are written to convey precise information. The words selected by the authors are usually those that suggest very specific meanings—ones that are generally agreed upon by all who write and read in the field. However, the language of the poet or other literary writer, as well as the language of many social scientists and newspaper writers, is intended to sway our feelings or to convince us of a particular point of view. Words chosen by such writers are frequently being used connotatively, and the connotative meanings may vary from individual to individual.

For example, what is your idea of a *liberal*? Ask your friends what they think it means to be liberal. Do the same for the word *conservative*. Is it "good" to be a liberal in politics and a conservative in religion? What does it mean to have *liberal* moral values? What about *radical*? *Conservative*? *Reactionary*? Are you to the *left* in some ways, to the *right* in others? What do *you* mean by *left* and *right*? What does your neighbor mean? What does a particular historian mean? Remember, something you might consider to be the greatest thing in the world, someone else might scorn:

Reprinted through the courtesy of the Chicago Tribune–New York News Syndicate, Inc.

Simple Connotations

Children might be introduced to the idea of connotative language by being taught denotative meanings of words with their connotative counterparts. For example, denotatively, a *chicken* is a fowl. Connotatively, *chicken* might mean cowardly (He's a chicken) or glamorous (What a chick).

Ask students to give the denotations and some possible connotations of the following words: *dog, monkey, yellow, pink, peach, apple.* Point out that denotations are scientific, literal meanings; where there is a *physical referent*, the denotation is synonymous with it. Connotations are emotional meanings—and may be pleasant or unpleasant.

A delightful verse that appeared in *The Saturday Evening Post* might serve to introduce young people to the idea of connotations and to the pleasant and unpleasant associations words used connotatively might suggest.

Semantics

Call a woman a kitten, but never a cat;
You can call her a mouse, cannot call her a rat;
Call a woman a chicken, but never a hen;
Or you surely will not be her caller again.

You can call her a duck, cannot call her a goose;
You can call her a deer, but never a moose;
You can call her a lamb, but never a sheep;
Economic she likes, but you can't call her cheap.

You can say she's a vision, can't say she's a sight;
And no woman is skinny, she's slender and slight;
If she should burn you up, say she sets you afire,
And you'll always be welcome, you tricky old liar.*

---

* Reprinted with permission from *The Saturday Evening Post*, © 1946 The Curtis Publishing Company.

Teaching Strategies

1. Ask students to suggest as many *animal names* as they can that are used connotatively. For example:

cat	duck	lamb	worm
kitten	goose	sheep	tiger
mouse	deer	monkey	fox
rat	moose	beaver	wolf

Have students use these words connotatively in sentences or phrases.

2. Ask students to suggest as many *growing things* as they can that are used connotatively. For example:

peach (He's a peach.)	lemon (The car's a lemon.)
peachy (Everything's peachy.)	potato (hot potato)
apple (apple of his eye)	pea (two peas in a pod)
plum (plum of a job)	violet (shrinking violet)
nut (What a nut he is.)	pansy (He's a pansy.)
egg (good egg, bad egg)	vegetable (He is a vegetable.)
banana (top banana)	

3. Ask students to suggest as many *colors* as they can that are used connotatively. For example:

green (with envy)	pink (glowing)
green (naive)	red (anger)
blue (sad)	red (communism)
white (with fear)	red (in the red—losing money)
white (purity)	rosy (happy)
yellow (cowardly)	brown (brown-nose)

4. Contrast the connotative meanings of colors with the ideas the visual image of the same colors represent, for example, in national and school flags. For example:

red (anger, communism)	red (valor)
white (with fear, purity)	white (purity, hope, truth)
blue (sad)	blue (justice, loyalty, sincerity)

Figurative Language

"Figures of speech" are a form of connotative, or nonliteral, language. Some of the most commonly used figures of speech are *similes, metaphors, personification,* and *allusions.* Such figures of speech are commonly found in literature and in slanted writing. Frequently, figurative language is used to clarify a difficult idea.

Similes

A simile is an analogy in which two dissimilar things are shown to be alike, at least in one respect. In a simile, the word *like* or *as* is used. For example:

> "*Words are like leaves,*
>   And where they most abound
>   Much fruit of sense beneath
>   Is rarely found. . . .
>
> "But *true expression,*
>   *Like the unchanging sun*
>   Clears and improves
>   Whate're it shines upon."

Addison, "Essay on Criticism"

"The kingdom of heaven is like to a grain of mustard seed . . ." (Matt. 13:31)

"The kindom of heaven is like unto leaven, which a woman took, and hid in three measures of meal, till the whole was leavened." (Matt. 13.33)

"The bluejay shouted like a noisy politician."

"Airplanes roar like demons tearing through the sky to strike at their foes."

Metaphors

Metaphors, like similes, are analogies, but the word *like* or *as* is not used.

They are two peas in a pod.

Theresa is a vegetable.

He is a peacock.

"Merry larks are ploughmen's clocks."

"All the world's a stage."

"Dry leaves are little brown kites riding the wind."

"The clouds are fairy castles in the sky."

Personification

Personification is the technique of representing a thing or an animal as a person. For example:

The flames ate the house.

Fear lit flames of horror in her eyes.

Money talks.

The ocean threatens with the voice of an angry giant.

The pages of my book speak to me with many voices.

Allusions

An allusion is an indirect reference to a person—real or mythical—or to a place or a thing. For example:

1. Someone once said, "The only thing wrong with Shaw's *Pygmalion* is its name." Although the title describes the play perfectly, most people do not understand the allusion.

Pygmalion, of course, was a Greek sculptor who carved an ivory statue of a maiden and then fell in love with it. Mere human women could not compete, in Pygmalion's eyes, with his own creation. He therefore prayed to the goddess Aphrodite for a wife who would resemble the statue. Aphrodite brought the statue to life.

In Shaw's play, Professor Henry Higgins is Pygmalion, and Eliza Doolittle is the statue—molded not from ivory, but from "a squashed cabbage leaf." It is fascinating to follow the allusion through the play, including the Epilogue, in which Shaw comments that Eliza should not marry the professor, but rather Freddie. Why does Shaw say this? Remember the *allusion*.

2. Research relating to mythology is interesting.

   a) Is *January* an appropriate name for the first month of the year? Who is *Janus*?

   b) Is *cereal* named appropriately? Who is *Ceres*?

   c) Was the ship *Titanic* appropriately named? Who is *Titan*?

   d) Have you ever been *tantalized*? Who is *Tantalus*?

   e) Where does *hypnotize* come from? Who is *Hipnos*?

3. Biblical allusions also abound.

   a) What was meant when Moishe Dayan was called a modern *David*?

   b) Who was *Job*, as in Job's Daughters?

   c) What does it mean to "raise *cain*"?

   d) Have you ever felt like *Daniel*?

   e) "East Pakistanis engage in mass *exodus*." Exodus?

   f) The *genesis* of the idea—Genesis?

4. Modern allusions are also common.

   a) Have you ever heard of anyone called an *Einstein*?

b) Did anyone ever say to you that "if you take that job, you'll be going to *Timbucktu*"?

c) He's met his *Waterloo.* To what does this refer?

d) She's a modern *Florence Nightingale.*

DIACHRONIC LINGUISTICS

One very enjoyable area of language that is often overlooked is the area of diachronic linguistics. Use your morphology to figure out what diachronic means. *Dia-* means "through," as in diameter (measure through), diathermy (heat through the skin), diagnose (to know, or see through). *Chron-* means "time," as in chronological (time order), chronic (lasting a long time), and chronometer (a highly accurate kind of clock). Diachronic, therefore, means through time, and diachronic linguistics is a description of language as it changed through time.

The English language has changed in several major ways. One such change has been in *sentence pattern.*[2] English has evolved as a language of very straightforward syntax—NV, NVAd, NVN, NVNN, NVNA, VLvN, NLvA, NLvAd, and transformations and elaborations of these patterns. *Sound patterns* of words have also changed, and correspondingly, so have many spellings. *Meanings* of some words have changed. *New words* have been added to our language.

The study of diachronic linguistics for students below the college level ought to be pure pleasure. There is no need to be overly technical about it. The major stress ought to be to make children and young people *aware* of the fact that *language grows and changes*—all living languages do. Such a concept cannot be taught in the abstract. Numerous examples are needed to make the point clear.

Students are fascinated by finding the many ways our language has grown and is presently growing. Language, like human behavior, changes continuously. Only dead languages, like Latin, do not change. Let us look at some simple and enjoyable ways of making this point.

Sound Changes

English has undergone a "great vowel shift" from Old English to Middle English to Modern English. This shift, though regular, is quite complex, too much so to hold the interest of most precollege students. However, if you are an English teacher, your class would enjoy comparing Chaucer in the original with modern translations of the same passages.

The consonant shift, however, is much easier to grasp and demonstrates some major changes in sounds of English. Frequently referred to as *Grimm's law*, after one of the brothers Grimm, who described the change, it is also often called the *First Germanic Consonant Shift*, the only Germanic consonant shift which affected English.

Broadly stated, what happened was:

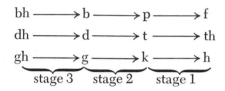

Each original set of consonants changed only once; for example, the *b, d, g* that resulted from the shift of *bh, dh, gh* did not shift further. Indeed, had they done so, the words formerly distinguished by these sounds would have fallen together as homophones, losing distinction and producing much confusion. The whole process is understood to have taken place in three stages; after *p, t,* and *k* had shifted, it was possible for *b, d,* and *g* to shift without producing homophones.*

Table 6.2   Sound and spelling changes occurring as a result of Grimm's law

Grimm's law describes these sound and spelling shifts which occurred in the Germanic languages, including the ancestor of Old English.		From the language named, English later borrowed a cognate and used it in more formal words, such as the following:	
Original	New	Language	Words
dent	tooth, teeth	Latin	*dent*al, *dent*ist, in*dent*
gno	know	Greek	dia*gno*se, a*gno*stic
pater	father	Latin	*pater*nal
mater	mother	Latin	*mater*nal
ped	foot, feet	Latin	*ped*al, *ped*estal, tri*pod*
centum	hundred	Latin	*cent*, *cent*ipede
pisces	fish	Latin	*pis*cary, *Pisces*
kardiakos	heart	Greek and Latin	*card*iac
canis	hound	Greek and Latin	*can*ine
corn	horn	Latin	*corn*ucopia
tris	three	Greek and Latin	*tri-* (*tri*angle, *tri*cycle)
host	guest (circular shift)	Latin	*host*

---

* Stuart Robertson and Frederic G. Cassidy. *The Development of Modern English*, 2d. ed. Englewood Cliffs, N.J.: Prentice-Hall, 1954, p. 29. Reprinted by permission.

Table 6.2 shows the alteration of some words according to Grimm's law. Note that these changes involve only consonant shifts. Some vowels shifted later.

Another interesting sound shift is one that is occurring today. If you listen to yourself—and other people—speaking, you will notice that very often in words of three syllables, the middle vowel, and therefore the middle syllable, is being dropped. We just do not say it. Of course, some people do—but enough do not. The change is widespread nationally. Here are some of the words that are changing:

rest*au*rant	fam*i*ly	prob*a*bly
om*e*let	av*e*rage	comp*a*ny
int*e*rest	min*e*ral	diff*e*rence
gen*e*ral	crim*i*nal	po*e*m

Try to think of other examples. Ask your students to help you.

Changes in Meaning

We can also look back to see how meanings of words have changed. Some common types of changes are *amelioration* and its opposite, *perjoration*; also, *generalization* and its opposite, *specialization*. Today is an age of both *euphemism* and *antieuphemism* and of *hyperbole*.

Amelioration

Meanings of some words have ameliorated, or elevated. For example, at one time, any youth was a *knight*, and a minstrel was what we consider a buffoon today. A *minister*, now a servant of God, was a common servant. If one was *enthusiastic*, it meant he was fanatical. And *nice* meant ignorant.

Pejoration

The opposite trend is perhaps more common. Pejoration means degredation. Meanings of more words seem to pejorate than to elevate. For example, a *villain*, rather than a scoundrel, was a person from a villa, a farm servant. *Lust* meant pleasure or joy. A *lewd* person was a lay person, unlearned, but not indecent or obscene. Chaucer once described someone as "lewd and nice," i.e., unlearned and ignorant. *Lewd* has pejorated, whereas *nice* has ameliorated. A *pirate* was one who adventured. And any boy was an *imp*. Today *propaganda* is pejorating, as is *criticism*. Can you think of other examples?

Generalization

Some words broaden, or extend, in meaning. Once upon a time, when one *shipped* something, one sent it by ship. Logical? But today, we "ship" by plane, truck, train, car, or any other way we can find. If we *sailed* the Atlantic, we *sailed*—but not today! We might "sail" to Europe, but does anyone think we're taking a sailboat?

At one time only men were described as *virtuous*. To call a lady virtuous was disastrous—like calling a woman *virile* today (the same root). And once, a *picture* was a painting only—not a photograph, a collage, a print, etc.

Specialization

Word meanings also change in the opposite way. And, no doubt, more words specialize than generalize. A *girl* used to be a young boy or girl. Starving meant dying, but today it is just one way of dying. *Meat* was any food, not just the flesh of an animal. And *coast* was any border.

When there are two or more words in our language that mean the same thing, all but one will drop out, or the words will diverge in meaning. At one time there were three words meaning "small animal": animal, beast, and deer. Today, *animal* is the general term, *beast* often means a brutal creature, and *deer* is a particular kind of small animal.

Divergence and specialization lead to preciseness in definition. For example, one speaks of a *pack* of wolves, but a *herd* of cattle, and a *flock* of sheep, a *school* of fish, and a *swarm* of bees. One speaks of the *aroma* of coffee, but the *bouquet* of wine, and the *fragrance* or *perfume* of flowers.

To call a person *fatherly* is different from calling him *paternal* (though the words are cognates). And *motherly* differs in meaning from its cognate, *maternal*.

Much new terminology is now being used in mathematics—in the new math. Also, new terminology is used in English classes—especially in relation to linguistics . In both cases many of the words are not new, but they are being used in specialized ways. In some cases the terms *are* new, possibly newly coined, e.g., grapheme, phoneme, and morpheme.

Euphemism and antieuphemism

If we wish to be delicate in our speech, we use euphemisms—at times. If we wish to be direct, and possibly harsh, we use antieuphemisms—at times. A euphemism is a pleasant term for what may be a very unpleasant idea. Since the idea is unpleasant, the euphemism remains a euphemism only for a time and then it, too, becomes unpleasant, and a new euphemism is needed.

Note the names for women's sizes: junior, misses, women's half-sizes, petites. Women's blouses are sized large, so that almost anyone can take size 12, 14, or 16, but skirts are smaller, so that most can take size 8, 10, or 12. Stretch stockings are not sized small, medium, large, and extra large, but short, average, long, and extra long. This pleases milady, for no woman wants to be considered extra large, but extra long is fine.

For awhile, one rarely used the term *to die*, but instead used *to pass away*. To die has returned, however, especially if we are speaking of a person who is not close to us. Cemetery has become memorial park. And sometime during World War II, "replacements" no longer were sent into battle; instead, "re-inforcements" went in. We all felt better about it. And the draft has become the selective service.

Another example is the word *symphony*, which caught on briefly as a euphemism for melting pot. What do the contributions of individual instruments of a symphony orchestra suggest to you that might be similar to contributions of various peoples in our society? Does *melting pot* suggest something quite different?

Hyperbole

Hyperbole is an overstatement, an obvious exaggeration. With some people, things are never fine or good, but *grand, superb, perfect, gorgeous, fantastic*—or *dreadful* or *horrid*. *Unique*, which used to mean one of a kind or without equal, has been replaced by *absolutely unique*. Some things are *quite unique*.

New Words Enter Our Language

How do new words come into our language? Chiefly by coining and by borrowing (stealing?).

Coining

We can coin new words in a variety of ways:

1. We *combine morphemes* in new ways:

   aquanaut   cosmonaut   astronaut   television

2. We *blend* the first part of one word with the last part of another:

$$
\begin{aligned}
smoke + fog &= \text{smog} \\
breakfast + lunch &= \text{brunch} \\
motor + hotel &= \text{motel} \\
boat + hotel &= \text{botel} \\
float + hotel &= \text{flotel} \\
skirt + short &= \text{skort} \\
slip + glide &= \text{slide} \\
twist + whirl &= \text{twirl} \\
flash + blush &= \text{flush (flush of pride)} \\
squeeze + crash &= \text{squash}
\end{aligned}
$$

3. *Acronyms* are words formed from the first (or first few) letters of several words:

UNESCO—*United Nations Educational, Social, Cultural Organization*

SNAFU —*Situation Normal: All Fouled Up*

What do these represent? In time, we forget because the acronym is enough to convey meaning.

WAVES	RADAR	NATO
WACS	SONAR	SCUBA
CARE	SALT	

4. Slang words or expressions come and go. Occasionally, however, one stays. What do these mean?

dinged   zapped   waxed   mushroom people

Her heels were on fire = she was in a hurry

Antsville = a place full of people

Pile up the z's = go to sleep and snore

Stable your horse = park your car

Slang is novel, fresh, and picturesque when it enters our language. Too soon, however, it brands its user as stereotyped and unimaginative—unless he has a *new* slang expression.

Borrowing

Fortunately, we do not have to spend Washingtons (American dollars) for the words we borrow from our neighbors around the world—or we would really be broke. Both the English and Americans have been heavy borrowers, and that is one reason our language is extremely rich and colorful.

Page through a well-illustrated dictionary. Whenever you see an interesting picture, check to see from which language the word came. Here are some samples:

American Indian	*Spanish*	*Italian*
pecan	patio	violin
totem pole	maize	cameo
moccasin	potato	volcano
tepee	chocolate	piano
toboggan	mosquito	opera

raccoon	taco	vest
chipmunk	llama	

French	*German*	*Hindi*
pork	dachshund	cheetah
venison	otter	bungalow
genie	wiener	shampoo
humor	dollar	pajamas
croissant	house	jungle
calendar	edelweiss	

Greek	*Scandinavian*	*Australian*
alphabet	sister	kangaroo
circus	teeter totter	boomerang
octopus	sky	

Arabic	*Russian*	*Eskimo*
candy	sputnik	kayak
algebra	babushka	igloo
sugar		

Turkish	*Persian*	*Japanese*
coffee	caravan	kimono
yogurt		

Teaching Strategies

1. Collect as many euphemisms as possible. Contrast them in meaning with the words for which they are substitutes.
2. Collect as many acronyms as you can. See if you can coin some new ones.
3. Make your own exercises, like the following one for mathematics, using words in your content area.

Greek	*Latin*	*Arabic*	*Hebrew*	*Chinese*
geometry	triangle	zero	abacus	tangram
tetrahedron	set	algebra		
labyrinth	tangent	zenith		
octagon	square			

Write the language from which the words for the following illustrations come:

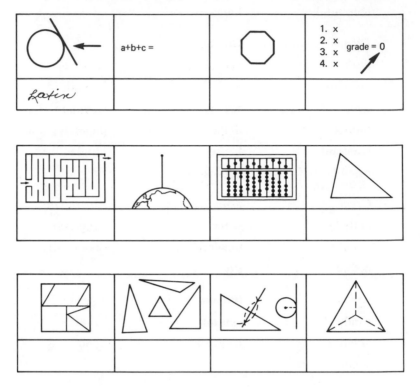

PHONIC SYLLABICATION

Sometimes students know a word orally, but are unable to pronounce it when they see it in print. Most English words are phonically regular, and if students know and can apply fewer than 20 phonic generalizations which have proved useful, they are able to decode these "regular" words.[3] Thus, they would be able to pronounce words they see in writing and, if they have them in their listening vocabulary, they would be able to derive meaning from the written symbol. They would save time by not having to refer to the dictionary so often.

Among the most useful phonic generalizations for secondary students to know are those that relate to syllabication. English and English language arts teachers might wish to teach these to their students directly. Teachers of other subjects may wish to study these so that when they are teaching new words to their classes, they can reinforce the use of these generalizations.

The methodology for teaching these generalizations progresses from teaching: (1) *auditory discrimination* of syllables, to (2) *visual discrimination* of syllables, to (3) actual syllabication according to three generalizations.

Teaching Strategies

1. Ask students to say several one-syllable words, then two-syllable words, then three-syllable words (auditory discrimination).

2. Ask students to number from 1 to 30 on a sheet of paper. *The teacher reads the following words*, each accompanied by its number. The student writes the number of syllables each word contains (auditory discrimination). Students *do not* see these words in print.

1. October	11. remote	21. rose
2. March	12. any	22. daisy
3. June	13. concern	23. complete
4. apple	14. elephant	24. statue
5. number	15. dinosaur	25. window
6. professor	16. coffee	26. piñata
7. main	17. pitcher	27. organ
8. linguistics	18. lamp	28. cello
9. ornament	19. carpet	29. phonograph
10. ten	20. garden	30. mouse

The teacher checks individual papers to see which students have made errors. If any student has made *more than three errors*, he needs extra help.

3. Next, the teacher writes the same 30 words on the board and explains that each time we have a *single vowel*, a *vowel pair*, or a final *vowel-consonant-e*, we have a syllable (visual discrimination). Students are asked to circle each vowel grapheme. (A *vowel grapheme* is composed of the number of vowels it takes to spell an unbroken vowel sound. In general, English vowel graphemes are spelled with *one vowel*, as in *cat, me,* and, *strong*, or with *vowel pairs*, as in *coat, main, meet, coin*, or with a *vowel and a final e*, separated by a consonant, as in *cake, Pete, cute,* and *hide*.)

1. Ⓞ c t Ⓞ b Ⓔ r	11. r Ⓔ m Ⓞ t ¢
2. M Ⓐ r c h	12. Ⓐ n Ⓨ
3. J Ⓤ n ¢	13. c Ⓞ n c Ⓔ r n
4. Ⓐ p p Ⅼ Ⓔ	14. Ⓔ l Ⓔ p h Ⓐ n t
5. n Ⓤ m b Ⓔ r	15. d Ⓘ n Ⓞ s ⓐ u r
6. p r Ⓞ f Ⓔ s s Ⓞ r	16. c Ⓞ f f Ⓔ Ⓔ
7. m ⓐ ⓘ n	17. p Ⓘ t c h Ⓔ r
8. l Ⓘ n g Ⓤ ⓘ s t Ⓘ c s	18. l Ⓐ m p
9. Ⓞ r n Ⓐ m Ⓔ n t	19. c Ⓐ r p Ⓔ t
10. t Ⓔ n	20. g Ⓐ r d Ⓔ n

21. r(o)s ¢   26. p(i)ñ(a)t(a)
22. d(a i)s(y)   27. (o)r g(a)n
23. c(o)m p l(e)t ¢   28. c(e)l l(o)
24. s t(a)t(u e)   29. p h(o)n(o)g r(a)p h
25. w(i)n d(o w)   30. m(o u)s ¢

4. Next, students are supplied with "hypothetical words" and are asked to circle each vowel grapheme and write the number of syllables the word contains (visual discrimination):

v = vowel   c = consonant   l = l   e = e

1. v c v c v e   _____   11. c c v c v v c l e   _____
2. c c v c c v v c   _____   12. v v c v c c   _____
3. v v c v v c c   _____   13. c v c c v c c l e   _____
4. c v c v v c v c e   _____   14. v c v v c v   _____
5. c c v c v v   _____   15. v c c v c c v v c v c   _____
6. v c c v c c v v   _____   16. v v c   _____
7. v c v c c v v c e   _____   17. v v c e   _____
8. c v c c v c v v c   _____   18. c v c l e   _____
9. v c v v   _____   19. v c v v c v c e   _____
10. c v c e   _____   20. c c c v c   _____

answers:

1. (v)c(v)c(v)c   3   *11. c c(v)c(v v)c⌢l(e)   3
2. c c(v)c c(v v)c   2   12. (v v)c(v)c c   2
3. (v v)c(v v)c c   2   13. c(v)c c(v)c c⌢l(e)   3
4. c(v)c(v v)c(v)c ¢   3   14. (v)c(v v)c(v)   3
5. c c(v)c(v v)   2   15. (v)c c(v)c c(v v)c(v)c   4
6. (v)c c(v)c c(v v)   3   16. (v v)c   1
7. (v)c(v)c c(v v)c ¢   3   17. (v v)c ¢   1
8. c(v)c c(v)c(v v)c   3   18. c(v)c⌢l(e)   2
9. (v)c(v v)   2   19. (v)c(v v)c(v)c ¢   3
10. c(v)c ¢   1   20. c c c(v)c   1

* A *final e* is pronounced only when it is preceded by a *consonant* + l (-cle), in which case the *e represents a schwa sound* and is pronounced before the *l*: tab*le* = tabəl, princi*ple* = principəl.

5. Next, students are supplied with "nonsense words" and asked to circle each vowel grapheme and then write the number of syllables the word contains (visual discrimination):

1. s p e e n o t	_____	11. v o n e	_____
2. r o a z z l e	_____	12. c r o y k l e	_____
3. n e a s e	_____	13. a w s e m m a b	_____
4. n e i s e	_____	14. s c h l a m p s	_____
5. d o a l l y	_____	15. p s y r d	_____
6. m o u s s o p t	_____	16. d o m i k	_____
7. d e m m i n	_____	17. p u b m y	_____
8. f a i t s u d	_____	18. b l y	_____
9. r o n d l e	_____	19. s a t h p h a	_____
10. b o i j a u d t a l	_____	20. a m n e s e	_____

answers:

1. s p(e e)n(o)t	2	11. v(o)n e̸	1
2. r(o a)z z l(e)	2	12. c r(o y)k l(e)	2
3. n(e a)s e̸	1	13. (a w)s(e)m m(a)b	3
4. n(e i)s e̸	1	14. s c h l(a)m p s	1
5. d(o a)l l(y)	2	15. p s(y)r d	1
6. m(o u)s s(o)p t	2	16. d(o)m(i)k	2
7. d(e)m m(i)n	2	17. p(u)b m(y)	2
8. f(a i)t s(u)d	2	18. b l(y)	1
9. r(o)n d l(e)	2	19. s(a)t h p h(a)	2
10. b(o i)j(a u)d t(a)l	3	20. (a)m n(e)s e̸	2

6. Next, students are taught the three phonic syllabication generalizations:

   a) *situation: v c c v* When two vowel graphemes are separated by two consonants, divide between the consonants: as-ter, sil-ver, tar-get, but-ler.

   b) *situation: v c v* When two vowel graphemes are separated by one consonant, the consonant may go with the first or the second vowel. Try it both ways. If you know the word orally, you will know which one is correct: liz-ard, lem-on, wag-on; ra-zor, spi-der, ti-ger.

   c) *situation: -c l e* When a word ends in consonant l-e, these three letters compose the final syllable: bi-ble, ea-gle, bun-dle, tur-tle, noo-dle.

7. Next, ask students to divide the *hypothetical words* and the *nonsense words* into syllables (visual discrimination):

answers:

*1. v́c v́c v c	3	11. c c v́c v v́/c l e	3
2. c c v c/c v v c	2	12. v v́c v c c	2
3. v v́c v v c c	2	13. c v c/c v c/c l e	3
4. c v́c v v́c v c ¢	3	14. v́c v v́c v	3
5. c c v́c v v	2	15. v c/c v c/c v v́c v c	4
6. v c/c v c/c v v	3	16. v v c	1
7. v́c v c/c v v c ¢	3	17. v v c ¢	1
8. c v c/c v́c v v c	3	18. c v/c l e	2
9. v́c v v	2	19. v́c v v́c v c ¢	3
10. c v c ¢	1	20. c c c v c	1

* Use ´c to indicate that division may come *before* or *after* the single consonant.

answers:

1. s p e e n o t	2	11. v o n ¢	1
2. r o a z/z l e	2	12. c r o y/k l e	2
3. n e a s ¢	1	13. a w s e m/m a b	3
4. n e i s ¢	1	14. s c h l a m p s	1
5. d o a l/l y	2	15. p s y r d	1
6. m o u s/s o p t	2	16. d o m i k	2
7. d e m/m i n	2	17. p u b/m y	2
8. f a i t/s u d	2	18. b l y	1
9. r o n/d l e	2	**19. s a t h/p h a	2
10. b o i j a u d/t a l	3	20. a m/n e s ¢	2

** The following are digraphs (one sound spelled with two letters) and are never divided between: *ph, sh, th, ch.*

8. Now we are ready for *real words*. To review the generalizations, do the following:

a) *Clue 1:* vc - cv

ram - page	floc - cule	mas - cot
vc - cv	vc - cv	vc - cv

har - dy	cal - cine	plain - tiff
vc - cv	vc - cv	vc - cv

When two vowel sounds are separated by two consonants, divide between the consonants.

b) *Clue 2:* v - cv or vc - v

E - gypt	par - a - noid	leg - um
v - cv	vc - v - cv	vc - v

lei - sure	rem - i - fy	frig - ate
v - cv	vc - v - cv	vc - v

When two vowel sounds are separated by a single consonant, divide either before or after the consonant.

c) *Clue 3:* - cle

cy - cle	poo - dle	ten - a - ble
ma - ple	snif - fle	tem - ple

When a word ends in -*cle*, divide before the consonant.

9. When a real word is to be taught in a content area and it is phonetic:

a) Write it on the board, perhaps in a sentence.

b) Ask the students to try to pronounce it.

c) If they cannot do so, ask how many syllables it has and where the syllabic divisions are. Mark them on the board. Then ask students to pronounce it. If they still cannot do so:

d) Reinforce appropriate vowel generalizations or consonant generalizations by listing several easy words that have the troublesome vowel or consonant grapheme.

e) Ask them to pronounce the word, or pronounce it for them. Have them repeat it orally.

f) Define it and/or use it in a sentence. Use an illustration if possible.[4]

SUMMARY

To help students build diverse and powerful vocabularies, many considerations are necessary. Words must be looked at in several ways—denotatively and connotatively. Techniques for building vocabulary in each of these areas are numerous.

Words rarely have only one *denotation*. Some words have over 100. It is not unusual for a person to think he knows the meaning of a word and not be aware of other nuances or meanings and, therefore, misinterpret or misrepresent a passage.

Of unsuspected difficulty sometimes are *simple words with specialized or technical meanings* in the content areas. The importance of using *context clues* was stressed. Students should be taught to examine words to see if the meanings they are associating with these words make sense in the sentence and paragraph in which they are found. Authors of textbooks frequently lead the reader by the hand to help him understand new words or new meanings of old words. Several techniques the teacher might use to guide students and to make vocabulary study enjoyable were given. The study of *morphology* develops word power rapidly. And it is interesting.

Symbols and *abbreviations* add variety, but may also burden the reader. We must be sure that students understand the symbols and abbreviations used in our books.

Different from word denotations are word *connotations*, the interpretive meanings of words. Young children can be taught to grasp *simple connotations*. In fact, they thoroughly enjoy working with connotations for animal names and growing things. Later, they can work with *figurative language: similes, metaphors, personification*, and *allusions*.

Diachronic linguistics is an area often overlooked. Yet to study some aspects of how language has changed is both pleasurable and helpful. Especially interesting are *sound changes* that have occurred in the past, such as the *First Germanic Consonant Shift*, and the present tendency to drop medial vowels in some three-syllable words. *Meaning changes* also fascinate some of our young. These changes can be classified today into certain patterns: *amelioration* and *pejoration, generalization* and *specialization, euphemism* and *antieuphemism*, and *hyperbole*. New words are continually being added to our language by *coining: combining morphemes* in new ways, *blending*, forming *acronyms*, and *slang*. The English and American languages have also borrowed heavily from languages around the globe.

Many secondary school students would benefit from being taught phonic syllabication generalizations. These generalizations can help them pronounce many polysyllabic words which already are in their listening vocabularies. Three generalizations were given and ways of teaching them were explained.

NOTES

1 Additional references include: Wilbur S. Ames. "The Development of a Classification Scheme of Contextual Aids," *Reading Research Quarterly*, **II** (Fall 1966): 57–82; A. S. Artley. "Teaching Word-Meaning Through Context," *Elementary English Review*, **XX** (1943): 140–143; K. L. Dulin. "New Research on Context Clues." *The Journal of Reading*, **XIII** (1969): 33–38; Constance M. McCullough. "Learning to Use Context Clues," *Elementary English Review*, **XX** (1943): 140–143.

2 See Carl Lefevre. *Linguistics and the Teaching of Reading*. New York: McGraw-Hill, 1964.

3 See Lou E. Burmeister. "Content of a Phonics Program Based on Particularly Useful Generalizations," in *Reading Methods and Teacher Improvement*, ed. Nila Banton Smith. Newark, Delaware: International Reading Association, 1971, pp. 27–39.

4 For further elaboration, see Arthur Heilman. *Phonics in Proper Perspective*, 2d ed. Columbus, Ohio: Charles E. Merrill, 1968.

SUGGESTED ACTIVITIES

1. Design four different kinds of vocabulary exercises or activities that would be useful for teaching words in your content area.

2. Design a bulletin board display using morphemes important in your content area.

3. Compose a chart using the following format, which includes bound morphemes important in your content area.

morpheme	meaning	words in my field using the morpheme	words in other fields using the morpheme

4. Design one exercise or activity to help students understand the process of language change (diachronic linguistics) as it relates to your content area.

5. Syllabicate the following nonsense words:

a n s a m	t r e f l e	w a u n m o p
d o m c l e	v o a g g a d	z e f g o n e
p a i s o d	b o l e	c l o o m p
t u n n o i k	u s m o u t h	d r e s c l e

REFERENCES FOR FURTHER READING

Altick, Richard. *Preface to Critical Reading*. New York: Holt, Rinehart and Winston, 1969, Chapters 1 and 2.

Ames, Wilbur S. "The Development of a Classification Scheme of Contextual Aids," *Reading Research Quarterly*, **II** (Fall 1966): 57–82.

Artley, A. S. "Teaching Word-Meaning Through Context," *Elementary English Review*, **XX** (1943): 68–74.

Burmeister, Lou E. "Content of a Phonics Program Based on Particularly Useful Generalizations," in *Reading Methods and Teacher Improvement*, ed. Nila Banton Smith. Newark, Delaware: International Reading Association, 1971, pp. 27–39.

Cole, Luella. *The Teacher's Handbook of Technical Vocabulary*. Bloomington: Illinois Public School Publishing Co., 1940.

Davis, Nancy B. *Basic Vocabulary Skills*. New York: McGraw-Hill, 1969.

Dulin, K. L. "New Research on Context Clues," *Journal of Reading*, **XIII** (1969): 33–38.

Fries, C. C. *Linguistics and Reading*. New York: Holt, Rinehart and Winston, 1963.

Hafner, Lawrence E. (ed.). *Improving Reading in Secondary Schools, Selected Readings*. New York: Macmillan, 1967, Section 5.

Harris, Albert J. *How to Increase Reading Ability.* New York: David McKay Co., 1970, Chapters 13, 14, 15.

Hayakawa, S. I. *Language in Thought and Action,* 2d ed. New York: Harcourt, Brace and World, 1964.

Herber, Harold. *Teaching Reading in Content Areas.* Englewood Cliffs, N.J.: Prentice-Hall, 1970, Chapter 8.

Karlin, Robert. *Teaching Reading in High School.* Indianapolis: Bobbs-Merrill, 1964, Chapter 5.

Karlin, Robert (ed.). *Teaching Reading in High School—Selected Articles.* Indianapolis: Bobbs-Merrill, 1969, Chapter 5.

Laird, Charlton. *The Miracle of Language.* New York: Harcourt, Brace and World, 1953.

McCullough, Constance M. "Learning to Use Context Clues," *Elementary English Review,* **XX** (1943): 140–143.

Olson, Arthur V. and Wilber S. Ames (eds.). *Teaching Reading Skills in Secondary Schools.* Scranton, Pa.: International Textbook Co., 1970, Section 5.

Pei, Mario. *The Story of the English Language.* Philadelphia: J. P. Lippincott, 1967.

Roberts, Paul. *Modern Grammar.* New York: Harcourt, Brace and World, 1968.

Robertson, Stuart and Frederic Cassidy. *The Development of Modern English.* Englewood Cliffs, N.J.: Prentice-Hall, 1964.

Schubert, Delwyn and Theodore Torgerson (eds.). *Readings in Reading—Practice, Theory, Research.* New York: Thomas Y. Crowell Co., 1968, Section 4.

Spache, George. *Toward Better Reading.* Champaign, Illinois: Garrard, 1963, Chapter 20.

Trela, Thaddeus M. *Fourteen Remedial Reading Methods.* Palo Alto, Calif.: Fearon, 1968.

Chapter 7

DEVELOPING LITERAL COMPRE-HENSION OF READING MATERIALS

What is the cognitive domain?

What are the seven levels of the cognitive domain?

What is the place of literal comprehension activities in the cognitive domain?

What are the four common literal level reading skills?

Which of these skills are important in your content area? When?

How can each of these be taught at the recall level? At the translation level? What are the possibilities for teaching such skills at higher cognitive levels?

INTRODUCTION

This chapter and the next two deal with the development of students' comprehension skills and abilities. Chapter 7 is concerned with literal comprehension. Chapter 8 deals with interpretation skills as well as those that relate to the application of ideas in practical situations. Chapter 9 presents ways of teaching what is commonly referred to as critical-creative reading.

These skills are considered to be cognitive skills. *Cognition*, or the processes of knowing and perceiving, relates to the intellectual development of a person or society. Much has been written lately about the *cognitive domain*, that is, the domain, or realm, of the intellect—that part of a person's development commonly referred to as his intellectual development. Cognitive qualities are measured on I.Q. tests and on many school tests.

It has long been an aim of teachers to develop students intellectually. There is an ever-evolving body of knowledge in most subject areas that the schools have felt a need to pass on to youth: to have them learn it, digest it, react to it, and possibly create with it.

Society often dictates that educated people know certain facts, and people are often judged by the amount and kind of knowledge they possess. Often, people succeed in business in relationship to their knowledge, their ability to *think*, to apply what they know to old and new situations, to judge, create, and evaluate intellectually.

There is little doubt that the intellectual development of students is important—both in general and in relation to subject matter areas. Yet though we have long talked about such development, it is only recently that a clear structure of the *cognitive domain* has been provided for our use.

If we understand the structure of this domain, we will be better able to understand what we are doing—or perhaps what we ought to be doing—in the classroom to foster our students' thinking ability. If we understand the various *levels of cognition*, we may be better able to balance our classroom activities in order to avoid an overemphasis on one or more levels and an underemphasis or omission of others.

THE COGNITIVE DOMAIN

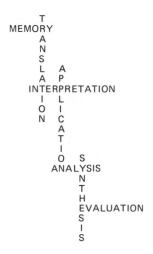

Benjamin Bloom is the senior author of a book titled *Taxonomy of Educational Objectives: Handbook I, Cognitive Domain.* Using this volume as source material, Norris Sanders wrote a very practical and lucid book, *Classroom Questions—What Kinds?* in which he outlined seven levels of the cognitive domain. In the discussion that follows, the seven levels are taken from Sanders. The descriptions of the levels are partly Sanders', but largely the work of the present author, who gathered her ideas from numerous sources. The seven levels are:

1. *Memory*—remembering or recognizing just what the author has said. Common types of questions or activities at the memory level relate to recalling or recognizing: (a) facts, dates, definitions, (b) main ideas as given by the author, (c) sequence of events, commonly called the story line, and (d) directions as given.

2. *Translation*—putting information or knowledge into another form. For example, a student might: (a) translate a Spanish passage into English, (b) paraphrase a definition or passage, (c) take information from a paragraph and put it into graph, map, or chart form; or he might do the opposite—take information from a graph, map, or chart and put it into sentence or paragraph form, (d) put a story into skit form or a play into story form, (e) actually follow directions exactly as given.

3. *Interpretation*—recognizing, or seeing, *unstated relationships,* such as: (a) given the cause, determining the effect; or, given the effect only, understanding the cause, (b) anticipation—what might happen next, (c) formulating a main idea when none is given—inductive reasoning, (d) making deductions

from generalizations supplied, (e) relating to characters—real or imaginary—and understanding what motivates them, (f) imagery—being able to live vicariously—being able to see, feel, smell, hear, and taste through the imagination.

4. *Application*—a relatively high level of cognition which involves the ability to *both* (a) recognize an instance when a principle applies and also (b) apply it with success. The college student taking a reading methods course might ask himself if he could recognize what kind of help each student in a class needs and whether he could successfully give this help. But that is not enough. He must go and do it.

5. *Analysis*—the knowledgeable dissection of something and the examination of the parts that compose the whole. We may analyze propaganda, for example, by answering such questions as: (a) Who is the author and whom is he serving? (b) What are his purposes? (c) What techniques does he use? (d) To what need is he appealing? Or, we may analyze poetry, noting (a) rhyme, rhythm, meter, (b) the period in which it was written and whether it is exemplary of that period, (c) mood and tone. Or, we may learn to recognize fallacies of reasoning. Or, we may reason deductively by using syllogisms or inductively by using necessary and/or sufficient conditions, etc. Or, we may look at the steps as outlined for a chemistry experiment and logically question what the result of following them would be—or we might recognize that if we did not follow them *exactly*, something disastrous might happen.

6. *Synthesis*—the integration, reorganization, or fusion of ideas, usually from various sources. J. P. Guilford, in *Structure of the Intellect*, uses the terms *convergent* and *divergent* production.[1] In *convergent production*, ideas or materials are integrated in a conventional way. In *divergent production*, ideas or materials are organized or produced in a unique, or unusual, way. Divergent production also includes elaboration and fluency.

7. *Evaluation*—the formulation of a standard and the judging of an idea or object in relationship to that standard. For example, if we decide what characterizes a good modern play, we can then critique a play according to these standards. Of course, new standards may be evolving.

Discussion

When we are teaching in the content areas, we may feel that our textbook and other materials at our disposal at least partially dictate the cognitive level at which we will expect our students to perform. It is true that sometimes the cognitive level is well determined by the material or occasion. For example, the following people might be best off to follow directions precisely as given: the girl who is baking a cake, the chemist who is performing a given experiment, the engineer who is building a bridge (memory-translation level).

At other times these same people might perform at higher levels: the girl who decides she would like to add poppy seeds to the cake, the chemist who is experimenting in the hope of discovering something new, or the engineer who is designing a bridge (analysis, synthesis, and evaluation levels).

It is often not only the material, but also the way *we* view the material that determine the level at which we expect students to perform. Do we view the ideas contained in a textbook as completely objective? If so, perhaps it is best to work at the lower levels. Or, do we think the author is biased, presents just one point of view, and is too general or incomplete? If so, we are likely to work at higher levels and to send our students in search of additional information.

The way we view our students may determine the levels at which we work. Perhaps we think that the brighter students should work at the higher levels and the less bright at the lower levels. Yet certainly the brightest students need to know some facts, and they must be able to understand exactly what an author is saying before they react to it. And the slowest students need these skills, too, but they must also learn to reason, analyze, synthesize, and evaluate as best they can, though certainly with simpler materials and ideas than the bright student would use. It may just be that it is *our* knowledge-ability and *our* point of view toward the material and students that determine the levels at which we work.

Literal Comprehension

It is the purpose of this chapter to discuss the four major literal comprehension skills and, when possible, to demonstrate ways of helping students achieve these skills. Brief suggestions will be made to indicate that some of these skills can and should, at times, be taught at higher levels also. The teaching of these skills at higher levels will be explained more completely in the following two chapters.

The reader of this book should recognize that as a teacher, he is the one who decides which reading skills are important—or which kinds of questions he will ask—to help develop the understandings he feels are important in his course at a particular time. No one else can do this for him, for only he knows his students and how they relate, or are able to relate, to the materials and ideas of his course.

The teacher should understand the full range of cognitive skills—or thinking levels and activities—so that his decisions are made wisely. He should also understand the capabilities of his students. His goals, or objectives, as well as his activities, should be designed so that they are appropriate to both his students and also the content of his subject. The following skills are considered to be at the literal level:

> following directions as given
>
> recalling facts, dates, etc.
>
> recognizing and recalling main ideas
>
> recognizing and recalling the pattern and sequence of ideas

Students can engage in these activities at what Sanders calls the memory and/or translation levels. At the *memory level*, they recall exactly what the author has said, in his words. At the *translation level*, they recall what was said, but they respond by using their own words or by engaging in some other type of "translation" activity, such as drawing an illustration, putting words into graph, map, or chart form, putting a story into skit form, actually following directions as given, etc.

FOLLOWING DIRECTIONS AS GIVEN

Following directions is obviously a very important skill, not only as it relates to reading, but also as it relates to many other in-school and out-of-school activities. Yet, students frequently learn to ignore directions for several reasons: directions are often poorly given, the same directions are repeated so often that students know they will be given again and again, and students learn to "mask" directions with the hope that someone else will do the job— and often someone else does!

Much of the student's behavior in relation to following directions is molded at home; however, a teacher cannot bemoan this fact. Positive action must be taken. What can a teacher do? Of utmost importance is establishing the practice of *giving directions only once* and expecting them to be followed. This is even a difficult procedure to follow in graduate level education courses, where teachers themselves ask over and over about simple directions that have been clearly stated—clearly enough stated so that 90 percent of the class understands. Some people just do not listen, expecting that they will be catered to.

Of course, it is necessary that the directions be given clearly and un-ambiguously. If they are complex, it helps to present them in written form.

With students who do not follow directions well, the following procedure can be used. First, be sure you have the student's attention. Second, present only one direction at a time, e.g., "Open your book to page 29." Wait for it to be followed. Then, present another single direction, e.g., "Read the title of the chapter." Wait for this to be done. Then, give another single direction, e.g., "Read the first main heading." Wait for this to be done. Give another single direction, e.g., "Formulate several questions that you expect to be answered in this section," etc.

After students are able to follow one direction at a time, give them two to be followed consecutively ("Open your book to page 29, and read the title of the chapter"). When this has been done, follow with, "Read the first main heading and formulate several questions that you think will be answered in this section," etc. When students are able to follow two consecutive directions well, give them three consecutive directions. Later, give them four and then five. If they wish, allow them to write the directions down.

Remember that when you give directions, you must have the attention of the students to whom they are given. The directions must be clearly stated and in the students' realm of understanding. It must be possible for the students to carry out the instructions.

Teaching Strategies

It can be interesting, enjoyable, and worthwhile to give students in a classroom a list of directions to follow. Be sure the reference materials are available so that they can find the answers. Time students when they are doing the exercise.

In English

1. Look up the word "genre" in your dictionary and write the first two definitions given.

   _____

   _____

2. Look in your dictionary to find in what year Thomas Gray was born and in what year he died. Write the dates here: born _____, died _____.

3. Complete the following sentence by inserting two adjectives that make sense in it:

   The _____ _____ building collapsed when the tornado struck.

4. Insert two common nouns and any additional words necessary to complete the following sentence:

   _____ and _____ tied in the race.

5. If all the words in the following sentence are spelled correctly, circle every third word in this complete item; if not, circle every second word: "The dinosaur is a prehistoric animal."

●

●

●

10.

time: _____

In mathematics

1. Circle names of objects that are three-dimensional and underline names of objects that are two-dimensional:

    circle   triangle   sphere   parallelogram

    square   cube   cone   hexagon

2. Put a box around the number that is the cube root of 64. If it is not given, put a triangle around each number:

    1   2   4   5   7   8   16

3. Draw an illustration of a pentagon in the box below.

4. If 5 zos 7 = 12,

    and 8 zos 9 = 17,

    and 12 zop 2 = 10,

    and 4 zop 1 = 3,

    what does 6 zos 8 zop 5 equal? _____

5. What real word does *zos* stand for?   _____

6. What mathematical symbol does *zos* represent?   _____

7. What real word does *zop* stand for?   _____

8. What mathematical symbol does *zop* represent?   _____

9. If quadruped means four-footed,
   quadrilateral means four-sided, and
   biped means two-footed, what is the
   word for two-sided?   _____

10. Octopus (really oct*oped*) means what?   _____

                                                    time: _____

In science

1. On what page(s) in your textbook will you find information about air pollution? _____

2. Circle names of members of the primate order. Cross out other names:

    man   elephant   monkey   spider   chicken

    lemur   zebra   orangutan   lion   ape

    deer   tiger   dinosaur   gorilla   dog

    (Common knowledge? Otherwise, a chart should be in sight.)

3. If 32° Centigrade equals 0° Fahrenheit, circle every word that starts with a vowel; if not, underline every word that starts with a *c* or an *s*. (Common knowledge? Otherwise, a chart should be available.)

4. Look at the chart in the front of the room. Find the planet which is nearest the moon. Write its name here: _____

5. Look in the Glossary of your textbook. Write the author's definition of the word polarize: _____

_____

●

●

●

10.

time: _____

In social studies

1. Look at the map on page 192 of your book. Circle the states that fought on the side of the South in the Civil War; underline the states that fought on the side of the North. Cross out the states that did not fight.

New York	Arizona	Louisiana	Florida
Alabama	Texas	Wisconsin	Iowa
Indiana	Maine	California	Alaska
Michigan	Kentucky	Missouri	Pennsylvania
Virginia	West Virginia	Ohio	Nevada

2. Using the same map, locate the states that fought for the South that are not listed in item 1. Write their names here: _____

_____

3. Find the jacket for the book *Black Like Me* on the bulletin board. Write the name of the author here: _____

4. Use your dictionary to find what the word *apartheid* means. Write the definition here: _____

_____

5. Use the Biographical Sketches part of your textbook to find the date of the original publication of *Uncle Tom's Cabin*, by Harriet Beecher Stowe. Write it here: _____

•

•

•

10.

time: _____

The first student finished with a perfect paper could write a set of directions appropriate to the content field for the next similar activity, perhaps to be held the next week. (Any one student would do this only once.) By writing such directions, the student would get practice in stating instructions lucidly and unambiguously. If the student does a poor job, it might be better for the teacher to allow the student's peers to correct him at the time of the activity rather than for the teacher to correct him before time.

Caution

Students should know that it is not always wise to follow directions. Recent court-martial trials indicate this is true even in the military.

When students follow directions as given, they may be operating on the literal level of thinking. If, however, they have carefully analyzed the impact of following the directions and have decided that the directions are worthy of being followed as given, they are reacting on a higher, nonliteral, level.

Table 7.1   Level of thinking used in following directions

Action	Reason	Level
Followed directions as given	It did not occur to student to do otherwise	Literal
	Interpreted and/or analyzed and/or evaluated directions and decided they were worth following explicitly	Interpretive (or higher)
Did not follow directions as given	Student was unable to do so; was too careless	Below literal
	Interpreted and/or analyzed and/or evaluated directions and decided they should not be followed or should be altered	Interpretive (or higher)

When directions are not followed, it may mean that the student has been careless or unable to follow them, in which case he has not reached the literal level of comprehension, which includes translation activities, i.e., carrying them out as given. Or, it may mean that he reacted to the directions in a negative, or partly negative, way and, therefore, did not do explicitly as directed. Your job? To find out at what level he was acting and what motivated him. You might use introspective-retrospective techniques to find out at which level he is thinking. See Table 7.1 to help you identify the level.

Consider the following directions. Would you follow the directions as given? Write an A in the blank if you would follow the directions as given, followed by a 1 for "literal level" or a 2 for "higher level." Write a B in the blank if you would not follow the directions as given, followed by a 1 for "below literal level" or a 2 for "higher level."

1. Buy Chek-X cereal. Research proves it's the best for your health. _____

2. Buy Chek-X cereal. There's a toy in every box. _____

3. Work this nuclear physics problem successfully, and you'll win $5000. _____

4. With just ten dollars worth of material you can make this beautiful evening dress (or bookcase). Buy today. Make it when you have time. _____

5. The price of ice cream is 78¢ per half-gallon; milk is 25¢ a quart; bread is 58¢ a loaf. Add the prices to get the total cost. _____

6. Divide the compound word moonlight into syllables between the two morphemes. _____

7. Do this chemistry experiment exactly as directed in your text-book. _____

8. Do exercise 4 in your grammar book, and hand it in tomorrow. _____

9. "Set the table," your mother tells you. _____

10. "Set the table," your wife (husband) tells you. _____

11. "You'll have to finish this project tonight," your boss tells you. _____

12. "Shoot those civilians in the ditch," your lieutenant in Vietnam tells you. _____

RECALLING FACTS, DATES, AND OTHER DETAILS

Recalling such details as facts, names, and dates can be important for several reasons. First, there are certain details that every educated person should know, and not knowing them marks a person as uneducated. Knowing certain facts is necessary for a person to be able to carry on an intelligent conversation.

Who is president of the United States? Vice-president? Who are your state senators? Who is prime minister of Canada? Of Britain? Who is president of France? Of Mexico? Who is the head of state in Italy, West Germany, Russia, China, etc?

What are some plays that Shakespeare wrote? Who wrote *Don Quixote?* What characterizes Romantic poetry?

Where is Tibet? Formosa? Baja California? Trieste? Cape Town? Bengal?

When was America discovered? When was the Revolutionary War fought? The Civil War? When was the atomic bomb dropped on Hiroshima?

Batting averages, golf scores, and leading football teams are facts important to some groups of people.

Knowing how much air should be in an automobile tire is important to most drivers.

Knowing when school begins and ends is important to many people.

Knowing how much $2 + 2$ is, 4×4, $3 - 1$, etc., is important. And knowing what H_2O stands for is also important.

"Etcetra, etcetra, etcetra," said the king in *The King and I*. Many facts are important to know. But such details also serve as building blocks for forming concepts, and some facts are important principally as basic information from which it is possible to make inductions. Then, the generalization, or the principle, that was induced becomes the important idea, and the facts are not important to remember any longer.

Details are best learned as they relate to the main idea they support. They may be remembered because they supply specific examples which make the principle or generalization more meaningful or because they supply supporting evidence for a conclusion.

The details may be the basic ideas that are used in formulating a generalization, as is true in inductive reasoning, and they may be remembered because they were the building blocks in recognizing a concept. On the other hand, a given generalization may be somewhat empty in meaning until concrete, supporting illustrations are recognized.

When it is important that details be remembered, they should be related to the main idea they support. When a main idea has been stated, students could be asked such questions as:

1. Give specific examples that support the given generalization—and any examples which do not. (expository: simple listing and contrast)

2. Give specific examples of factors the author said caused the effect. (chronological: effect → cause)

3. Give specific examples of factors the author suggests might follow if a certain action is taken. (chronological: cause → effect)

4. What specific visual images combined to give the general impression you observed? (spatial)

5. What details supplied by the author would you include in sketching a picture of plantation life? (spatial)

6. What planets would you have to include to sketch a map of our universe? (spatial)

Additional examples of these types of activities are given in the sections of this chapter on main idea and sequence. Questions of detail are at the literal level only if the student *recalls* details given. If the student culls from his background of information details that support or contradict a given generalization, he is thinking above the literal level (see Chapters 8 and 9).

Unfortunately, knowledge of details is frequently overstressed in our schools. Too many questions that are asked in the classroom deal with facts. It is easy to ask factual questions and easy to grade the response. But how important is it for the student to know the fact? What insights into human nature will it give him? Does it help him get a "feel" for history? Does it give him some perspective to help him think more logically, humanly, or spiritually? There should be some value in knowing the fact for it to be important enough for the student to be quizzed about it.

A good strategy for you would be to think about your course. What facts, dates, and names are important? These you might help students learn. Which are there to round out main ideas but in themselves are relatively unnecessary to know? These could be discussed in relation to the main idea or to formulating a concept, but need not be stressed or remembered. For example, in studying this book, it is important for you to know that new words have entered our language in several ways, e.g., through a blending of the first part of one word with the final part of another. You might remember a few examples, but to remember them all is unnecessary. It is the principle that is important, especially if you are going to teach English. A more important principle of language growth for you to remember if you are a science teacher is that many new words have entered our language by combining morphemes, or even by direct borrowing. The social scientist might also find acronyms of vital interest and importance. But facts, in themselves, are rarely as important as is indicated by the stress put on them in our schools. And time spent on them is time taken away from other kinds of intellectual activities.

RECOGNIZING AND RECALLING THE MAIN IDEA

Main idea is a term usually applied to the central thought of one or a few consecutive paragraphs—or of a unit composed of an integrated collection of sentences that form part of a complete work, such as a chapter, essay, or short story. The skill of recognizing and/or formulating a main idea is related to the skill of recognizing and/or formulating the central thought of a unit—such as the sentence, a collection of discrete but related items, or the theme of an essay, chapter, or story.

When a reader *recognizes* or *recalls* a main idea *that is stated for him* or *that is a stereotyped concept* encompassing details that are supplied, he is reading or thinking at the literal level. However, when he must *formulate* a main idea by synthesizing details, possibly in a unique way, or by recognizing patterns of thought, or by reasoning inductively in any other way, he is thinking at a level higher than the literal. Sometimes it is difficult to know what level of thought was required of the reader for him to arrive at the main idea. Often, it may not be necessary to make such fine distinctions. We can work in a variety of ways to help students develop the ability of recognizing and recalling the main idea.

Family Names—Classifying

Teaching Strategies

We might, for example, begin finding or using family names for a series of discrete items.[2] In sequencing the development of this skill from easy to difficult, we might progress in this way:

1. Provide a list of family names. Also group like items (requires inductive *or* deductive *recall*).

blends	acronyms	combined morphemes		
a) CCC	WPA	NATO	RADAR	<u>acronyms</u>
b) telephone	amorphic	trilateral	astronaut	<u>　　　　</u>
c) brunch	skort	floated	smog	<u>　　　　</u>

2. Group like items, but do not supply family names (requires inductive *recall*).

a) square	circle	triangle	rectangle	_____
b) sphere	ellipsoid	cube	cone	_____
c) algebra	trigonometry	geometry	calculus	_____

3. Supply family names. List items ungrouped (requires inductive *or* deductive *recall*).

Wisconsin	Chicago	Florida	France
Mexico	El Paso	Cailfornia	Oneonta
Russia	Milwaukee	Canada	Utah

I. *cities*	II. *states*	III. *nations*
A.	A.	A.
B.	B.	B.
C.	C.	C.
D.	D.	D.

4. Do not supply family names. List items ungrouped (requires inductive *recall* if stock response is given—planets, stars).

| Jupiter | Sun | Moon | Saturn |
| Mars | Polaris | Earth | |

5. Supply family names. List no items (requires deductive *recall*).

I. *flowers*	II. *fruits*	III. *vegetables*
A.	A.	A.
B.	B.	B.
C.	C.	C.
D.	D.	D.

Syntactical Synthesis[3]

To teach students to recognize the central thought (kernel) of a sentence, proceed as follows:

Teaching Strategies

1. Teach them to recognize the subject (noun) of a sentence. Have them underline the noun (N) on each of a series of sentences.

   a) <u>José</u> threw the ball over the fence.

b) The grass has turned brown.

c) The mountain range runs for 250 miles.

d) Gas is escaping from the furnace.

2. Teach them to recognize the verb (V) of a sentence. Have them underline the V with two underscorings.

a) José threw the ball over the fence.

b) The grass has turned brown.

c) The mountain range runs for 250 miles.

d) Gas is escaping from the furnace.

3. Give them experience with a variety of patterns to help students recognize common kernels (N = subject noun, N_2 = predicate noun, V = verb, Lv = linking verb, A = adjective, Av = adverb).

a) Gregory is reading.   (N V)

b) Maria sang loudly.   (N V Ad)

c) Rick made a homerun.   (N V N_2)

d) Nadia named her horse "Star."   (N V N_2 N_3)

e) The matador made the bull angry.   (N V N_2 A)

f) Charlotte is a cat.   (N Lv N_2)

g) The bull is irate.   (N Lv A)

4. Next, combine the two processes of underlining kernels of sentences and finding family names to literally induce the main idea of a paragraph:

The factories of the South spin and weave cotton cloth and make it into clothing. They make iron, steel, and machinery from iron ore. They make fertilizer for farms from phosphate rock. They make furniture from their lumber. And they make rayon and paper from their cotton and wood pulp.

Find the family names for the:

N's: factories, they, they, they, they,   = factories

V's: spin, weave, make, make, make, make, make   = make

N_2's: cloth, clothing, iron, steel, machinery, fertilizer,
         furniture, rayon, paper   = various products

Main Idea: Factories (of the South) make various products.

5. When there are elaborations of sentence length or of several sentences, underscore kernels only in basic sentences:

To some, a home is a haven (removed from the hectic pace of the outside world. It is the place where family members enjoy one another and also where each may pursue special interests, sometimes in solitude and at other times with one or more family members or friends). For other families, it is always "<u>open house</u>," (with visitors made welcome at any time without advance planning or preparation).

Find the family names for the:

N : home, it	= <u>home</u>
V : is, is	= <u>is</u>
N₂: haven, open house (contrast, no family name. We have a contrast paragraph.)	= <u>haven, open house</u>

Main Idea: Home for some is a haven; for others, an open house.

Placement of Main Idea Statement[4]

Teach students that when stated, the main idea, or central thought, of a paragraph can be found anywhere within the paragraph. The following symbols might be used to exemplify this. The horizontal line in each symbol indicates the place of the main idea.

▽ = main idea at beginning of paragraph

△ = main idea at end of paragraph

⧖ = main idea at beginning and end of paragraph

◇ = main idea within paragraph

○ = main idea not stated

Give students experience with all of these types of paragraphs. Select paragraphs from reading materials available to your students. Ask students to underline the main idea and to draw the symbol that illustrates the location of the main idea. For example:

Some words that formerly stood for a particular action or thing have gradually become more inclusive in meaning. Such a word is *companion* (Latin, *com*, together + *panis*, bread), literally "a bread-sharer." Closely related is *company*, a general term which today is not restricted to "a group that shares bread." A *lord*, literally "loaf-keeper," has vastly wider responsibilities than keeping loaves. *Companion*, *company*, and *lord* all go beyond the restricted association of bread; the meanings of these words have become generalized. The process is generalization.[*]

⧖

---

[*] T. C. Pollack, *et al. The Macmillan English Series—English 12.* New York: Macmillan, 1964, p. 176. Reprinted by permission.

The three general ways of speaking that you have been studying are called the casual, consultative, and deliberate keys. Each of us is most at ease in the casual key, enjoying a drifting conversation with friends and acquaintances. When we speak in the consultative key, we explore a problem with another person, asking for information, making explanations, and attempting to reach a fuller common understanding. We are consulting with others. Before using the deliberative key, we frequently deliberate, planning our ideas and putting them in a helpful order for our listeners. We frequently must say more in order to be understood by a large audience than we would need to say in speaking to just one or two people, for our listeners do not have the chance to interrupt us with questions or show us that they are following our thoughts.*

Before we take up thermodynamics itself, it is appropriate for us to look into the three different mechanisms by which heat may be transferred from one place to another. . . . When we place one end of an iron rod in a fire, the other end becomes warm as a result of the conduction of heat through the iron. Conduction is a very slow process in air; a stove warms a room chiefly through the actual movement of heated air, a process called convection. Neither conduction nor convection can take place appreciably in the virtual void of interplanetary space. Instead, the heat the earth receives from the sun arrives in the form of radiation. These mechanisms all illustrate a fundamental fact: the natural direction of heat flow is from hot bodies to cold ones.†

Grip the metal so the layout line is just below the vise jaws when shearing it to a line. This will leave sufficient metal to finish by filing or grinding. When cutting, it is best to hold the metal in the vise without using vise jaw caps. This provides a better shearing action between the vise jaw and the chisel. Advance the chisel after each blow so that the cutting is done by the center of the cutting edge.‡

---

* Bernard Tanner, *et al. English 9.* Menlo Park, Calif.: Addison-Wesley, 1968, p. 10. Reprinted by permission. Copyright © 1968 by Addison-Wesley Publishing Co., Inc. All rights reserved.

† Arthur Beiser. *The Mainstream of Physics.* Reading, Mass.: Addison-Wesley, 1962, p. 200. Reprinted by permission.

‡ John R. Walker. *Modern Metal-Working.* South Holland, Ill.: Goodheart-Willcox, 1970, Unit 8, p. 1. Reprinted by permission.

Even though we do not have a 20-cent coin, we often use the symbol $.20 to mean 20/100 of a dollar (or 20¢) just as we use the symbol $.25 to represent the value of our quarter. We use the mark $.45 to mean 45/100 of a dollar (or 45¢) because it is easy to write and to use in computation. When we deal with money, we use decimal symbols as abbreviations for fractions with 100 as denominator. For example, a symbol like $2.47 is an abbreviation for 2 dollars and 47/100 of a dollar. Since 2 + 47/100 is 247/100, we say that $2.47 is an abbreviation for 247/100 of a dollar. Explain why $23.51 is a symbol for 2351/100 of a dollar. Which of the symbols $23.51 and 2351/100 of one dollar is easier to understand and to use? *

Other activities that help students recognize main ideas are:

1. selecting the best title from a list

2. matching a picture or illustration with a paragraph that describes it

3. selecting from a list of statements the one that best expresses the main idea

4. writing a series of headings for a series of paragraphs.

SEQUENCE

Sequence, as it relates to reading, refers to the order in which ideas are presented. "What ideas did the author relate first, second, third, etc.?" is a sequence-type question. Sequential patterns of discourse can be classified in one of the following three ways—chronological, spatial, or expository.

These are pure forms. In practice, however, almost all speech or writing is a combination of these patterns. We classify a passage according to the predominant pattern followed.

Chronological Order

Chronological order is time order. There are several time order patterns. The most obvious pattern progresses from beginning to end (first, second, third, fourth, fifth, etc.). Another chronological pattern is the reverse (fifth, fourth, third, second, first). Another common chronological pattern is known as the flashback pattern, in which either the end or the climax is given first, followed by a beginning-to-end sequence.

* Charles Brumfiel, *et al. Arithmetic: Concepts and Skills.* Reading, Mass.: Addison-Wesley, 1963, p. 247. Reprinted by permission.

Much fiction is written in a forward-moving chronological pattern, although some, like *Rebecca* and *Good-bye Mr. Chips*, is written using the flashback technique. If you are asked to relate what you did during the past week, you might choose to go backwards: Friday, Thursday, Wednesday, Tuesday, etc.

History books are usually written in chronological order. So are biographies and autobiographies. Many literature anthologies are organized according to "periods" or "ages" of literature—the Elizabethan Age, the Romantic Age, the Victorian Age, etc.—and these "ages" are set in the book in chronological order.

The chronological order pattern can be related to a student's experience in terms of his daily schedule (from the time he arises until he retires), and in terms of his weekly or yearly schedule. The progression of seasons is chronological, as is the progression of a lifetime. The steps of baking a cake, building a bookcase, performing a science experiment are in chronological order. Examples abound which we can use in clarifying this pattern to students.

Some paragraphs are written in chronological order, as is the following:

> Caesar now moved toward sole power. When Pompey and his followers fled to Greece, Caesar first made himself secure in Italy and Spain; then he defeated Pompey in Greece. He moved over into Africa, put Cleopatra on the throne of Egypt, and made Egypt an ally of Rome. In Asia Minor he drove out a dangerous tribe of barbarian invaders who had attacked Roman provinces. It was after this victory that he sent home his famous three-word message: Veni, Vidi, Vici—"I came, I saw, I conquered." *

When the chronological order pattern is important for students to recognize—for example, in understanding a chapter of a book—ask them to page through the chapter, noting main headings. Ask them if these headings, which represent main ideas, are given in chronological order. Ask them to jot down the main headings in the order of their presentation.

Translation level activities

After students have jotted down the main headings of a chapter, they can be taught to put these major ideas into another form, i.e., other than the simple recall-level listing form. Other common forms that could be used for the chronological pattern are: outline, flow chart, time line, and tree chart.

---

* Anatole Mazour and John M. Peoples. *Men and Nations: A World History*. New York: Harcourt, Brace and World, 1961, p. 115. Reprinted by permission.

Outline

The outline is versatile and can be used for recording any organizational pattern. Roman numerals are usually used to indicate major headings; capital letters are used for first-order subheadings; and arabic numerals are used to indicate second-order subheadings. (A newer form utilizes arabic numerals throughout, with decimals to indicate subheadings.)

The outline is more than a simple listing. There never are fewer than two main points nor more than five main points. Similarly, there are never fewer than two nor more than five subpoints of any one order. Outlining means *dividing* and *classifying*. Nothing can be divided into fewer than two parts. And anything classified into more than five divisions becomes unruly and is lacking in organization.

A time order outline might look like the following:

> Title: Specific steps are followed in a controlled experiment.
>   I. A question is asked.
>   II. A hypothesis is formulated.
>   III. A plan of attack is followed.
>   A. First . . .
>   B. Second . . .
>   C. Third . . .
>   IV. Results are acted upon.
>   A. Results are observed.
>   B. Results are tabulated.
>   C. Results are interpreted.

Using the newer form, our outline would look like this:

> Title: Specific steps are followed in a controlled experiment.
> 1.0 A question is asked.
> 2.0 A hypothesis is formulated.
> 3.0 A plan of attack is followed.
>   3.1 First . . .
>   3.2 Second . . .
>   3.3 Third . . .
> 4.0 Results are acted upon.
>   4.1 Results are observed.
>   4.2 Results are tabulated.
>   4.3 Results are interpreted.

Which form do you prefer?

Flow chart

Sometimes a flow chart will clarify and illustrate the chronological pattern
better than will an outline. For example, instead of using the preceding outline, we might have drawn a flow chart like that in Fig. 7.1.

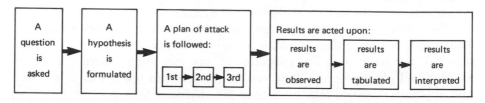

Fig. 7.1   Specific steps are followed in a controlled experiment.

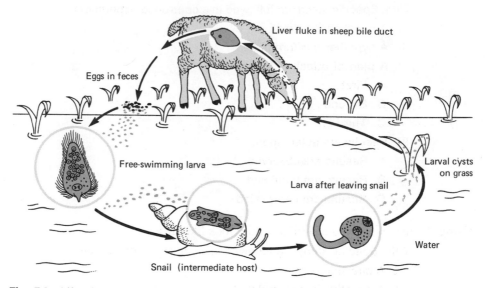

Fig. 7.2   Life history of a sheep liver fluke. (Reprinted by permission from William H.
Gregory and Edward Goldman, *Biological Science for High School*, Boston: Ginn and Co.,
1965, p. 270.)

Figure 7.2, which shows another type of flow chart, is based on the paragraph that follows.

The life history of the liver fluke is an interesting example of the dependence of
parasites upon intermediate hosts. The eggs, which are produced in large
numbers, are eliminated in the feces, or waste matter, of the sheep. Water is
necessary for the survival and development of the fertilized eggs. In a swampy
pasture they produce free-swimming larvae that infect certain snails. The snail

is thus the intermediate host. In the snail's body changes occur in the fluke larvae that result in the production of other larvae. These escape from the snail and form cysts on blades of grass. When a sheep eats the infected grass, the cycle starts again.*

Time line

For recording other kinds of information, a time line might be useful. A typical time line is shown in Fig. 7.3.

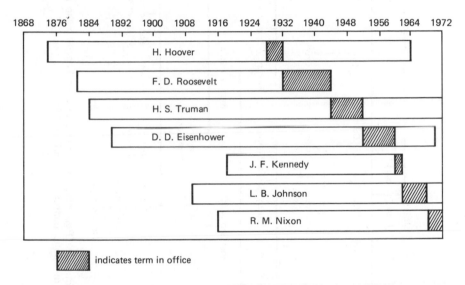

Fig. 7.3   Life spans of presidents of the United States with terms in office from 1928 to 1972.

Tree chart

For recording genealogy, a tree chart is useful. Figure 7.4 on the following page shows the derivation of modern English in tree chart form.

Spatial Order

In spatial, or descriptive, order, the pattern of discussion is from area to area, or region to region. For example, a classroom can be described in relationship to its seating pattern, its pattern of windows, chalkboard space, bulletin board space, bookcases, etc. A garden can be described from its focal point, e.g., a

* William H. Gregory and Edward Goldman. *Biological Science for High School*. Boston: Ginn, 1965, p. 270. Reprinted by permission.

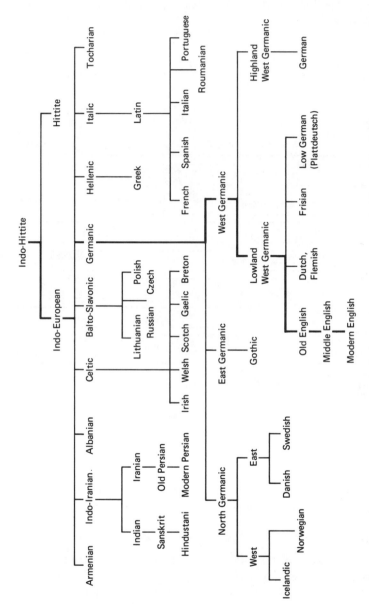

Fig. 7.4 The ancestry of modern English. (Reprinted by permission from *Teaching the English Language in Winsconsin*, Madison: Department of Public Instruction, 1967, p. 128.)

birdbath, and then in concentric circles around it. Rainfall in the United States can be described starting at the West coast and moving eastward. Similarly, the strengths and weaknesses of political parties are often described in relationship to regions of our country—the Deep South, the Midwest, the Far West, etc. All of these orders are spatial, since space, or area, is the unifying factor.

Students can easily give you examples of spatial order. Ask them what route they take in coming to school, or what route they followed on their last trip, or what route they would follow if they could go anywhere they wished. Ask them to describe the location of various animals in the zoo or products in a store.

Spatial order patterns are commonly found in most types of writing. Where did the American troops fight during World War II? requires a spatial-order answer, although it might also be organized chronologically. Where were American fighting men found in Vietnam in December 1971? must be answered spatially. Where would I look if I lost my golfball in an open field? must also be answered spatially—and by using a definite pattern, for example:

This item is similar to one found on a commonly used I.Q. test.

Translation level activities

To make sense out of a spatially oriented discourse, the reader or listener must recognize the pattern. To help him recognize and recall the pattern, several formats are useful. Among them are the outline, sketches, maps, floor plans, etc.

Outline

Any type of order can be recorded in outline form. The following outline demonstrates its use with spatially oriented ideas.

Title: The area surrounding the prisoner of war camp

  I. Between due east and due south was a vast swampland.

  II. Between due south and north by west were soldiers stationed
  at close intervals.

  III. Between north by west and north by east was a mountain range.

  IV. Between north by east and due east was a river.

Sketch

Drawing a sketch—or studying one that is provided—often helps us to
visualize a descriptive passage. Following are several examples.

Closterium is a common desmid. Fission occurs along isthmus dividing plant
into two semicells. Crystals in the vacuoles at each end of plant are continually
agitated.[*]

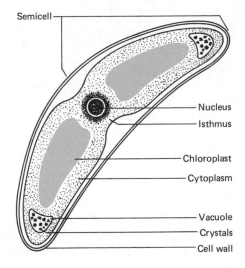

Living conditions such as temperature, pressure, amount of light, and kinds of food available are different at each level of depth in the ocean. The animals found at each level show a great variety of ways of adjusting to the different conditions.°

° Text and illustration from *Science Is Explaining* by Wilbur L. Beauchamp, *et al.*, p. 209. Copyright © 1963 by Scott, Foresman and Company. Reprinted by permission.

A figure is symmetrical or has symmetry if corresponding parts are alike in size, shape, and position. An isosceles triangle is symmetrical; a scaline triangle is not. Symmetry is one of the basic principles of design, because a harmonious balance between parts of a figure is an important element in beauty. Practically all living things exhibit symmetry. A leaf, like the one illustrated, has approximate *line symmetry*. That is, you can draw a line through the figure so that the designs on either side of the line are congruent. This line is called the *axis of symmetry*.°

Map

Maps can be used to translate a discourse into a visible pattern. We have maps of college campuses, cities, states, nations, and the world. It is possible to map almost any region. And a map usually clarifies a spatial organizational pattern better than can words. Figure 7.5 shows one example of how a map can be used to depict spatial organization.

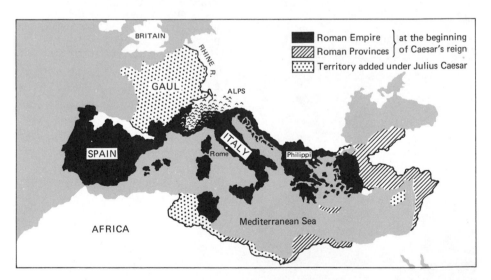

Fig. 7.5 The Roman Empire in 44 B.C., at the time of Julius Caesar. (From *Adventures in Appreciation*, Laureate Edition, by Walter Loban and Rosalind A. Olmstead, © 1963 by Harcourt Brace Jovanovich, Inc. and reproduced with their permission.)

° Text and illustration from Frank M. Morgan and Jane Tartman. *Geometry*. Boston: Houghton Mifflin, 1963, p. 200. Reprinted by permission.

Floor plan

Drawing a floor plan helps the reader visualize spatial organization. For example:

> The Aintree comes with a spacious loft, providing additional space for sleeping.
> The main level contains a basic living ell with a kitchen tucked in behind a
> free-standing bar. A large bedroom lies behind, with space for the luxury of a
> full bath across a narrow hall.°

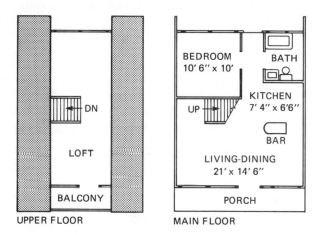

Expository Order

In expository writing the unifying factors are not time or space, but ideas and/or facts. Expository writing can be organized in the following kinds of patterns: cause to effect, effect to cause, question to answer, general statement to factors or details (deduction), details to general statement (induction), etc.

Students use these patterns regularly in their daily lives. For example, if you ask them why they chose the lunch they had, they might answer that it was nutritious, it did not have too many calories, and they like it. Or, ask them what kind of a car they would buy—if they could buy one—and why. Or, ask them what the following adds up to: "I have not studied since the last exam. I have another exam today" (cause to effect). Ask them why they got an A (B, C, D, F) on the last exam.(effect to cause). There are numerous examples that can be used to explain expository order.

The following is a typical expository passage of the deductive type (generalization stated first, followed by factors which compose it).

° Text and illustration from Lindal Homes, 10411 Empire Way South, Seattle, Washington. Reprinted by permission.

How can you assure a good credit rating? Specialists in consumer credit point to the "three C's" of a good credit rating—character, capacity, and collateral.

CHARACTER. How good is your reputation concerning payment of bills? When you are able to negotiate credit on your good name, you have established credit on the basis on your character. Among the personal traits that make you a good credit risk are your willingness, intention, and habit of meeting your financial obligations, plus the stability of your job and family and the continuance of your health.

CAPACITY. How prepared are you to meet financial obligations? Your ability to meet financial obligations is affected by your income. Is your income regular? Will it last over the length of time covered by your period of indebtedness? What other commitments might stop you from making regular payments?

COLLATERAL. What is your net worth? What assets do you have to guarantee financial responsibility? If you own property or other assets that may be transferred to the lender in the event you cannot pay your debts, you are securing your debt. Property used as security is called collateral. If you have the confidence of another person as to your character and your capacity to repay a loan, and he is willing to act as a co-signer on a note, he is offering his own character and capacity to you as collateral.*

Translation level activities

Such a pattern can be outlined easily. For the expository pattern, outlining is an exceptionally satisfactory translation activity. However, there are other visual patterns that are also highly useful. Among them are charts and various kinds of graphs.

Outline

The preceding passage can be outlined as follows:

Title: The "three C's" of good credit rating

I. Character	or	1.0 Character
II. Capacity		2.0 Capacity
III. Collateral		3.0 Collateral

---

* Dora S. Lewis, *et al. Housing and Home Management.* New York: Macmillan, 1969, p. 146. Reprinted by permission.

Whole chapters in student textbooks should be surveyed by the students before they read them. After such a survey, when they note only main headings, students should be asked to formulate an outline—either mentally or on paper. This might be done as a class-wide or group activity if several texts are being used, and the outline written on the board. This survey step, either done by the student himself or as a group activity, should be one of the initial steps in all reading assignments except those that are narrative.

After the headings are listed, students should be encouraged to anticipate what will be discussed under each heading. Students should be taught to ask questions about each heading. Then when they read silently, they should seek answers to these questions. After they have found the answers, they discuss them in class or recite them silently to themselves. They then review the complete chapter and possibly translate their knowledge, using an outline, another visible pattern, or a mental pattern. (In Chapter 5, SQ3R, a similar technique, was discussed in more detail.)

Chart

Charts are especially useful for making comparisons and are frequently seen in many types of readings materials. To reinforce your memory about this section of this chapter, fill in Table 7.2.

Table 7.2   Sequence at the literal level

Sequential patterns	Appropriate translation activities

Graph

Graphs are very useful for recording expository information. Among the most common are map graphs, pie graphs, bar graphs, line graphs, and pictographs.

A *map graph* can be used to show basic relationships. The main idea, or theme, is stated in the center, and each major subdivision is written on an arm:

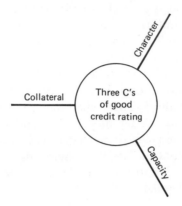

The *pie graph* can be used when the whole of something can be broken into weighted parts (Fig. 7.6). When sketching a pie graph, the student should try to use no fewer than two or more than five major divisions whenever possible, as illustrated in Fig. 7.6(b). He should draw heavy lines to indicate major divisions. Subdivisions should be indicated with lighter lines. He should also make sure that the circle of a pie graph is always fullfaced, i.e., never askew. The visual image is distorted if the circle is not flat.

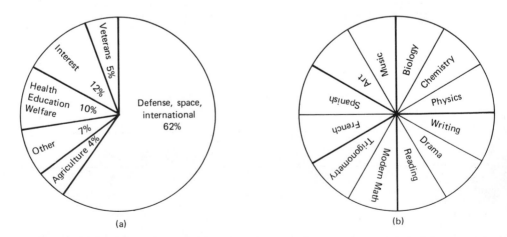

Fig. 7.6 Pie graphs: (a) expenditure of tax dollars; (b) factoring of students according to their electives.

The *bar graph* is useful for recording quantities, e.g., inches of rainfall according to area or date, production of manufactured items, average temperatures, etc. (Fig. 7.7).

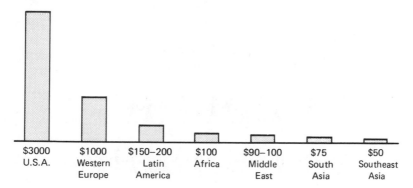

Fig. 7.7   Per capita annual income in various parts of the world in 1966. (From *Background Papers for Social Studies Teachers* by Leonard S. Kenworthy. © 1966 by Wadsworth Publishing Company, Inc., Belmont, California 94002. Reprinted by permission of the publisher.)

The *line graph,* a smoothed-out bar graph, is useful for many purposes, including comparisons, as in Fig. 7.8.

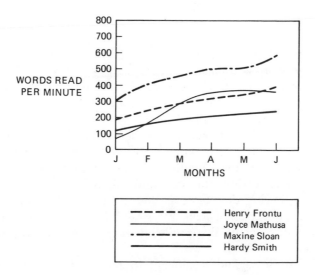

Fig. 7.8   Reading rate of four students in reading-improvement class, January to June 1972.

A *pictograph* is a type of bar graph in which illustrations are used instead of bars. They're usually more colorful and appealing than are bar graphs, but they serve the same purpose. Figure 7.9 is an example of a pictograph.

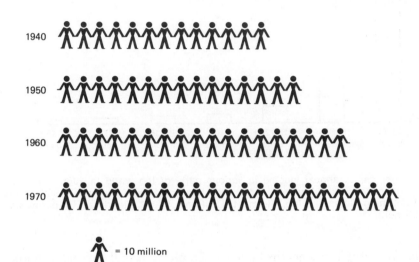

Fig. 7.9 Population of the United States from 1940 to 1970.

SUMMARY

At the beginning of this chapter, the *cognitive domain,* as delineated by Sanders from the work of Benjamin Bloom and others, was briefly explained to serve as an introduction to this chapter and Chapters 8 and 9. The seven levels of the cognitive domain are: *memory, translation, interpretation, application, analysis, synthesis,* and *evaluation.* These levels are listed in hierarchical form, starting with the level which is least demanding intellectually.

Chapter 7 deals with the importance of, and ways of, teaching memory- and translation-type activities. Traditionalists consider these to be literal level activities. Four such reading comprehension skills have been discussed here. They are: (1) following directions as given, (2) recalling facts, dates, etc., (3) recognizing and recalling main ideas, and (4) recognizing and recalling sequence. Ways of teaching these skills at the memory and translation levels were explained.

Frequently, students find it difficult to *follow directions,* or they have learned to circumvent directions. Teachers must both give directions clearly and establish the practice of avoiding needless repetition. At times, teachers might make a game of following directions while keeping the content of the directions subject-centered. Students must be alert to the fact that some directions should be followed exactly as given, whereas others can be altered somewhat, and still others should not be followed at all.

Recalling facts, dates, and other details is another literal comprehension activity. Some facts are important for all educated people to know; others are needed to help the student generalize. Some facts are important as tools, e.g., mathematics tables, etc. However, many teachers overstress the importance of details.

Recognizing and recalling main ideas is a basic skill for higher level comprehension. Although this skill is usually at the literal level, a student lacking this skill cannot move up the ladder in cognition. Techniques for developing this skill are: *classifying* (finding family names), *finding kernels of sentences, finding kernels in paragraphs and synthesizing like parts of speech, locating the main idea* in a paragraph, and others.

Recognizing and recalling sequence is another basic skill. Three patterns were explained, as were translation level activities for recording each pattern. The *chronological pattern* lends itself to the following types of translation forms: *outline, flow chart, time line,* and *tree chart.* The *spatial pattern* can be recorded in *outline form* and in *sketches, maps,* and *floor plans.* The *expository pattern* also lends itself to *outline* form, plus *charts* and *graphs* of various types, such as *map graphs, pie graphs, bar graphs, line graphs,* and *pictographs.*

The teacher's job is to know both the content of the materials being studied and the cognitive skills necessary for understanding the content, as given here and in other chapters. In addition, of course, he must know the students. Only then can the teacher decide which skills are essential to develop in order to help the students master the concepts. Usually, it is important to work not only at the literal level, but also at higher levels.

NOTES

1 J. P. Guilford. "Frontiers in Thinking that Teachers Should Know About," *The Reading Teacher* (February 1960): 176–182.

2 For a wealth of examples of such activities, see Rachel Salisbury. *Better Work Habits.* Glenview, Illinois: Scott, Foresman, 1966.

3 For the basic ideas included in this section, the author is indebted to Dr. Theodore L. Harris and associates in the Laboratory of Research in Basic Skills at the University of Wisconsin, 1966–1968.

4 See John L. Edwards and Nicholas J. Silvaroli. *Reading Improvement Program.* Dubuque, Iowa: Wm. C. Brown Co., 1969, pp. 29–35.

SUGGESTED ACTIVITIES

1. Name, in order, and briefly describe the seven levels of the cognitive domain as given by Sanders.

2. Name four literal level reading activities, and briefly describe each.

3. Design a microteach session for following directions in your content area.

4. Describe three instances when it is necessary to follow directions as given and three instances when it might be wiser to alter directions or not follow them.

5. Design five different types of activities for teaching young people to recognize and recall main ideas in your content area.

6. Design a microteach session for helping young people recognize and recall sequence in one of the following orders: chronological, spatial, or expository.

7. In a content area textbook, locate one graph, map, or chart for each organizational pattern (chronological, spatial, expository) and write four literal level questions about each. One of the four questions should be of each type: following directions, detail, main idea, and sequence.

8. Anticipate two ways in which the teaching of main idea and sequence can be done on a level higher than literal.

REFERENCES FOR FURTHER READING

Bloom, Benjamin, *et al. Taxonomy of Educational Objectives: Handbook I, Cognitive Domain.* New York: David McKay, 1956.

Bond, Guy L. and Miles Tinker. *Reading Difficulties: Their Diagnosis and Correction.* New York: Appleton-Century-Crofts, 1967, Chapter 11.

Dawson, Mildred (ed.). *Developing Comprehension, Including Critical Reading.* Newark, Delaware: International Reading Association, 1968.

Dechant, Emerald V. *Improving the Teaching of Reading,* 2d ed. Englewood Cliffs, N.J.: Prentice-Hall, 1970, Chapter 13.

Edwards, John L. and Nicholas J. Silvaroli. *Reading Improvement Program.* Dubuque, Iowa: Wm. C. Brown Co., 1969.

Guilford, J.P. "Frontiers in Thinking that Teachers Should Know About." *The Reading Teacher,* **23** (February 1960): 176–182.

Hafner, Lawrence (ed.). *Improving Reading in Secondary Schools, Selected Readings.* New York: Macmillan, 1967, Section 4.

Harris, Albert J. *How to Increase Reading Ability.* New York: David McKay, 1970, Chapter 6.

Herber, Harold (ed.). *Developing Study Skills in Secondary Schools* (Perspectives in Reading #4). Newark, Delaware: International Reading Association, 1965, Chapters 5, 6, 7.

Herber, Harold. *Teaching Reading in Content Areas.* Englewood Cliffs, N.J.: Prentice-Hall, 1970, Chapters 5, 6, 7.

Karlin, Robert. *Teaching Reading in High School.* Indianapolis: Bobbs-Merrill, 1964, Chapters 6 and 7.

Karlin, Robert (ed.). *Teaching Reading in High School—Selected Articles.* Indianapolis: Bobbs-Merrill, 1969, Chapter 6.

Marksheffel, Ned D. *Better Reading in the Secondary School.* New York: The Ronald Press, 1966, Chapter 11.

Salisbury, Rachel. *Better Work Habits.* Glenview, Illinois: Scott, Foresman, 1966.

Sanders, Norris. *Classroom Questions—What Kinds?* New York: Harper & Row, 1966.

Weiss, M. Jerry. *Reading in the Secondary Schools.* New York: Odyssey Press, 1961, Section 5.

Chapter 8

INTERPRETING AND APPLYING IDEAS IN READING

What interpretive level skills are important in content area subjects? How can these skills be taught?

What are application level activities?

Can we help students see opportunities that may arise in the future to use what they have learned in our classes?

INTRODUCTION

The purpose of this chapter is to explore and suggest ways of helping students *interpret* printed materials and *apply* ideas they have gained through reading. Chapter 9 deals with the development of the skills called *analysis, synthesis,* and *evaluation,* often referred to as critical-creative reading.

The major difference in thought process between functioning at the levels discussed in Chapters 8 and 9 is this: to function at the analysis, synthesis, and evaluation levels requires the use of formal logic and/or a conscious knowledge of the thought processes being used. To function at the interpretation and application levels does not. Few students (or even teachers) are prepared to use logical argumentation of a formal type, yet most can be taught to think beyond the very obvious "common sense" level.

When the questioning technique is used for teaching, *it is important to note that the form of a question does not determine the level of thought required to answer it.* The same question, in fact, asked of various students might elicit simple recall from some, interpretive reasoning from others, and analytic, synthetic, and evaluative judgment from others. Yet their answers might be similar.

What appears to be a complex evaluation question, for example, might draw a memory level response from a student who listened to his parents discuss the matter the night before. Another student might answer it by fusing ideas and seeing relationships without consciously knowing how he did so. Still another student might have formulated standards against which he judged the worth of the ideas presented. The teacher who uses *introspective-retrospective techniques* could identify the level of thought used by a student. ("How did you arrive at that answer? What makes you think so? Who advocates that point of view?")[1]

Sometimes it is extremely difficult to identify the cognitive level used unless we control conditions, as can be done in research. Sometimes it is not too important to know the level of thought used.

Understanding, then, that we lack some precision in our classification system because we cannot control all variables, e.g., a student's past experience, let us proceed. In this chapter, we shall examine the levels of interpretation and application. In Chapter 9, analysis, synthesis, and evaluation will be discussed.

INTERPRETATION

For a student to work at the interpretation level, he must be aware of *relationships* that exist between the ideas expressed in the materials at hand and something within his own bank of ideas—the ideas he has stored in his memory from past readings and experiences. Only part of the relationship exists in the immediate source; the other part comes from within him.

The idea external to the material at hand is what allows the student to go beyond literal comprehension of the ideas presented by the author. If we recognize this fact, we also recognize the importance—to the individual student —of using a variety of materials in the classroom. And we recognize the importance of helping the student relate ideas in the presently used materials with those in other materials and with past experiences in order to facilitate interpretation.

The following are types of activities which might be interpretive. (They will be at a lower level if the activity is simple recall from a previous experience. They will be at a higher level if formal logic or scientific evidence is used in the thinking process.)

1. *cause-effect relationships*, when only one is given
2. *anticipation* of what is to follow or inferring what has come before
3. *inducing main idea or theme* when they are not stated
4. *classifying*—convergently or divergently—without prompts or stereotypes
5. *making comparisons*—likenesses and differences
6. *inferring time, place, mood*
7. *inferring motives* of characters or real people
8. *responding to imagery*—living vicariously, having mental pictures—being able to touch, smell, see, hear, taste through the imagination
9. *empathizing*—a deeper vicarious experience than achieving imagery.

If we analyze these nine discrete listings, we can see that the first four are closely related and the last four are closely related. In accordance with our principle of outlining as set forth in the previous chapter, we have three broad categories of interpretive level activities. The first and third categories happen to have *four* identifiable components, and the second has *two*. (Thus, we have *from two to five main points* and *from two to five* subpoints.)

We might call the general categories relations, comparisons, and insights. Thus, our outline would look like this:

Title: Interpretive Thinking Skills

1.0 Perceiving unstated relationships

    1.1 Anticipating and "retrospecting"

    1.2 Recognizing cause-effect relationships

    1.3 Classifying convergently and divergently

    1.4 Inducing main idea and theme

2.0 Making comparisons

    2.1 Seeing likenesses (analogies)

    2.2 Seeing differences (contrasts)

3.0 Achieving insights

    3.1 Inferring time, place, mood

    3.2 Inferring motives of characters and real people

    3.3 Responding to imagery

    3.4 Empathizing with characters and real people

Even the subpoints might be *paired*. Do you see similar types of thinking processes between activities related to points 1.1 and 1.2, between 1.3 and 1.4, between 2.1 and 2.2, between 3.1 and 3.2, and between 3.3 and 3.4?

    Let us look at kinds of activities related to each of the pairs of subpoints.

Anticipating and "Retrospecting"/Cause-Effect

What will follow? or What will come next? are anticipation questions. What came before? or What preceded this action? are retrospective questions. If a cause-effect relationship is to be established, the following types of questions would be appropriate for seeking the cause: What caused the situation to exist? What factors led up to the necessary conclusion? When looking for effect, on the other hand, the following types of questions would be appropriate: What is likely to happen if the following conditions exist? What is likely to happen now that we have performed this action?

    In anticipation and retrospective activities, a cause-effect relationship has not been established. Sequence is being considered: what follows, or will follow, a situation—or what normally precedes, or has preceded, a situation—are different questions from those that establish or assume (at the interpretive level) a cause-effect relationship.

    For example, a person can become a drug addict only if drugs are available to him. Yet the mere availability of drugs does not mean that a person will become an addict. The availability of drugs is a necessary, but not a sufficient, condition to establish or even assume a cause-effect relationship. However, availability of drugs must *precede* addiction.

    In content area subjects, the following kinds of questions can be used to encourage anticipation and retrospection or to help students observe factors that might be found "traveling together," which would give us leads to the possibility of the existence of a cause-effect relationship.

Teaching Strategies

In mathematics

1. *Biography:* What do you think preceded Einstein's success as a mathematician? Check his biography to see if you are correct. Were these conditions necessary and sufficient to cause his success? Could you, with the same conditions available, be equally successful if you took advantage of them? Is an "X" factor operating? If you think so, attempt to define it. Is it available to you?

2. *Word problems:* Read a word problem such as the following:

   > You and your friends are planning a picnic. Your job is to bring hot dogs, buns, and potato chips for the crowd. Sixteen people are expected, and you have five dollars to spend. At the grocery store you find that hot dogs are 89¢ a dozen, buns are 45¢ a dozen, and potato chips are 79¢ for a large bag. Do you have enough money to buy enough hot dogs and buns so that everyone will get at least two, and still have enough money for a bag of potato chips? What is the exact cost?

   Anticipate the approximate cost $(3 \times .90) + (3 \times .50) + .80 - 2.70 + 1.50 + .80 + .80$. Then figure the exact cost. Then compare the two. If there is a large discrepancy, it is possible that the "exact cost" answer is wrong, since the arithmetic in it was more difficult than the arithmetic in the approximate-cost computation.

3. *Visual problems:* Is the total area of circles A and B and of the triangle C greater, equal to, or less than the area of square D?

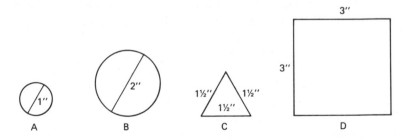

   Anticipate the answer before computations are made. After the computations are completed, compare the "exact" answer with the anticipated answer. If there is a sizable discrepancy, repeat the operations.

In science

1. *An experiment:* Look at this pineapple plant. Do you think it was given too much water before it died? Too much or too little sunlight? What else might have caused it to die? Can you suggest ways of setting up an experiment to see which of these factors or which combination of these

factors may have caused the plant to die? (Such discussion might precede an actual experiment with pineapple plants and/or might be used in a preliminary discussion to help students relate to a botany experiment in their manuals.)

2. *An experiment:* What do you think would happen if you reversed the order of some of the steps in the following experiment, doing step 4 *before* step 3? What would happen if you used the wrong proportions? (This would be a higher-level question *if* formal scientific reasoning was used. It would be at a lower level *if* it was recall.)

3. *Biography:* Having studied the discoveries made by the Curies, attempt to place the discoveries in chronological order. Check the biography to see if you are correct.

In social studies

"The reforms have worked just as well as we predicted—and even better than we expected," says one top American official here.

> —Peter R. Kann in the *Wall Street Journal.*

New Yorker: One top and very *candid* American economic official.[2]

1. *Current events:* What do you think will happen if our population doubles by the year 2000? If we attain zero population growth by the year 2000?

2. *Current events:* How did our city (or other area) become so polluted? Give three major reasons. Discuss their interaction.

3. *Biography:* From what you know about the background of the President, discuss factors which may have caused him to make his recent decision.

In English

1. *Fiction:* Read to the climax of the story. Then close your book and write an ending. Compare your ending with the author's.

2. *Mystery:* Read the last chapter of the book. Write a beginning. Compare your beginning with the author's.

3. *Character analysis:* What do you think was Hamlet's fatal flaw? What were his greatest strengths?

Classifying/Inducing Main Idea and Theme

Classifying, or grouping, items, sentences, paragraphs, or ideas into generally agreed upon categories is a convergent thinking activity. The same is usually true if the activity is selecting from several choices the main idea of a paragraph or the theme of a longer work. Certainly exceptions can be stated, but in general this is true. Further, such activities are usually at the literal level and were amply discussed in Chapter 6.

However, *formulating* a main idea and classifying items or ideas when such classification patterns are not simply recalled are interpretive level activities—at least. For example:

1. Compare the thought processes involved in selecting the main idea in the two passages that follow.

First passage

Once in power, Caesar showed himself a statesman as well as a politician and general. He made vast reforms and planned even more. His first attention went to the provinces. He granted citizenship to many provincials. As governors he chose trained men and paid them a fixed salary. Other officials were sent to check on the governors, removing those who did not rule well. Land which had been seized by wealthy men was regained and divided among landless farmers and veterans. This move established groups of Romans throughout the provinces, and thus spread Roman culture and influence. Caesar also gave membership in the Senate to many provincials.

Caesar secured laws to relieve poor farmers and men who could not pay their debts. He improved the roads so that armies as well as traders could move quickly to all parts of the empire.*

Second passage

. . . Caesar's first attention went to the provinces. He granted citizenship to many provincials. As governors he chose trained men and paid them a fixed salary. Other officials were sent to check on the governors, removing those who did not rule well. Land which had been seized by wealthy men was regained and divided among landless farmers and veterans. This move established groups of Romans throughout the provinces, and thus spread Roman culture and influence. Caesar also gave membership in the Senate to many provincials.

Caesar secured laws to relieve poor farmers and men who could not pay their debts. He improved the roads so that armies as well as traders could move quickly to all parts of the empire.*

2. Take the following items and put them into two groups.

| grapefruit | cucumber | banana | onion |

The convergent—middle-class—way of grouping these is according to function:

Fruit	*Vegetable*
grapefruit	cucumber
banana	onion

---

* Anatole G. Mazour and John M. Peoples. *Men and Nations: A World History.* New York: Harcourt, Brace and World, 1961, p. 115. Reprinted by permission.

In fact, on commonly used I.Q. tests, such a grouping pattern is the only one for which the student is given credit. In what other ways could these four items be logically grouped? According to shape? Color? Sorry, no credit! Why not? Because that's not the way *middle-class* children think —another reason that commonly used I.Q. tests are unfair to culturally different children.

3. In how many ways can the following items be grouped:

or these:

a b c d e f g h i j k l m n o p q r s t u v w x y z

or these:

monkey	cactus	grape	diamond
gold	dinosaur	lime	daisy
whale	mouse	ruby	rose

Might your classification system depend on whether you are teaching phonics or science, whether you are playing "Twenty Questions," or the way *your* mind works? If you were taking an entrance exam for the only graduate school you could possibly attend, and it had been devised and would be scored by a Zuni Indian, how would you group them?

After items are grouped, and possibly put in outline form, a title, thesis statement, or theme telling what the whole is about should be induced. Possibly a summary statement should be composed.

Activities, then, that might be engaged in are:

1. inducing these statements, or themes
2. summary or précis writing
3. testing for card stacking (Is only one point of view presented?)
4. headline writing

Two examples of heading writing follow.

COMPUTERS
TO FORM
OWN UNION

—Headline in the *Amsterdam News.*

New Yorker: It'll be fun to watch them collect dues.[3]

KING FAISAL
LEAVES S.F.
—IN 3 PLANES
—Headline in the *San Francisco Chronicle*.
New Yorker: Kings do things right.[4]

Making Comparisons

Activities that help the student focus on similarities and differences are important not only academically but also practically. How does a student decide which suit or golf clubs he wants to purchase? How can he determine which car he prefers? How does he decide where he will travel or what sport he will engage in or which book he will read?

Usually, such decisions are best made by comparing alternatives, not just by zeroing in on one item as though blindfolded.

Fox, chief of the Police Department's juvenile aid division, told a workshop on gang control that policemen and gang members have many things in common. Among them he said were:
Both usually come from families.
—Dayton (Ohio) *Daily News*

New Yorker: That's enough. We don't need to hear the others.[5]

In mathematics

1. Are the distances the *same or different* that a horse would have to run if he were always in the inner lane rather than the outer lane of the Derby racetrack? If they are different, what is the measured distance?

2. Which three of the following geometric figures are *most alike*: square, circle, oval, sphere? Why?

3. *Compare* the cost of a trip to Mexico City, Honolulu, and Jamaica in regard to air fare, hotel rooms in first-class hotels, second-class hotels, and food.

In science

1. Are the hibernating habits of a black bear and a hampster the *same or different?*

2. Which four of the following animals have eating habits which are *most alike*: monkey, ape, lemur, orangutan, gibbon, chimpanzee?

3. *Compare* the use of helium with other gases used to inflate and provide lift for balloons in regard to cost and safety.

In social studies

1. Are the philosophies of Nixon and Eisenhower the *same or different* in regard to world trade?
2. Which two of the following countries are *most alike* in the quality of their contribution to peace talks in the 1970-1972 Vietnam negotiations: France, England, West Germany?
3. *Compare* the Roman and Greek Empires' contributions to modern thought in theology and art.

In English

1. Are there more *likenesses or differences* between the dramatic literature of France and England during the seventeenth century?
2. Which four of the following authors are *most alike* in philosophy: Wordsworth, Keats, Shelley, Byron, Coleridge? In form?
3. *Compare* Shakespeare and Cervantes in regard to quantity of writing which survives and their sense of humor as reflected in their major works.

Inferring Time, Place, Mood/Inferring Motives of Characters and Real People

Activities related to the identification of reasons for a thought occurring to a person or for a person (or fictional character) participating in a particular activity relate to inferring motives of characters and real people.

In literature and social studies

Inferential skills are especially important in reading literature and social studies, including current events, as well as in daily living. When only partial information is given and the reader must place the ideas in time (or era) and/or area, he is making inferences. When he must assess the mood (or emotional feelings) or tone (general effect or atmosphere), he is dealing with this skill. For example, one might infer *time* and *mood* from the following episode:

> Mr. Anders, the schoolmaster, tried to comfort his pupils. He said that air-raid shelters were found in every country, but they were only a precaution. He was sure they would never be used.
> "Norway's safe from war," he said. "Our country's been at peace for over a hundred years. We've no quarrel with anyone and no one has a quarrel with us. Let's not worry about a thing as unlikely as war."
> There was a knock on the classroom door. Uncle Victor came in. He was a great favorite with all the children. When he visited the school he always told a sea story, and so today they settled back for one of his salty tales. But it was no sea story that brought Captain Lundstrom on this occasion. He whispered a few words to Mr. Anders and then spoke to the class.

"Now that we're building bomb shelters, we ought to have an air-raid drill," he said. "We want to teach everyone to go in orderly fashion to the shelters and not to be crowding the doorways."

"Just like a fire drill," Mr. Anders said." *

And from the following passage, the reader can infer *time* and *place*:

The exuberance of the age carried over into every field of human endeavor. The universities were full of intellectual vitality and disputation, fruitful in sifting truth. In this age schoolmen dared to apply the rationalism of Aristotle to the elucidation of articles of faith; in this age pagan philosophy and Christian theology came to terms, and eminent theologians established the principle that there is no quarrel between faith and reason. In this age intellectual giants fought with razorlike logic to subdue their adversaries before a university public numbering thousands. In this age every art flourished to an astounding degree. We have from this period a vast, vigorous, anonymous literature: the *Nibelungenlied, Aucassin and Nicolette, Reynard the Fox*, the *Fioretti*—to give only a sampling.†

From the following poem, we can interpretively read the *eternality of time* (unimportance of literal time) and the *universality of place* (unimportance of literal place):

OZYMANDIAS

I met a traveller from an antique land
Who said: Two vast and trunkless legs of stone
Stand in the desert. Near them, on the sand,
Half sunk, a shattered visage lies, whose frown,
And wrinkled lip, and sneer of cold command,
Tell that its sculptor well those passions read
Which yet survive, stamped on these lifeless things,
The hand that mocked them, and the heart that fed:
And on the pedestal these words appear:
"My name is Ozymandias, king of kings:
Look on my works, ye Mighty, and despair!"
Nothing beside remains. Round the decay
Of that colossal wreck, boundless and bare
The lone and level sands stretch far away.

Percy Bysshe Shelley

---

* From the book *Snow Treasure* by Marie McSwigan. Copyright 1942 by E. P. Dutton & Co., Inc. Renewal © 1970 by Kathryn McSwigan Laughlin. Published by E. P. Dutton & Co., Inc. and used with their permission.
† Ruth Mary Fox. *Dante Lights the Way*. Milwaukee: Benziger Bruce & Glencoe, 1958, p. 4. Reprinted by permission.

To demonstrate the eternality and universality of this poem, the reader might suggest other names for Ozymandias, e.g., Hitler, Joseph McCarthy. Who else? Personalities from literature might also be used.

Inferring motives of characters and real people is of utmost importance if we are to understand what is going on in literature and the real world. Sometimes a motive is not explained, and sometimes a motive is given, though it may not be the true one. Note, for example, the importance placed on motive in determining the penalty for a crime. Recall the debates and discussions related to Senator Edward Kennedy's delayed report to the police of the tragedy at Chappaquiddick.

Awareness of motive can be taught to the very young and can be developed more fully as students mature. For example, why did the stepmother in *Cinderella* treat her daughters and her stepdaughter differently? Why did Charlotte befriend the pig in *Charlotte's Web*? Why did Brutus assist in the slaying of Caesar? Why did Hamlet at one time treat Ophelia as if she were insane?

Motives can be related to authors and the themes of their works. What, basically, was William Golding trying to explain in *Lord of the Flies*? What was Huxley saying in *Brave New World*; Cervantes in *Don Quixote*? And, of course, motives can be related to acts of senators and representatives in Congress, to the President of the United States, and to deeds of your acquaintances, etc.

In science

Not to be forgotten, however, is the importance to the scientist of inferring time and place of the development of such things as rock formations, the continental drift, various species of animal and plant life, etc., and also of inferring motives of scientists (including himself) as they relate to the kinds of research they pursue and the value they give to the research of others.

In mathematics

The mathematician is also concerned with inferring moods and motives of people when he designs a bridge or a highway. He may be interested in ancient or comparative architecture because it suggests the possibility of improving the present, making a home or a community a more desirable place in which to live. He may see mathematical patterns in music and art and from these be able to infer the mood and/or the era of the creator.[6] Like the scientist, he should also be concerned with inferring his and others' motives in relation to specific areas of interest.

Responding to Imagery/Empathizing with Characters and Real People

When a reader responds to the imagery of a passage, he mentally sees, feels, hears, touches, or smells in accord with the description. He lives vicariously— possibly in a different age or place.

Closely related to this is the ability to empathize. Empathy suggests the totality of experience. When one empathizes, he becomes another person, or he is so much the other person that there is an intimacy of feelings, thoughts, and motives. Different from sympathy, which suggests a spontaneous emotion in time of misfortune, empathy suggests involvement with another person or fictional character to the extent of vicarious, or imaginative, identification. Such responses are probably best classified in both the cognitive and affective domains.

Some examples of passages replete with imagery are given below. To which physical sense, or senses, do each appeal or relate?

1. "The atmosphere churned. The dirt of years, tobacco of many growings, opium, betel nut, and moist flesh allied themselves in one grand assault against the nostrils." [7]

   _____ smell

2. The anthropologist stared in amazement as he viewed before him the ruins of the ancient civilization of Zandu. He could not wait to walk among the ruins.

   _____

3. "Long ago a primitive hunter caught a large fish. It was so large that he wanted to be able to tell people about it after he had eaten it. He found a forked stick that fit his fish. . . . Then he ate the fish.

   "Later this hunter's friend caught a fish and boasted that his fish was just as long as the hunter's. How could the hunter prove him wrong (or right)?"*

   _____

4. "To 1½ cups papaya pulp add juice of 1 lemon, ½ cup sugar, and beat into 2 stiffly whipped whites of eggs. Cook. Serve with whipped cream."[8]

   _____

It is impossible in a brief exposition to exemplify empathy. Yet surely you can recall a person who can read your thoughts—who can predict your actions and is on your side. You, no doubt, remember going to a movie and imagining yourself to be the hero—if you are a man, or the heroine—if you are a woman. You have probably felt the same way when you have read some books.

---

* Robert E. Eicholz, _et al._ _Modern General Mathematics._ Menlo Park, Calif.: Addison-Wesley, 1969, p. 135. Reprinted by permission. Copyright © 1969 by Addison-Wesley Publishing Co., Inc. All rights reserved.

APPLICATION

To work at the application level, a level higher than interpretation, one must *wtihout prompts* recognize a situation in which a previously learned principle applies and utilize the principle successfully. This is frequently called *transfer of learning.*

You are learning about the teaching of reading in this course. If you were in a classroom, could you recognize a situation that calls for the teaching of a particular reading skill or level of comprehension and also teach it with success? If so, you are functioning at the application level—at least. All content area subjects provide ample opportunity for working at the application level.

Perhaps one reason that most students find word problems in mathematics harder than simple process problems is that word problems are usually at the application level. Success in working a word problem is not determined simply by properly performing the arithmetic task, but rather by first properly identifying the task. Such identification requires the singling-out of that task from all others as the appropriate one to solve the problem. It also often requires recognition of the fact that some information is irrelevant. Cognitively, this is a high level activity.

Look at the following problems:

1. A cubic mile of sea water contains about 38 pounds of gold.
    a) How many cubic miles of water would be needed to have 1596 pounds of gold?
    b) One pound of gold will make a thin wire about 900 miles long. The distance around the earth is 24,902 miles. With the gold from 1 cubic mile of sea water, how many feet of wire would you have left after you wrapped it around the earth once? *

2. How many stamps does David have in his collection if 16% of them are less than one year old and 25% of those that are older than one year, or 26 in number, are Japanese?

What thought processes are required of the student if he is to successfully work problems 1 and 2? Is there any irrelevant information included?

Similar types of activities are found in science materials.

In social studies, predicting how a segment of the population will vote is an application level activity. Similarly, predicting how individuals or groups will act in any circumstance is at the application level. What one must do in making such predictions is draw from past knowledge that which is appro-

---

* Robert E. Eicholz, *et al. Modern General Mathematics.* Menlo Park, Calif.: Addison-Wesley, 1969, p. 109. Reprinted by permission. Copyright © 1969 by Addison-Wesley Publishing Co., Inc. All rights reserved.

priate to the solution of the problem and use it effectively in making realistic predictions. Such activities will be at higher cognitive levels if more than common sense reasoning is used. Can you think of other social studies activities that might be considered application level activities?

In English, students frequently study grammatical principles, possibly the Latin type or modern linguistic type. Many students do well on such activities. Yet, how many of them use these principles in their writing? Frequently, there is little transfer! Like the girl who stayed after school to write on the board "I have gone" 500 times and on completion of that task wrote a note to the teacher saying, "I have went home," many students fail to see the relevance of grammar to their own writing. Reaching the application level is a difficult task for many, and direct teaching is frequently necessary to effect transfer.

Do students sometimes read literature, and possibly even identify the theme, without pondering its relevance to life, or to their lives? If so, they have not reached the application level. So, too, of history and the arts, and of science and mathematics, and of all that is "learned." Sometimes information is compartmentalized and used only in specific situations—without being generalized. Such is the case when a student spells well in English class, but poorly in all other classes.

Teaching for transfer is essential. Expecting a student to transfer—and helping him to do so—is also important. The teacher's task here is difficult. Too many prompts lower the level of the activity—possibly to the literal level. Too few prompts make the transfer impossible for some students. When a new principle is learned, the teacher might ask the class to suggest occasions when this principle might be used in the future. Thus, transfer when the occasion arises might be facilitated.

Application level activities might also revolve around the use of appropriate reference materials. Questions might be asked which require students to use research techniques. At the application level, students would be required to decide which resources are most appropriate for answering a question, and they would be required to use these resources in finding the answer.

Such reference materials range from indexes of materials (the *Reader's Guide to Periodical Literature*, the *Art Index*, etc., the card catalog) to reference materials (encyclopedias, almanacs, dictionaries) to types of literature (textbooks, various genre of literature, e.g., biography, poetry, essays, novels, etc., newspaper articles, magazines and journals) to community, state and national resources (community leaders and archives, etc.). More information about reference indexes and materials is given in Chapter 11.

SUMMARY

Reading comprehension abilities called *interpretation* and *application* have been explained in this chapter. Basically, the thought processes involved in *interpretive activities* require the reader to see a relationship when only part of the relationship is given. The other part is supplied from the reader's background of experience. This related experience may have been gained through reading, listening, or otherwise observing—either consciously or subconsciously. For the activity to be interpretive, the reader himself must grasp, or formulate, the relationship. Otherwise, the activity is at the memory or translation level.

The following types of interpretive activities were explained and exemplified: *perceiving unstated relationships* (anticipating and retrospecting, recognizing cause-effect relationships, classifying convergently and divergently, inducing main idea and theme), *making comparisons* (seeing likenesses and differences), *achieving insights* (inferring time, place, mood, motives of characters and real people, responding to imagery, empathizing with characters and real people).

Application level activities require the reader to both *recognize* a situation in which a previously learned principle applies and *use* the principle successfully. Commonly, this is called *transfer* of learning.

Word problems in mathematics are frequently more difficult than simple process problems because many of them require the student himself to identify from all he has previously learned the process to be followed in solving a specific problem. In addition, the student must carry through the process successfully.

In all classes, students frequently compartmentalize their knowledge and use it only when directly guided to do so. Teachers must exert efforts to help students see when previously learned knowledge or principles might apply to a present situation and also to understand that what they are learning at the present time may be used in the future. Too much guidance, however, lowers the level of activity; too little makes it impossible. To strike a balance takes experience.

NOTES

1 See William S. Gray. "New Approaches to the Study of Interpretation in Reading." *Journal of Educational Research,* **LII** (October 1958): 65–67.

2 *The New Yorker,* March 13, 1971, p. 136.

3 *The New Yorker,* April 3, 1971, p. 93.

4 *The New Yorker,* June 26, 1971, p. 88.

5 *The New Yorker,* January 23, 1971, p. 65.

6 "Donald in Mathmagic Land." Glendale, California: Walt Disney Educational Material Co., 1960. Junior-Senior School Level, 26 minutes.

7 Thomas Burke. "The Chink and the Child," in *The Golden Argosy*, ed. Van H. Cartmell and Charles Grayson. New York: The Dial Press, 1955, p. 67.

8 Bertha Munks. *Florida's Favorite Foods*. Tallahassee: State of Florida Department of Agriculture, 1957, p. 129.

SUGGESTED ACTIVITIES

1. List three different types of interpretive level activities, and indicate sub-activities which belong with each.

2. Name two characteristics of all application level activities.

3. Design a two-minute microteach session showing how you might teach either anticipation or retrospection in your content area.

4. Design a ten-minute microteach session showing a way in which you could teach divergent classification in your content area.

5. Using a chapter in your content area textbook, write six different types of interpretive level questions.

6. Using the same chapter, write two application level questions.

7. Compare the relative merits of literal level activities with those of the interpretive and application levels.

REFERENCES FOR FURTHER READING

Beery, Althea, Thomas C. Barrett, and William Powell (eds.). *Elementary Reading Instruction: Selected Materials*. Boston: Allyn and Bacon, 1969, Chapter 7.

Bond, Guy L. and Miles Tinker. *Reading Difficulties: Their Diagnosis and Correction*. New York: Appleton-Century-Crofts, 1967, Chapter 15.

Dawson, Mildred (ed.). *Developing Comprehension, Including Critical Reading*. Newark, Delaware: International Reading Association, 1968.

DeBoer, John and Martha Dallman. *The Teaching of Reading*. New York: Henry Holt, 1970, Chapter 6.

Hafner, Lawrence E. (ed.). *Improving Reading in Secondary Schools, Selected Readings*. New York: Macmillan, 1967, Sections 4 and 10.

Harris, Albert J. *How to Increase Reading Ability*. New York: David McKay, 1970, Chapter 16.

Herber, Harold (ed.). *Developing Study Skills in Secondary Schools* (Perspectives in Reading #4). Newark, Delaware: International Reading Association, 1965.

Herber, Harold. *Teaching Reading in Content Areas*. Englewood Cliffs, N.J.: Prentice-Hall, 1970, Chapters 5 and 6.

Karlin, Robert. *Teaching Reading in High School*. Indianapolis: Bobbs-Merrill, 1964, Chapters 6 and 7.

Karlin, Robert (ed.). *Teaching Reading in High School—Selected Articles*. Indianapolis: Bobbs-Merrill, 1969.

Marksheffel, Ned D. *Better Reading in the Secondary School*. New York: The Ronald Press, 1966, Chapter 8.

Olson, Arthur V. and Wilber S. Ames (eds.). *Teaching Reading Skills in Secondary Schools*. Scranton, Pa.: International Textbook Co., 1970.

Otto, Wayne and Richard J. Smith. *Administering the School Reading Program*. Boston: Houghton Mifflin, 1970.

Sanders, Norris M. *Classroom Questions—What Kinds?* New York: Harper & Row, 1966, Chapters 4 and 5.

Schubert, Delwyn G. and Theodore L. Torgerson (eds.). *Readings in Reading: Practice, Theory, Research*. New York: Thomas Y. Crowell Co., 1968.

Spache, George. *Toward Better Reading*. Champaign, Illinois: Garrard, 1963, Chapters 4, 16, and 18.

Chapter 9

ANALYZING, SYNTHESIZING, AND EVALUATING IDEAS THROUGH READING

What is the basic difference in thought processes between analysis-synthesis-evaluation activities and interpretive level activities?

Are there important analysis type activities in all content areas?

Are there times when synthesis level activities should be encouraged?

What are the two steps in evaluation?

INTRODUCTION

Analysis, synthesis, and evaluation activities are frequently referred to as critical-creative thinking abilities. Much has been written and spoken about such abilities, yet the frequency of their use in many classrooms is appallingly scarce. There are several reasons for this.

For students to think at these higher levels, they must use a wide variety of materials. And it is necessary for the teacher to help them find the common core of such materials as well as relate their previous experiences to ideas gained in their present reading materials. Normally, not all students in the same classroom will have read the same things, nor will they have had the same experiences. A skillful teacher is, indeed, necessary. This is true even at the interpretive and application levels, but greater knowledge and skill on the part of the teacher are necessary to help students function on these higher levels.

Frequently, students attach a halo to the printed word, thinking that anything that is in print must be true. On the other hand, some of these same students find it extremely difficult to suspend judgment of ideas in materials long enough to know what the author is saying if the author's ideas and opinions differ from theirs. The reader becomes emotional, and does not even know what the author has said.

When controversial issues are being studied, the teacher's first questions should be at the literal level. When the teacher is satisfied that the students have grasped the author's ideas, then—and only then—should students be asked to react at higher levels. One important kind of activity here is to ask the student to put himself in the author's place—to recognize and think from the author's value system and to see if what the author has said makes sense in this value system. Then, the value system itself should be evaluated.

For example, making extensive trips into outer space and spending millions or billions of dollars on them makes sense to many middle- and upper-class citizens. They may have an insatiable curiosity about what lies beyond our planet. And, in addition, they may be able and willing to postpone immediate satisfaction with the hope that in time at least some of their questions will be answered. From their point of view, money spent on space travel is well spent.

On the other hand, those who are starving or who are living in the midst of race tumult and those who empathize with these people probably feel that immediate internal reform in our country is far more important. From their point of view, it would be far better to spend the tax dollar on urban renewal and on improving race relations and job opportunities.

Students in a class should be taught to examine both points of view, looking for the rationale behind each. They should attempt vicarious empathy with those who feel differently. Each of these points of view is perhaps legitimate— as it relates to a subculture.

Within a society such as ours the basic problem may be one of establishing priorities. The subcultures interact with and affect one another. Indeed, if the destitute decide to blow up NASA, our space program would be set back considerably. It is also possible, however, that our space program may, in time, immeasurably benefit the needy.

Other examples abound and may help clarify the growing realization that various value systems function within our society. Thirty years ago, many teen-agers listened to jazz only when their parents were out. It was the same with rock-and-roll not too long ago. And today and tomorrow it is sure to be something else.

Certain very traditional moral values within our society are widely questioned today, particularly values that relate to premarital sex. Parents may have one value system, but if they do not attempt to listen to their adolescent sons and daughters and attempt to see their point of view, communications will very likely cease. They may thus give up the chance of converting their children—or of being converted themselves.

The classroom atmosphere must allow for divergence in opinions. There must be freedom of expression. The teacher must learn to refrain from making judgments, e.g., praising one student for his opinion and rejecting others. Instead, students should be encouraged to test their ideas, to think further about them. They might, however, be evaluated on their logic, or lack of it.

Another important point must be made; that is, that critical reading (analysis of propaganda, of semantics, authenticity of sources, etc.) should not be carried out in a predominantly negative way. Unfortunately, the word "critical" has pejorated in American usage, for "critical" suggests fault-finding. (Even the word "propaganda" has pejorated.) Persuasive language and techniques are not all bad. The word "critic" more nearly suggests the meaning intended here. An art critic, for example, is not a fault-finder. He is a judge. Part of his job is to identify and describe the best.

Analysis (plus synthesis and evaluation) is a good word for our idea at the present time. Sometimes, a student might simply be asked to pick out the best characteristic of an article or advertisement, etc., or the most useful idea. If he is to create, these useful ideas or characteristics will come in handy. (For example, if a student is to become a commercial artist, which activity will help him most: (1) picking out the ten most useful ideas or characteristics from a group of advertisements and combining them, or (2) picking out the ten most worthless ideas or characteristics and doing what with them?)

ANALYSIS

In analysis (one of the three highest levels in the cognitive domain), a complete statement is broken, or separated, into its component parts for individual study. In addition, a student thinking on the analysis level "must be conscious of the intellectual process he is performing and know the rules for reaching a valid and true conclusion." [1] Lower levels of thinking do not require the student to be aware of the precise thought process being used.

The area of *semantics*, as discussed in Chapter 6, belongs at the analysis level. If a student is *aware of how words work*—for example, by being aware of multiple denotations, connotations, hyperbole, euphemism, etc.—he is consciously aware of some techniques used for persuasion. Similarly, being able to consciously distinguish between vague and precise use of language and to judge the effectiveness of language are analytical techniques.

Related to the area of persuasion are the following additional activities:

1. making judgments related to the authenticity of a source of information
2. distinguishing between fact and opinion
3. analyzing propaganda
4. detecting fallacies of reasoning

Each will be explained in the following sections.

Authenticity and/or Choice of a Source of Information

Who is the best person to make an accurate and unbiased statement about a subject? Such a question is a good starting point for judging the authenticity of a source of information. For example, multiple-choice items such as the following might be supplied. The student is to check the source that is *likely* to be the best one from the three supplied.

1. The poem "Grazing Grass" is a modern classic.

    _____a. John Ciardi, poetry editor of the *Saturday Review*

    _____b. Jim Jonski, mannish gym teacher at Fordheights Secondary School

    _____c. Geraldine Sloan, glamorous actress

2. Switzerland has the highest per capita income of any country in Europe.

    _____a. Elaine Brooks, bank teller

    _____b. Jonathan DeLonge, star basketball player

    _____c. Dr. Gordon Kline, professor of economics, Townheights University

3. The human body needs five main classes of nutrients: vitamins, fats, minerals, carbohydrates, proteins.

    _____a. James Greene, business manager of Taco House Restaurants

    _____b. Svelta Smith, director of Slymnastics Spa

    _____c. Ross Jones, high school general science teacher

4. Two negatives do not make a positive in English.

    _____a. Virginia Karbunki, mathematics teacher

_____b. Marchance Hubbard, high school principal

_____c. Juanita Duran, English teacher

5. Modern mathematics is on its way out.

_____a. Jim Brown, high school student

_____b. Henry Osborne, editor, *Mathematics for Today's Students*, 1945

_____c. Jerome Slomowicz, chairman of research, USOE

6. This sundae contains only 250 calories.

_____a. Roberta Fatma, only 15 and already 175 pounds

_____b. Velma Hodges, home economist

_____c. Walter Smithsona, soda jerk

Such activities should be used to spur class discussion—to get students *thinking about* the importance of selecting appropriate sources for specific kinds of information. Such an exercise is not meant to be graded, but rather to introduce discussion and possibly debate—to lay the foundations for an analytical task which is, indeed, difficult and, certainly, is not a simple multiple-choice activity.

Such an activity might be further extended by asking such questions as: (1) What makes him think so? Which evidence seems to support the judgment best? and (2) Why does he want me to think so? Which person would be least prejudiced by selfish motives? The following exercise exemplifies this strategy.

In *part 1* of each question, check the person who is likely to be the best qualified to make the given statement. In *part 2*, check the person who is likely to be least biased by selfish motives. In *part 3*, check the evidence which best supports the judgment.

Astroturf is as safe to use on a football field as is grass.

1. *Who said so?* Which person is best qualified to make this statement?

_____a) Hugh Jefferson, Patterson High's football coach

_____b) John Harwick, professor of health and physical education at State University

_____c) Gary Johnson, president of the school board

2. *Why does he want me to believe him?* Which person seems least biased by selfish motives?

_____a) Harry Eagleson, owner of Eagleson's Garden Shop

_____b) Jim Smith, president of Smith's Carpet Store

_____c) Oscar Henderson, chairman of research for the department of health and physical education at State University

3. *What makes him think so?* What evidence best supports his judgment?

_____a) "There were no serious accidents on the astroturf field at State University this year."

_____b) "A survey of 20 universities—ten using astroturf and ten using grass—showed no significant differences in accident rate or seriousness over the past three years."

_____c) "Astroturf is as thick as grass, and more regular. It should therefore be as safe as grass to use."

The student must recognize the fact that even so-called authorities often differ in their points of view and judgments. Two Ph.D.'s in reading might differ radically in their recommended approaches to beginning reading instruction, and a third might advocate a third approach. Several biographers might shed altogether different light on the same subject. Well-trained and prominent newscasters may differ in their interpretation of current events. Two textbooks on the same subject may differ radically. Even two medical doctors may recommend different treatments for the same malady.

Therefore, the student must be encouraged to compare sources of information on the same subject. He should be encouraged to compare the backgrounds and biases of the authors and to make his own judgments or *withhold judgment* until he has more information.

Teaching Strategies

1. Compare two or more biographies of the same person, or a biography with an autobiography

2. Compare several advertisements for competing products

3. Compare Chamber of Commerce materials from several geographical areas

4. Compare campaign speeches with the carry-through

5. Compare the same event as reported in a local paper or two with the report of it in the *New York Times*, the *Christian Science Monitor, Time, Newsweek*

6. Compare a theme as presented in a novel, a play, an opera, a poem, an essay; for example, compare *Of Thee I Sing* by Cole Porter with articles and editorials about Spiro Agnew, Lyndon Johnson, Richard Nixon, and Harry Truman as vice-presidents

7. Compare the discussion of the American Civil War in textbooks written by a northerner, a southerner, and a European

8. Compare several editorials about our space program—one advocating the pro point of view, another the con

9. Compare a textbook discussion of an event in history with a biographical and/or fictional account

10. Compare television offerings in your community with those in New York City and London.

Fact versus Opinion

Students must learn to distinguish between a statement of fact and a statement of opinion. A statement of fact can be either verified or proved false. A statement of opinion, however, is an expression of personal feeling, and it cannot be objectively proved to be true or false. Opinions may be swayed by emotions or reason. Facts are based on actuality. (Of course, what is considered a fact today may not be considered as such tomorrow.)

The following exercise exemplifies how students might learn to distinguish between fact and opinion.

1. John H. Glenn was born in 1921.

2. John H. Glenn was the first American to orbit the earth in space.

3. John H. Glenn is the greatest of all American astronauts.

Can the date of John H. Glenn's birth be verified? Can it be proved that he was, or was not, the first American to orbit the earth in space? Can it be objectively determined that he is, or is not, the greatest American astronaut?

The first two statements can be proved true or false by consulting official records. However, the third is a matter of judgment, or opinion.

Which of the following are statements of fact (i.e., they can be proved true or false by using objective evidence)? Which are opinions?

__F__ 1. Richard Nixon was born in 1913.

_____ 2. Richard Nixon was the 37th president of the United States.

_____ 3. Richard Nixon promoted more reforms than any other president since F. D. Roosevelt.

_____ 4. Two plus two equals four.

_____ 5. Adding is easier than subtracting.

_____ 6. Seven minus four equals eight.

_____ 7. Algebra is less enjoyable than geometry.

_____ 8. Geometry is more useful than algebra.

_____ 9. Trigonometry should be taught in college.

_____10. Everyone needs three years of high school mathematics.

_____11. Chaucer is the greatest English poet.

_____12. Cervantes is the greatest author Spain has ever produced.

_____13. *Hamlet* has been produced more often than any other Shakespearean play.

_____14. "It is me" is incorrect grammatically.

_____15. Water freezes at 32°F.

_____16. Water freezes at 32°C.

_____17. Babies develop coordination at different rates.

_____18. Science is fascinating.

_____19. The space an object occupies is known as its volume.

_____20. Einstein was the greatest of modern mathematicians.

Propaganda Techniques

Some propaganda techniques can legitimately be classified in the area of figurative, or connotative, language. True, most propaganda techniques involve more than a word—they utilize phrases, sentences, paragraphs, and also illustrations. However, basically the *language* (or illustration) of propaganda is designed to sway, to influence people.

Propaganda can be good or bad. It can serve useful purposes in persuasion. But it can also be tricky: it can fool the naive. Students should be made aware of propaganda techniques so that they are able to evaluate persuasive arguments logically. The following types of propaganda techniques will be explained briefly: bad names, glad names, testimonial, transfer, plain folks, card stacking, and band wagon.

Bad names

Bad names are those expressions whose connotations are unpleasant. The terms are employed to incite hate, to cause fear, dislike, or distress. It is not difficult to think of many bad name (sad name) expressions. Here are a few:

communist	itchy
lemon	cheap
yellow	skinny
un-American	fat

Glad names

Glad names, on the other hand, are expressions with pleasant connotations. Sometimes called "glittering generalities" or "purr words," glad names are used by advertisers to describe *their* products, though they may use sad names to describe the products of their competitors. Glad names are used by all of us to convince others of our opinions or to sway them to our point of view. Some glad names are:

marvelous	smooth
supercalifragilisticexpealidocious	economical
All-American	slim
glamorous	pleasantly plump
healthful	

"Tell me frankly, am I a reliable source or an unconfirmed rumor?" (Copyright Field Enterprises, Inc., reprinted by permission of Publishers-Hall Syndicate.)

Testimonial

A testimonial is a tribute; at its best, an affirmation or declaration of gratitude for a statement honestly recommending a person, theory, or thing. Testimonies are given by people who are grateful for their religion, their government, their university, or their favorite sportsman. Our progress in space is a testimony to our society. On the other hand, our racial problems testify to apathy or to negativism in our society, as does pollution.

In advertising, a testimonial is often rendered by a glamorous movie star, a famous athlete, a zesty barking dog or a purring cat, or possibly by a plain folk. In most cases, the testimony is well paid for.

Transfer

In the transfer technique, a highly regarded person, symbol, or concept is somehow related to the idea or product that is "being pushed." Many students "buy" professor's ideas if attached to the idea are the words "research proves . . . ." Or, we buy toothpaste because "dentists endorse it" or because it contains some ingredients that sound very scientific. The eagle or the American flag may be pictured on a dictionary to help increase sales. Or, a picture of a baby or a movie star may attract us to a magazine.

Careful now—not all propaganda is bad! Much is good.

Plain folks

We are all familiar with the politician who kisses babies and parades his family in front of the public. And we have all seen pictures of candidates with holes in the soles of their shoes—a technique that may, however, backfire in time of prosperity. The affluent Stevenson was thus pictured—to play down his intellectual image. A friend of mine, a staunch Democrat, clipped this picture and pasted it to her door with the inscription: "Don't let this happen to you—vote for Ike."

The plain folks technique is gaining popularity in advertising today. Note the increasing number of ads in magazines, newspapers, and on T.V. in which average looking people, rather than the ultraglamorous, appear.

Card stacking

Card stacking is a technique we all use—not just advertisers, politicians, governments, etc. Not at all! What does the child who comes home with a poor report card tell his family? Does he present both sides fairly? What about the local Chamber of Commerce? And the woman whose favorite plant lost —or won—at the local floral show? What about you when you did not get that raise or that "A"?

The old art of debate forced sides to deliberately card stack. Each side presented only the best of one point of view and the worst of the other point of view. And what does a lawyer do in presenting his case? Card stacking is probably as old as man and is with us to stay. But we should be alert to it.

Band wagon

It is the rare person who is not anxious to "be with it," to join the crowd. Nowadays, almost everyone wants to go to college, even those who would benefit more from doing something else. We all pick up the latest slang, use it until we tire of it, and then discard it, as does the rest of our crowd—for the newer slang or jargon.

The constant plea, *everybody's doing it*, should trigger us to serious thought and careful analysis and evaluation. *Is everybody doing it? And do we wish to be one of these anonymous everybodies? Perhaps we should dare to be different.*

Everybody smokes pot. Or, all the kids smoke pot. Nonsense! Hippies don't conform. Nonsense—they conform with one another—with the other so-called "non-conformists." They are on the band wagon.

It's modern to engage in premarital sex, or extramarital sex, and, of course, we all want to be modern. We may want to be modern, but does all of this go along with it?

Where would we be if everybody did the same thing? Perhaps the prediction of Huxley's *Brave New World* would be borne out.

Teaching Strategies

1. The most obvious, and perhaps, overused, way of analyzing propaganda is to examine *advertisements*. Naturally, they are full of "selling techniques." Certainly, students—even young children—should learn to examine sales pitches on T.V., on billboards, in newspapers, and in magazines. Look for "truth in advertising." Contrast truthful ads with those that abound with "tricks." The following questions should be asked:

   a) Who is the propagandist?

   b) Whom is he serving?

   c) What is his aim in writing on (speaking about) this subject?

   d) To what human interests, desires, emotions does he appeal?

   e) What techniques does he use?

2. Examine *editorials* or *features* in newspapers and *essays*. Can you find evidence of card stacking or of a balance in presenting and weighing all sides of the issue? Are other propaganda techniques used or avoided?

   In science the topics might relate to space travel, ecology, recent discoveries, etc. *In mathematics*, to the "floating dollar," comparative prices, rise in the cost of living, etc. *In social studies*, candidates for office, evaluations of the performances of those who hold office, the race problem, etc. *In English*, to drama critiques, school language programs, book reviews, etc.

3. Compare the reports of the *same sports event* in several newspapers and/or news magazines, especially in the newspapers of two home towns or the two local schools. Is there card stacking? What about bad names, glad names, etc.?

4. Compare a *news* article with an *editorial* on the same subject. Is the news article more factual, the editorial more emotional?

5. Compare a *poem* and *a short story* on the same theme.

6. Compare *biographies* (or a biography and an *autobiography*) about the same person by different authors.

7. Compare several *textbooks* on the same subject.

8. Compare *people* in the public eye. Which use emotional language? Which are more literal in their choice of words? Which card stack?

9. Which of the following expressions would you choose to use if you were describing a friend? an enemy?

> yellow—cautious
>
> curious—busybody
>
> colorful—gaudy—flashy
>
> lies—white lies—fibs
>
> patriotic—chauvinistic
>
> janitor—engineer

Have the class form in random groups and play the "run" game (Chapter 6, p. 102). This time, each group in turn must suggest pairs of words, like the above, and tell which they would use in describing a friend and which they would use in describing an enemy.

10. Write two paragraphs describing the same person, place, product, or event. One paragraph should be slanted favorably; the other, unfavorably. Then write another as factually as possible, presenting both points of view.

11. Compare the impact of the following philosophy with that of modern linguists, especially as it would affect children in a classroom: Henry Higgins (from *My Fair Lady*, i.e., *Pygmalion* by G. B. Shaw): "Why can't the English teach their children how to speak:/ Norwegians learn Norwegian; the Greeks are taught their Greek./ . . . Why can't the English teach their children how to speak?/ This verbal class distinction by now should be antique."

Fallacies of Reasoning

There are eight fallacies of reasoning secondary students should understand. Each will be explained briefly here, and examples will be given.

Mistaken causal relationship

A mistaken causal relationship is the error of assuming that something is the cause of an effect when it is not. Frequently, such a fallacy occurs in relationship to correlation: two factors are found to correlate to a high degree and, therefore, it is assumed that one causes the other. For example:

1. It is well known that most successful people have large vocabularies (success and size of vocabulary correlate). Therefore, many people assume that the large vocabulary caused the success. And, therefore, many schools

spend an abundance of time on vocabulary, *per se*, working on vocabulary exercises divorced from the content of the course (vocabulary workbooks, etc.).

The fact may be that the two factors interact—the more successful a person is, the more experiences he has, and the larger his vocabulary is likely to be. Moreover, both success and a large vocabulary may be caused by high intelligence, insatiable curiosity, and drive. These may be the real causes of *both* the success *and* the large vocabulary.

2. Children who know the alphabet before they enter school are likely to be better readers than are children who do not know the alphabet when they enter school (knowledge of the alphabet upon entering school correlates with success in reading). Many school systems assume this means that knowledge of the alphabet, *per se*, causes the success in reading. Their first efforts with children are to teach the alphabet. This is an over-simplification.

    The basic question is *why* did the children know the alphabet. This gives the basic cause for their success in reading. They were both *interested* enough and *intelligent* enough to learn the alphabet. They had good *visual discrimination, auditory discrimination, sequential sense*, and possibly *motor skills*. Finally, *somebody cared* enough to teach them the alphabet. These are the factors that the school should develop, for they are the real causes of success in reading. Knowledge of the alphabet, of course, is one of the basic skills, though not the cause, of success.

3. Chanticleer, the rooster in an old folk tale, got to thinking he was a very important individual because early every morning he crowed—and, behold, the sun came up.

4. This pamphlet tells of many people who have been cured of various diseases by taking Zelt's patent medicine and of several unfortunate people who have suffered through failure to take it. I find it must be the medicine to cure me.

Statistical fallacy

A statistical fallacy is a result of the error of applying the wrong statistic to a situation or of misinterpreting the statistical finding. For example:

1. Graduates of Harvard University earn an average of $30,000 per year, whereas graduates of Wisconsin earn $20,000 per year. True? Possibly! But what *average* was used? Was it the mean, median, or mode?

    If several graduates of Harvard are millionaires, possibly because of family background rather than education, and the *mean* average was used, the result is misleading. The *mean*, or arithmetic, average emphasizes extremes, which may be irrelevant for our consideration. The *median* average is the one to use here.

2. A teacher reported that students in his class earned the following grades: 60, 61, 62, 65, 65, 66, 67, 68, 70, 98. The average of these grades is 68.2. He reported that it was discouraging to find that 8 out of 10 students made below-average grades.

His next-door neighbor reported his pleasure with his students, for 8 out of 10 of his students made above-average grades! The grades in his class-room were: 60, 61, 62, 65, 65, 66, 67, 68, 70, 20. His average was 60.3.

3. Salaries of beginning teachers have skyrocketed. Whereas in 1950, a beginning teacher could expect to earn $2200, and in 1960 he could expect $4500, today he is likely to receive $7000. (What about comparative costs of living?)

4. Graphs are frequently used for recording statistical findings. It is pos-sible to construct such graphs in misleading ways. For example:
   a) I am a teacher of a speed-reading course and wish to demonstrate the success of the course. I might use a graph such as this (Fig. 9.1):

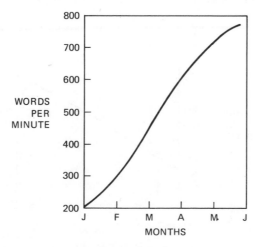

Fig. 9.1   Gain in rate of reading from January to June.

b) I may be the speed-reading teacher's worst enemy (Fig. 9.2):

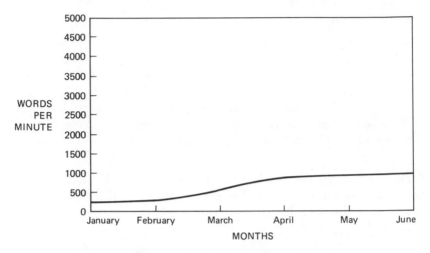

Fig. 9.2   Gain in rate of reading from January to June.

c) Somewhere in between may lie the truth (Fig. 9.3):

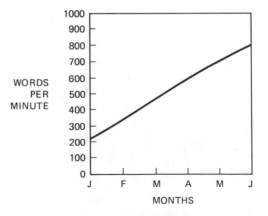

Fig. 9.3   Gain in rate of reading from January to June.

5. Pie graphs must be drawn full-circle to avoid distorted impressions. Note the false visual impression given in Fig. 9.4(a).

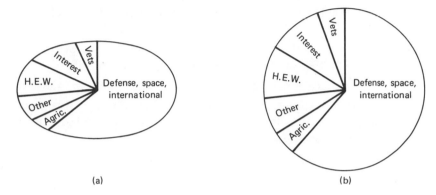

(a)   (b)

Fig. 9.4 How the tax dollar is spent.

False analogy

An analogy is false when the two things being compared are different in an area essential to the purpose of the analogy. For example:

1. Q: Do two negatives make a positive in English?
   A: Yes! In mathematics, so too in English, two negatives make a positive. Multiply -2×-4, and the result is $+8$, a positive number. It's true in mathematics and true in English. Two negatives make a positive.

   Q: When I say, "I don't have no money," what do you think I mean?
   A: You're loaded!

   Q: And what do I mean when I say, "I'm not unhappy?"
   A: You're blissful.

2. Q: Is motorcycle riding dangerous?
   A: No—the death rate of motorcycle riders is slightly below that of the general public. (The comparison should be made between age-mates.)

3. Since no individual can relieve his economic distress by increased expenditure, neither can a nation.

4. "A majority can never replace the man. . . . Just as a hundred fools do not make a wise man, an heroic decision is not likely to come from a hundred cowards." (Adolf Hitler)

Oversimplification

An oversimplification results from failure to examine all possibilities. There frequently is some truth in an oversimplification, but not enough. For example:

1. Maria argued that she was a poor reader because all of her family was poor in reading.
2. "Germany will be either a world power or will not be at all." (Adolf Hitler) (The "either-or" fallacy. Are there just two possibilities?)
3. "Either the husband is boss or the wife is." (The "either-or" fallacy.)
4. "Nothing can have value without being an object of utility. If it be useless, the labor contained in it is useless, cannot be reckoned as labor, and cannot therefore create value." (Karl Marx)

Stereotyping

Stereotyping is the process of overemphasizing characteristics that groups of people or objects are thought to have in common and underemphasizing the uniqueness of individuals. Redheads are ill-tempered; mothers-in-law are bossy; professors are absent-minded; Mexicans are lazy.

Stereotyping includes giving stock, or conventional, responses: the *only* valid way to group grapefruit, bananas, onions, and cucumbers is according to function, i.e., fruits versus vegetables. Nonsense!

The importance of *breaking the stereotype* cannot be overemphasized if we are to progress in our democratic society and if we are to foster creativity. We must value the uniqueness of the individual and see people as multi-faceted. Since creativity is a form of synthesis, dependent on analysis (analysis is breaking apart, synthesis is putting together), if what students see as parts of a whole are stereotypes, nothing unusual will emerge as the parts are put together.

1. What is the most obvious way to group the following people? How many other ways can they be grouped? Do you have to know a great deal about them as individuals to group them in a variety of ways?

Jackie Robinson	Charles Percy	Barbra Streisand
Ethel Waters	Langston Hughes	George Wallace
Rod McKuen	Lee Trevino	Spiro Agnew
Sandy Koufax	Pearl Bailey	Ted Kennedy
James Baldwin	John Connally	Edward Brooke

2. Are women stereotyped professionally in the United States? Figure 9.5 shows the percentage of female doctors in various countries.

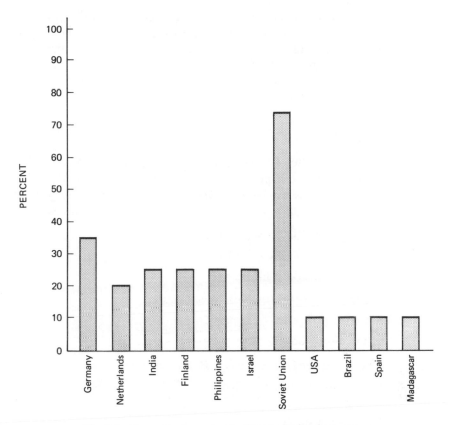

Fig. 9.5   Percent of women doctors in various countries.

Ignoring the question

Ignoring the question is the act of digressing into an irrelevant argument to make a point. All students and teachers are familiar with this technique. When a student does not know the answer to the question asked, he writes the answer to another, with the hope of getting some credit. Not only students use the technique, however. For example,

Q. How can inflation continue while unemployment keeps rising?

A. The course of inflation is like that of a ship entering a strange harbor, the momentum carries it forward even after the captain has signaled "slow" to the engine room. Key business indicators alert economists to the changing course of inflation, but like the myriad signal flags on a ship, the general public is not aware of their meaning. The unemployed dock workers are on the pier eagerly waiting to unload the cargo, but the tidal currents make the ship's progress toward port seem painfully slow. The experienced harbormaster knows the ship is coming in, but he is unable to communicate the certainty to those waiting to serve. Mid-course corrections by the captain only cause the uninformed to doubt his ability to bring the ship in successfully.

—*United States Investor*

New Yorker: Next question.[2]

Begging the question

Begging the question relates to *deductive reasoning* and, more formally, to syllogistic reasoning. It is the process of assuming that a generalization, or premise, is true when it has not been proved to be, and when it may, indeed, be false. Any deduction from such a generalization is faulty. For example,

1. Major Premise: I dislike boring subjects.
    *minor premise: Philosophy is boring.
    Conclusion: I dislike philosophy.

2. *MP: I get D's only when I have a lousy teacher.
    mp: I got a D.
    C: I had a lousy teacher.

3. Of course he voted for Nixon. He's a Republican, isn't he?
    *MP: All Republicans voted for Nixon.
    mp: He's a Republican.
    C: He voted for Nixon.

4. Of course she's selfish. She's a woman, isn't she?
    *MP: _____
    mp: _____
    C: _____

5. Evidence was produced that a certain statesman, although he denied that he had done so, had read a certain secret document. The evidence was met with a rebuttal: "How could a man of his character have told an untruth?"
    MP: _____
    mp: _____
    C: _____

---

* true?

6. "Oh . . . ," said the Cat: "We're all mad here. I'm mad. You're mad."
    "How do you know I'm mad?" said Alice.
    "You must be," said the Cat, "or you wouldn't have come here."

    (Alice in Wonderland)

    MP: _____

    mp: _____

    C: _____

7. We have assumed that he is a Communist because he said he is not. We
    know that Communists are taught to deny party membership.

    MP: _____

    mp: _____

    C: _____

Sometimes both the major premise and the minor premise are true, but a
valid conclusion cannot be drawn because the premises lack a balanced relationship or do not supply enough information. For example:

1. MP: All dogs have tails.

    mp: My monkey has a tail.

    C: No conclusion.

2. MP: Everyone in the assembly voted for Costanga.

    mp: My father voted for Costanga.

    C: _____

3: MP: If I get an A in this course, I'll be off probation.

    mp: I got a B in the course.

    C: _____ (No conclusion. The MP isn't "Only if I get
           an A"—I may be off probation if I simply pass the course.)

Circular arguments are also related. For example:

1. Capital punishment for murder is justified because it is right to put to
    death those who have committed murder.

2. In a debate Jerome asserted that some of his opponent's facts are not true,
    and he challenged him to prove them. The opponent, Marcus, replied that
    facts are facts and cannot be false and that since Jerome himself has called
    them facts, it is absurd to question their truth.

3. "Analogue . . . is something having analogy to something else."

Hasty generalization

An error in *inductive reasoning*, a hasty generalization is a conclusion drawn with insufficient evidence. It is difficult to conclude that a small sample is typical. At best, it is chancy to generalize from limited evidence. Limited evidence, instead, might lead to a hypothesis which could be further tested. For example:

1. I've been in El Paso for a week, and it has rained every day. There is some reason other than shortage of rain that makes it a desert.
2. Huberto, Walter, and Jim got A's in physics. This indicates that boys are smarter than girls.
3. Seventy percent of our homeroom voted for Nancy for senior president. She'll win!
4. Harry S. Truman, with a broad smile, was pictured in 1948 holding a morning paper whose headlines shouted, "Thomas E. Dewey Elected President."

SYNTHESIS

Synthesis is the act of combining, or unifying, separate elements into a coherent whole. At the simplest level, synthesis is the act of compounding: two items may be put together to form one. For example, we have looked at morphological synthesis:

$$air + port = airport$$
$$car + port = carport$$
$$ex + port = export$$
$$im + port = import$$
$$able + port = portable$$

Other examples abound. Flour and water can be synthesized to make paste, but the right proportions must be used. In how many ways can two flowerpots be used together? In how many ways can sterling silver and turquoise be used together? One way might be in the making of jewelry, and how many designs are possible? The answer, of course, is that there are sometimes an infinite number of ways of combining just two items!

Inventive chefs use common, ordinary ingredients to synthesize gourmet delights, whereas an uninventive cook, using the same variety of ingredients, may repeat the same menu week after week. Knowledge and availability of an unusual spice or other ingredient may add sparkle to an otherwise mundane menu. And unusual combinations of ingredients found in every kitchen can add glamor. Baked Alaska, for example, is made from ice cream, egg whites, sugar, and a few other ingredients everyone has at home.

Look at the varieties of architecture used in the world today. Each springs from the synthesis of a variety of materials. Frequently, the same materials are used, but in different proportions and combinations.

You might even try to recall the many different kinds of very simple objects you have seen. How many clock designs have you noticed? How many watches? How many chairs? Bookcases? Pillows? Dresses? Each results from a unique synthesis.

But we have been talking about material things. Actually, material objects, except those that are supplied by nature, are the result of human thought objectified. And the thought is a synthesis—the unification of ideas culled from various sources.

Subjective thought, however, is also a synthesis. Conversation, unless it is simple recall from a single source, is based on the synthesis of ideas. Research papers, classroom discussions, examinations, etc., offer an opportunity for encouraging synthesis, though too often they result in simple recall because we as teachers ask for such responses. *The kinds of questions asked, or the kinds of activities engaged in, determine the thought processes that will be used.*

Why not encourage activities requiring synthesis? We cannot do so if we use a single source, however, and if we do not relate to the student and his background of experience. We cannot do so if we have decided what the answers are and if unusual responses are not welcome in our classrooms. We cannot do so if we do not allow students to go off on tangents and if we do not allow individualized study and informal sharing of ideas. We cannot do so if we praise responses that agree with ours or if we look with approval on those who "choose" to read what we think they should choose to read. Encouraging synthesis is, indeed, a formidable task. Many of us must reorganize ourselves in order to do it.

A very important point must be made here. If we wish to encourage the objectification of thoughts or objects that are useful in a positive way, we must be alert to discourage an excessive amount of fault-finding at the analysis level and to encourage the search for facets or ideas of a positive nature. Instead of asking only what is wrong, we must also learn to ask *what is right.*

We all know people who get along with a wide variety of individuals because they can see something to admire in each. And we know others who have a limited circle of friends, all of whom fairly well agree with them. We all know people who can read a book or go to a lecture and be happy they did so because they got *one useful idea from it.* And we know those who cannot find the useful idea because they dwell on all the others. Too often, of course, we may fall asleep waiting for that one usable idea. The creative person is possibly the one who persists until he finds it.

The purpose of this discussion is not to argue that we need not be alert to dangers—fallacies of reasoning, ineptitude, etc. Rather, we must, in addition, look for the positive. Critical reading need not be predominantly negative. If we are to create (synthesize), we must create with something or with some ideas. If we stress fault-finding in analysis, what will our creations be?

There are, of course, two basic kinds of synthesis. From J. P. Guilford we get the terms *convergent production* and *divergent production*.[3] Convergent production results from synthesizing ideas or materials in a typical way. Certain ideas add up to a best answer or generalization, or at least a conventional one. However, these same ideas, possibly plus or minus others, might add up to something quite unusual or unique. This is divergent production.

Some authors consider both convergent and divergent production to be creative acts. Margaret Mead argues that the child who synthesizes in a way that results in a convergent response has performed a creative (for him) act, though his response does not add to the world's wealth of ideas. Others argue that only divergent production is truly creative, for only divergent production adds variety of concepts, ideas, and/or products.

What kinds of activities encourage synthetic thinking in content area classrooms? Among them are the following:

1. "production of a unique communication"
2. "production of a plan, or proposed set of operations"
3. "derivation of a set of abstract relations."[4]

Let us look at each of these in more detail.

Production of a Unique Communication

A unique communication can be a message on a postcard, an essay, a short story, a poem, a book, etc. As it relates to the teaching of reading, this communication should evolve at least partially from ideas gained through reading. In addition, or instead, the communication itself could serve as reading material for the student and/or his classmates.

For the communication to be on the synthesis level for a student, it must be the result of his original thought, not simply a form of recall or translation. In addition, the student must be able to logically or artistically justify the process and/or the product of his thought.

Some characters in literature are like real people. The author has put them together so that they are believable. After reading a book, we feel we know such personalities. Others are stereotypes—like cardboard. If we know the type, we know what the character will do. Such stereotypes may serve a purpose, even in the best literature, for there can be too many multifaceted (real) people in a story. Yet, the evolution of a "real person" requires synthesis on the part of an author. The description of a stereotype, or cardboard, personality requires recall of obvious dimensions.

Teaching Strategies

In social studies

In a social studies class, a panel discussion could be held with each participant representing a real individual. The participant would have to study this person well—to know his philosophy and his way of reacting. The participant would have to recall the person's activities and analyze his reasons for acting as he did. In addition, the participant would have to be able to predict logically how he might react to a timely issue.

1. Individual writers of the American Constitution might discuss their feelings about the Civil War.

2. Writers of the Monroe Doctrine might discuss their judgment of our involvement in the World Wars, Korea, and/or Vietnam.

3. Several senators, representatives, governors, the president, and/or vice-president might discuss a current issue.

4. A hippie or a drug addict might be impersonated and tell how he feels about a particular issue or living condition. Several might interact—a hippie and a nonhippie, for example.

5. A Negro might be impersonated by a white and a white by a Negro. They might converse about civil rights, etc.

6. A boy might pretend he is a woman looking for a high-level job. And a girl might be the male employer.

In English

Similar panels, or dialogues, could be held in other classes. In literature, several authors might discuss modern poetry. Cervantes might talk with his contemporary, Shakespeare. Or, characters from different plays or stories might interact. This need not be stern stuff; it might be entertaining.

> The other night she was seen on television as plain—if that is possible—
> Jane Eyre opposite George C. Scott's Heathcliff.
> > —Kevin Thomas in the *Los Angeles Times*.
>
> *New Yorker*: It's possible, but it's sort of complicated.[5]

In science

Madam Curie might tell what she thinks of the atom bomb. And the geographer, Columbus, might talk to Balboa. Two modern biologists or chemists might debate an issue. An executive of a detergent firm might talk with the president of National Wildlife or with Albert Schweitzer.

In mathematics

Einstein might talk with Frank Lloyd Wright about triangles or arches. A modern mathematician might carry on a dialogue with an old-fashioned arithmetic teacher. A topologist might demonstrate figures in space and talk with Euclid about the beginnings of geometry.

In all subjects, students might write short research papers debating an issue, answering a question, or predicting what will happen in the future. The important thing is that the answer should not be copied.

The teacher must be skilled in assigning topics that require original thought. This may mean that he relates the topic to a local or a hypothetical situation. Or, it may mean that he limits the input; for example, the teacher may briefly present several positions or ideas and require the synthesis within the hour. There are, of course, obvious advantages and disadvantages to such an assignment.

Production of a Plan of Operation

Can a student plan the steps that should have been followed (post-mortem) or that might be followed in carrying out an activity? Post-mortems are sometimes simple, as in playing bridge. After the cards have been played, it is easy to say what should have been done and to find logical arguments for such action. While one is playing, it is not as simple.

Answering the question "How should we have proceeded?" in a situation in which we did poorly may help us act more intelligently in the future. A teacher asks himself this question when a student does not work up to capacity level. Even though the student may no longer be in the teacher's class, answering such a question may help the teacher when working with other students.

A student who fails a course might be encouraged to design a plan of action for passing it the next time. And he might follow his plan!

Representatives in the student council might draw up a plan for a school-wide election. Or, they might design a course of action to follow in requesting more "student power."

Students can be involved in proposing courses to be offered by the school. And they can be involved in choosing topics to be covered in old and new courses. Students, individually or in groups, might design their own reading lists and be allowed to alter them as they progress.

Students might formulate hypotheses and test them in the school and community. Some students work on projects to raise money for scholarships or for camperships or for band trips, etc. Students might suggest plans that they think would be successful. Girl Scouts sell cookies, some groups wash cars, others clean up neighborhoods. Surely other plans might work—and possibly better. The ideas may come from the youngsters.

Plans should also be related to course work. Students plan how they will solve mathematics problems. It should not all be done for them. They plan how they will find information they need to answer different kinds of questions. They hypothesize whether or not an act of the president will work.

Derivation of a Set of Abstract Relations

The derivation of the Pythagorean theorem—that the square of the hypotenuse is equal to the sum of the squares of the legs—is an example of what is meant by the derivation of a set of abstract relations in mathematics. Here, the thought process is inductive.

On the other hand, a set of abstract relations may also be deduced. Such is the case when a student, without prompts, proves a geometric theorem. Usually, the thought process in such a case will be *convergent* production; i.e., he will follow a conventional path in proving the theorem.

It is important to note here that the *set of relationships* may be arrived at inductively or deductively. If they are arrived at *inductively*, individual items or subpoints are used in formulating a generalization. Many items may be observed, and where similarities are found, the items are grouped together. Unlike items are in another group. In divergent production, items will be grouped in unique, but in logically or artistically justifiable, ways.

In deductive reasoning, the generalization, or principle, is given, and the set of items, or subpoints, must be derived. At the synthesis level, this means that the subpoints must be related to one another. In divergent production, a unique item may be identified or a unique relationship may be found to exist.

Teaching Strategies

The following kinds of activities are appropriate.

In science

1. Derive a set of scientific principles that will tell us what the best date is for our next trip to the moon or for a class fieldtrip.

2. Derive a set of scientific principles that will tell us in our hometown how deep each of a variety of seeds should be planted.

3. Derive a set of scientific principles that will tell us the best place in a given region to build a paper mill (etc.).

4. Describe at least five different scientific characteristics by which a diverse group of people might be grouped, e.g., race, blood type, etc.

5. Describe at least five different scientific characteristics by which a diverse group of animals (flowers, meteorites, etc.) might be grouped.

In mathematics

1. Derive a set of mathematical principles that will tell us how to compute the cost of living in a specific geographical area.

2. Derive a set of mathematical principles that will tell us how much it costs the average student to attend your school.

3. Derive a set of mathematical principles that will tell us how to compute the comparative cost of driving a new Cadillac and a new Volkswagen to the second nearest city in the closest state to you.

4. Describe at least five different mathematical characteristics by which diverse geometric objects can be classified.

5. Describe at least five different mathematical characteristics by which numbers can be classified.

In English

1. Derive a set of linguistic principles that will tell us how to formulate phonics generalizations or what appropriate English is in a specific situation.

2. Derive a set of literary principles that will tell us if a new book is likely to become a classic.

3. Derive a set of literary principles that will tell us if the author of an article uses the card-stacking technique and if so, if it is a legitimate use of the technique.

4. Describe at least five different linguistic characteristics by which a diverse group of words can be classified.

5. Describe at least five different literary characteristics by which a diverse group of literary pieces can be classified.

In social studies

1. Derive a set of economic principles that will tell us where people with certain jobs or professions are likely to live in your community.

2. Derive a set of ethnic principles that will tell us where certain groups of people are likely to live in your community.

3. Derive a set of principles that will tell what new products should be produced in your community.

4. Describe at least five different sociological characteristics by which a racially diverse group of people may be classified.

5. Describe at least five different cultural characteristics by which we can classify ancient civilizations.

EVALUATION

The highest level of the cognitive domain is evaluation. The common meaning of the term "evaluation" differs from its use in this chapter. Students who "evaluate" frequently do so by recalling what someone else has said. They know a book is a classic because it is on all the lists. They know a Broadway play is mediocre because they read the review in *Time* or *Newsweek*. They know the President's new policy will not work because the newscaster said so, and they can parrot the reasons. This is not what we mean here by evaluation.

Our definition of evaluation includes two steps, both of which must be performed by the student himself. First, *he must set up standards* against which he will judge the value of an idea, or complex of ideas, or an object. Second, *he must judge the "goodness of fit"* between the standards and whatever it is that is being evaluated.

Sometimes, there is a gradation in the evaluation system. Teachers, for example, set up standards against which they judge the quality of a student's work. These standards are frequently complex and include such factors as objective cognitive judgments (from tests, etc.), subjective cognitive judgments (from essays, class discussions, etc.), affective involvement of the student (from class observations, etc.), effort, and improvement, etc. Students are judged against such criteria and a grade results: A, B, C, D, or F, and possibly a summary comment is made.

Those charged with hiring personnel in a large company also set up standards against which they judge candidates for positions. Some people are hired, and others are not. Some start at excellent salaries, whereas others get the minimum. So, too, the candidate for a position decides what the job must offer for him to accept it. The consideration frequently includes location, salary, working conditions, possibility for promotion, etc. The candidate, then, compares the job description with the criteria he has set up and takes the job that offers the "best fit."

So, too, some students enter college as "honors" students. Others enter in the regular program. Others enter on probation. Some can enter one university, college, or school but not another. The "goodness of fit" factor is operating in all of these situations.

What is required of students if they are to think evaluatively is that *they* set up the criterion and then judge against it for goodness of fit. Although discussed here as the highest level of the cognitive domain, such evaluation activities also occur at the analysis and synthesis levels.

In setting up such criteria, students must recognize certain principles. One is that there are some *universal truths* against which ideas may be evaluated. That is, there are some factors that every thinking person accepts as true or valuable. It is difficult to give an example of such truths. They might be facts that are observable, e.g., the earth spins on an axis, in some climates certain vegetation flourishes and others do not, the air gets thinner as we ascend a mountain, etc.

Few, if any, values are universal. *Values relate to particular cultures* and subcultures. Certain mores, strange to us, make sense to others. Shirley MacLaine, for example, explains in *Don't Fall Off The Mountain* that in some countries tact is more important than truth, and the worst sin one can commit is to cause a person to lose face. Margaret Mead explains that in some cultures a woman must bear a child to be considered marriageable. Even in our society, the value of an object or idea frequently relates to an age group or to a socio-economic strata.

Another consideration relates to *individual taste*. Some objects or ideas are of value to one person but not to another. My house might be great for me, but if I had ten children it might be too small, in the wrong location, and too fancy. A Rolls-Royce might be the only car for the Queen of England, but for her husband, a snappy Porsche is better. For some students, direct instruction in improving their rate of reading may be extremely valuable. For others, it would be the worst thing. One book might be the ideal one for one child, but dull for another.

Thus, when standards are being formulated, the student must keep in mind the *purpose* of his evaluation. Is it to judge against universal truths? Is it to judge according to a special culture or subculture? Is it to judge according to an individual's tastes or needs?[6] Each will require a different set of standards.

Following is an edict which came from the office of General Douglas MacArthur at the end of World War II. It contains criteria set up by the Allies against which all newscasting and newspaper reports originating in Japan would be judged during the initial period of the Allied occupation. If there was the slightest deviation, the right of the offending station or paper to broadcast or publish was suspended. This memorandum exemplifies a real-life situation in which standards were carefully formulated for the purpose of evaluation in order to protect the Allies.

OFFICE OF THE SUPREME COMMANDER FOR
THE ALLIED POWERS

19 September 1945

AG 000.73 (18 Sept. 45) CI
Memorandum for: Imperial Japanese Government
Through: Central Liaison Office, Tokyo
Subject: Press Code for Japan

1. News must adhere strictly to the truth.
2. Nothing shall be printed which might, directly or by inference, disturb the public tranquillity.
3. There shall be no false or destructive criticism of the Allied Powers.
4. There shall be no destructive criticism of the Allied Forces of Occupation and nothing which might invite mistrust or resentment of those troops.
5. There shall be no mention or discussion of Allied troop movements unless such movements have been officially released.
6. News stories must be factually written and completely devoid of editorial opinion.
7. News stories shall not be colored to conform with any propaganda line.

8. Minor details of a news story must not be overemphasized to stress or develop any propaganda line.

9. No news story shall be distorted by the omission of pertinent facts or details.

10. In the make-up of the newspaper no news story shall be given undue prominence for the purpose of establishing or developing any propaganda line.

For the Supreme Commander

HAROLD FAIR,
Lt. Colonel, A.G.D.
Assist. Adjutant General [*]

Teaching Strategies

Following are some examples of evaluation activities that might be used in content area subjects:

In Science

1. Assume that you are an industrialist in your community and have been accused of allowing your industry to pollute the air or water, etc. Prepare a set of criteria by which you could attempt to justify your action.

2. Assume that you are a private citizen suffering from industrial pollution. Determine a set of criteria by which you could attempt to justify the suspension of the industry's permit to carry on business.

3. Set up three important criteria against which you might evaluate the relative worth to you of each experiment in the laboratory manual. Judge against the criteria, and number in order of importance the ten most valuable experiments.

4. Set up five criteria that could be used in evaluating the importance of specific vitamins to the health of the human body. Judge the importance of each vitamin in relationship to the criteria, and tell which are necessary for human consumption and the quantity that is necessary.

5. Imagine that you are in charge of the scientific branch of the U.S. space program. If the astronauts could bring back only 80 pounds of materials from their first trip to Mars, tell what would get first, second, third, fourth, and fifth priority—and why.

In Mathematics

1. You are in charge of awarding a Pulitzer Peace Prize to the most outstanding mathematician in the world during the past decade. Set up criteria against which you would judge contributions of all candidates. Name five

---

[*] William J. Coughlin. *Conquered Press: The MacArthur Era in Japanese Journalism.* Palo Alto, Calif.: Pacific Books, 1952, pp. 149–150. Reprinted by permission.

candidates, and list them in order according to their worthiness to receive the prize.

2. You have decided to author a book on biographies of great mathematicians of all times. You can include only 12, however. Tell what criteria you would use to judge whether or not a mathematician should be included. Name, in order of importance, the 12 you would select.

3. Set up criteria—including cognitive and affective—against which you would judge the comparative worth of modern mathematics and traditional mathematics programs.

4. Set up criteria against which you could judge the relative worth of the metric and yard systems. Tell which system the U.S. should officially adopt for the future.

In Social Studies

1. Set up five criteria against which you can judge whether or not the ecology program in your community is making satisfactory progress. State the relative strengths and weaknesses of your community's program, and make three recommendations for immediate action, and three for near-future action.

2. Set up four criteria that could be used to justify polygamy (either polyandry or polygyny). Set up four that could be used to justify marriage for life. Set up four that could be used to justify serial monogamy.

3. Set up criteria that could be used to justify capital punishment. Set up criteria that could be used to invalidate capital punishment. Weigh them. Which do you favor? Why?

4. Set up criteria to help you determine when you should and should not obey orders. Are yours the same as those of your classmates? Why might they be different?

In English

1. Set up eight criteria against which you could judge which one of five plays should be next year's senior class play at your school. List in order the best three to present. Compare these with your classmates' choices.

2. You can select 100 paperback books for your classroom library. Set up criteria that will enable you to judge the 100 best books to buy. Write the list.

3. A local radio station has offered to give your class 20 minutes of time once a month for four months. Your students are to read poems during this time. Have students set up criteria to enable them to select the poems for each program. List the poems that would be read on each program.

4. A new Broadway play is to premier in your town, and one of your students is to serve as the critic for your local paper. He is to be selected in competition with other students in your class. Tell how the choice will be made.

5. Along with your class, set up criteria for assigning a grade to a composition. After the students have written their next theme, have each paper graded by three different students. Compare grades.

SUMMARY

Critical-creative reading and thinking are defined in this chapter as requiring the skills of *analysis, synthesis,* and *evaluation.* Such cognitive abilities require the reader or thinker to reason using techniques of formal logic or at least to be consciously aware of the thought processes he is using.

Analysis requires the examination of parts of the whole. Common analytical procedures in reading involve knowledge of semantics and persuasive techniques, including propaganda, judging the authenticity of a source of information, differentiating among facts, opinions, and values, and recognizing fallacies of reasoning. Although it is important to be aware of both ineptitude and danger, analytical activities should often stress the positive.

Synthesis is the act of combining, or unifying, elements into a coherent whole. Compounding is a simple form of synthesis. Useful synthetic activities involve the production of a unique communication, production of a plan of operation, and derivation of a set of abstract relations—inductively or deductively. Synthesis at times involves *convergent production;* at other times, *divergent production.*

Evaluation requires the *establishment of standards* and also a judgment as to the *goodness of fit* of the idea or object being evaluated in relationship to the standards. It is necessary for the evaluator to keep in mind the fact that there are three principles governing evaluation: (1) some ideas may be judged against *universal truths,* (2) some must be judged as they relate to *values of a particular culture or subculture,* and (3) some are judged as they relate to *individual taste.* Each requires the recognition of different types of criteria against which the goodness-of-fit test is made.

NOTES

1 Norris M. Sanders. *Classroom Questions—What Kinds?* New York: Harper and Row, 1966, p. 98.

2 *The New Yorker,* March 6, 1971, p. 69.

3 J. P. Guilford. "Frontiers in Thinking What Teachers Should Know About." *The Reading Teacher,* **23** (February 1960): 176.

4 Benjamin Bloom, *et al. Taxonomy of Educational Objectives—Handbook I: The Cognitive Domain.* New York: David McKay, 1956, pp. 168–172.

5 *The New Yorker*, June 12, 1971, p. 95.

6 Norris M. Sanders, *op. cit.*, pp. 144–146.

SUGGESTED ACTIVITIES

1. Name five different types of analysis level activities.

2. Pick two different types of analytic activities and design an exercise or activity for each in your content area.

3. Describe two instances when convergent synthesis is preferable to divergent synthesis, and two instances when divergent synthesis is more desirable.

4. Design a five- to ten-minute microteach session to introduce one aspect of synthesis in your content area.

5. Name two necessary characteristics of evaluation level activities.

6. Give two examples of each of the following: (a) a universal truth, (b) a value that relates to a particular culture or subculture, (c) a consideration that relates to individual taste.

7. Design a set of criteria against which you could evaluate the worth of an idea, article, or book in your content area.

8. Design a microteach session in which you would explain to students how they might: (a) select ideas from a variety of sources, (b) synthesize these ideas into a meaningful whole, and (c) evaluate the worth of the synthesis.

9. Compare the relative value of the seven levels of activities in the cognitive domain in your content area. Which level is most important, least important? Are all important? Why?

10. Discuss with your classmates the relative amounts of affective involvement students are likely to expend when they are working on literal level activities with the amounts of affective involvement expended when they are working on higher level cognitive activities. Which activities do you prefer? Why?

REFERENCES FOR FURTHER READING

Altick, Richard. *Preface to Critical Reading.* New York: Holt, Rinehart and Winston, 1969.

Bartley, W. W. III. "Lewis Carroll's Lost Book on Logic." *Scientific American.* **227**, No. 1 (July 1972): 39–46.

Beery, Althea, Thomas C. Barrett, and William Powell (eds.). *Elementary Reading Instruction: Selected Materials.* Boston: Allyn and Bacon, 1969, Chapter 7.

Dawson, Mildred (ed.). *Developing Comprehension, Including Critical Reading.* Newark, Delaware: International Reading Association, 1968.

DeBoer, John and Martha Dallman. *The Teaching of Reading.* New York: Henry Holt, 1970, Chapter 6.

Hafner, Lawrence E. (ed.). *Improving Reading in Secondary Schools, Selected Readings.* New York: Macmillan, 1967, Sections 4 and 10.

Harris, Albert J. *How to Increase Reading Ability.* New York: David McKay, 1970, Chapter 16.

Herber, Harold. *Teaching Reading in Content Areas.* Englewood Cliffs, N.J.: Prentice-Hall, 1970, Chapters 5 and 7.

Karlin, Robert. *Teaching Reading in High School.* Indianapolis: Bobbs-Merrill, 1964, Chapter 6.

Karlin, Robert (ed.). *Teaching Reading in High School—Selected Articles.* Indianapolis: Bobbs-Merrill, 1969.

King, Martha, Bernice Ellinger, and Willavene Wolf (eds.). *Critical Reading.* Philadelphia: Lippincott, 1967.

Marksheffel, Ned D. *Better Reading in the Secondary School.* New York: The Ronald Press, 1966, Chapter 11.

Massialas, Byron and Jack Zevin. *Creative Encounters in the Classroom.* New York: John Wiley, 1967.

Olson, Arthur V. and Wilber S. Ames (eds.). *Teaching Reading Skills in Secondary Schools.* Scranton, Pa.: International Textbook Co., 1970.

Sanders, Norris M. *Classroom Questions—What Kinds?* New York: Harper & Row, 1966, Chapters 6, 7, 8, 9.

Spache, George. *Toward Better Reading.* Champaign, Ill.: Garrard, 1963, Chapters 5 and 16.

Torrance, E. Paul and R. E. Myers. *Creative Learning and Teaching.* New York: Dodd, Mead, 1970.

Chapter 10

IMPROVING SPEED OF COMPREHENSION IN READING

What is the fastest rate at which anyone can read?

How can we teach students to skim effectively?

How important is flexibility of reading rate? How can we help students improve their speed of comprehension?

What mechanical devices can be used to improve a student's rate of reading? How useful are they?

INTRODUCTION

Most young people and adults wish they could read more rapidly than they do—and most could with the proper training. The *average* high school senior reads about 250 words per minute. With training, he could probably read about 500 words per minute. The question is, *should* he read 500 words per minute. And if so, when?

Copyright © 1972 United Feature Syndicate, Inc. Reprinted by permission.

A favorite joke of mine is, I am sure, pure fiction. During one of the famous Nixon-Kennedy debates, Nixon purportedly asked Kennedy if he had read a certain book. Kennedy, known for his ability to read rapidly, responded, "Of course I've read it, but at 1200 words per minute. . . . So you'll have to tell me what it's about."

Phenomenal reading rates have been reported, and sometimes it seems that a major restricting factor in speed reading is the inability to turn the pages fast enough.

VARIOUS RATES

Scanning and Skimming

It is, of course, possible to *skim* at rapid rates, and a reader can *scan* even more rapidly. *Scanning* is used when the reader wishes to quickly locate a word, fact, date, name, etc. His eyes glance rapidly over a page, or pages, to pick out the one detail he is seeking. He may scan an index, table of contents, page of a telephone book, or dictionary. He may quickly scan to find a section or idea he wishes to read more carefully. To be able to scan is very useful, and students should be taught this skill.

Skimming is more thorough than scanning, for in skimming, the reader quickly views an entire section of printed material. He skims to get an overall view of the material—to summarize it, to grasp the sequence of events, to write an outline, to get the author's point of view, to see if the topics included suggest complete coverage or card stacking, and to see if he wishes to read the material more thoroughly.

He may skim material in order to *preview* it so that he begins his reading with a framework, an "advanced organizer." Or he may skim in *review*, as an aid toward reconstructing what he has read.

Teaching Strategies

When textbook or other expository reading is done, the teacher should encourage students to skim both in preview and review. Students can be taught to skim and to see the value of skimming in a variety of ways. For example:

1. Have students open their textbooks to the beginning of a chapter. Together, read the title. Ask them to formulate a purpose or purposes for reading. Together, read the main headings of the chapter and the summary. Ask them to help you write an outline of the chapter on the board.

2. Have students open their textbooks to the beginning of a chapter. Tell them they will have three (or five) minutes to preview the title, formulate a purpose or purposes for reading, and grasp the main ideas so that they will be able to write an outline or summary. When time is up, have them close their books and then write the title, purposes for reading, and the outline or summary. Either discuss the result or collect the papers and grade them. Repeat this activity often.

3. After students have read a chapter, ask them to review it in a survey fashion, as suggested above. Ask them to write a summary or outline. If they previewed the chapter before reading it, ask them to compare their initial summary or outline with their final one.

4. Have the students preview, as suggested in items 1 and 2. Ask them if there appears to be card stacking. Ask what the author's point of view appears to be.

5. Ask individual students to preview an article they are considering reading. After doing this, and before they read the article, ask them if they think it will suit their purposes.

6. Ask students to preview two sets of similar materials—two articles, two essays, two chapters, two books. Ask them to explain the ways in which the materials appear to be alike (which topics do they include in common, what is the point of view, etc.), and in which ways they are different (which topics does only one include, etc.). Ask them which they would prefer to read if they could read only one, and why.

7. Ask students to preview two sets of related but dissimilar materials. Ask them if they know anything about the authors or if they can conclude anything about the authors from the main ideas or the sequence of the ideas that have been presented.

Rates Used for Complete Coverage of Material

How fast is it possible to *read*? When is it desirable to read at a very rapid rate? Is it ever preferable to read at slower rates? If so, when? These are important questions to consider. Let us begin with the first question. How fast is it possible to *read*? To answer this question, it is necessary to consider two basic concepts. One relates to the mechanics of reading; the other, to the ability of the reader to assimilate ideas.

The mechanics of reading

How do a reader's eyes move when he is reading? Do they move smoothly, as they do when he watches a bird in flight or an airplane come in for a landing? Or do they start, stop, start, stop, start, stop, etc.?

Pair off with a friend and ask him to face you while he reads a book. Watch how his eyes move. Then have him watch your eyes. Or, try the peep-hole test: cut a hole in the middle of a sheet of paper on which there is writing, and peep through the hole as he reads. Another possibility is that you use a mirror to watch his eyes.

Do his eyes move smoothly? If they do, he is not reading! As a matter of fact, he is reading words only when his eyes are stopped. When his eyes are stopped, or fixed, on a word, a part of a word, or a phrase, then, and only then, is he taking in the visual image. Then his eyes move on to another word or phrase, and he has another fixation, during which time he again takes in the visual image. And then his eyes move on again to another word or phrase.

In continuous reading, *the fixation may last as briefly as one-sixth of a second*, and probably much longer. His *eye-span* includes the number of letters or words he can read during one fixation. George Spache states that an eye-span in continuous reading can be no wider than the length of *three words*. Thus, in one-sixth of a second, the fastest reader can read three words. After reading the three words, the reader's eyes must move on to the next phrase. This eye movement, called a *saccadic sweep*, takes the best reader about 1/30 of a second. Then he is ready to read another three words, etc.

So the total amount of time it takes to read three words and move on to the next phrase is 1/6 + 1/30 second, or 6/30 (1/5) of a second. Therefore, in

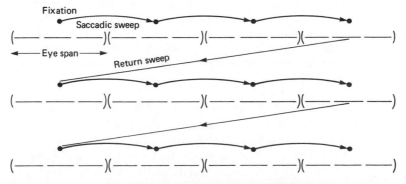

Fig. 10.1 Eye movements in reading.

one second, a speedy reader can read 15 words, and in one minute he can read 900 words.[1] He will read fewer words if lines are not composed of a number of words exactly divisible by three, for he then must make another fixation for the extra word or two.

Figure 10.1 shows this pattern of eye movements. At the present time, at least, there appears to be an upper limit in reading speed of about 800–900 words per minute, dictated by the mechanics of reading.

The student's assimilative ability

However, yet unanswered is the question of the upper limit which is set by an individual's ability (or desire) to assimilate ideas. Too many people neglect to seriously consider this factor when discussing speed of reading or attempting to help students increase their speed of reading. Frequently, these people are unaware of, or ignore, the fact that *eye movements are symptoms* of the mental processes that the reader uses while reading. That is, poor eye movements usually are not the *cause* of slow reading but, instead, they are the *effect*, or *symptom*, of some malady, restricting force, or even mental set.

> Jane was an excellent student in high school—a math major who studied everything thoroughly. She enjoyed poetry, essays, the classics. Everything she read she pondered. She could tell you everything the author of the history book said, and she could (and would) react to it and critically analyze it. But there was one thing she never did unless forced to, and that was read fiction and biography. She was moved to tears if asked to give a book report on such a book because she *hated* reading such books.
>
> Have you ever heard this story before? I can't believe it's that rare. It is a real story. And it wasn't until Jane took her first Education course in reading in graduate school that she learned about how to teach students to vary their rates of reading, and she taught herself. One thing she had to learn was that it is sometimes unnecessary, or even undesirable, to remember *everything* in a book. In a month and a half, she taught herself to read fiction at a rate at which she could enjoy it. And she began devouring the books she had missed—about one a day.
>
> Some students have the opposite problem. They read *everything* rapidly. They must learn to slow down when reading math and science.

It does not make sense to assume that all ideas can, or should, be assimilated at the same rate. Some ideas are more difficult to understand than are others. Some must be understood thoroughly, whereas others need be understood only in general ways. This suggests that students should use different rates of reading for various types of materials and/or when reading for different purposes. Despite the fact that we have for years given lip-service to this idea, the accumulated evidence suggests that most students, in fact, do not vary their rates of reading. Moreover, there is some evidence that suggests that they can be taught to use flexible rates.[2]

The presence of some factors might inhibit a student from reading as rapidly as desirable. Among them are: poor near-point visual acuity, poor visual fusion, poor vocabulary and word attack skills, excessive attention to details, lack of interest in the reading material, inadequate background of information which relates to the material, and low intelligence. (See Chapter 1 for a discussion of these factors.)

There is little point in stressing rate if one or more of the inhibiting factors is present. If the student's vision is poor, a correction can be made in most cases. If his vocabulary or word attack skills are inadequate, these skills must be built. If the reading material is dull to the reader, in some cases other material can be substituted. If not, interest should be built. A background of information also can be built. Perhaps nothing can be done about intelligence. It would, of course, be folly to expect a student with a low I.Q. to read as rapidly as one with a high I.Q.—all else being equal.

Flexibility of rate

Flexibility of rate is the keynote to reading success. Some things should be read slowly, others rapidly, and others at a moderate rate. There is no point in reading something too rapidly for proper ingestion and digestion of the ideas. Nor is there good reason for reading anything so slowly that the train of thought is lost.

The *difficulty of the material* (for the reader) and his *purpose for reading* it should determine the rate used. Speed in itself is neither a virtue nor detriment; neither is a slow rate, in itself, a virtue or detriment.

The rate must be appropriate to the reader, the material, and the reader's purpose. Poetry might be read over and over. It might be read orally. To compute the words per minute makes little sense. Poetry should be pondered. It has its own rate. Rushing through it makes as much sense as rushing through a symphony.

But when one loses himself in a novel or textbook, rate might be a virtue. When the reader lives vicariously, he forgets he is reading words or phrases. Ideas come through "loud and clear" as he flashes through (at less than 900 w.p.m.). He is in orbit, and his fastest rate comes in handy when he is reading for escape or when he is reading something he already knows quite a lot about. No point in dawdling!

Other rates come in handy, too. Sometimes a sentence must be read over and over before it makes sense to the reader. It is not always bad to regress. At other times, a steady moderate rate is best.

When should a student read at fast, medium and slow rates? Table 10.1 might serve as a guideline.

Table 10.1   Guide to determining proper reading rate

Rate	Difficulty of material	Purpose for reading
fast	independent level	to get general idea, main points, for pure enjoyment, especially of plot, escape
	instructional level	to thoroughly preview, get main headings, main ideas, sequence, to review
medium	independent level	to read to remember sequence for later recall, to appreciate style of writing, for greater depth of understanding than would be possible at a faster rate
	instructional level	to note important details, to formulate main ideas, to interpret, to classify
slow	independent level	to mull over ideas, to absorb and analyze thoughts, to anticipate uses for ideas, to promote tangential thinking
	instructional level	to examine thoroughly, to analyze, criticize, react to ideas, evaluate ideas, to solve problems, to follow directions

CLASSROOM ACTIVITIES THAT HELP BUILD SPEED OF COMPREHENSION

In many cases, a teacher can help students improve their speed of comprehension. First, students must be made aware of the fact that fast reading is not necessarily poor reading. The teacher might explain that - - - we - - - do - - - not - - - think - - - in - - - single - - - words. We think - - - in phrases - - - or in sentences. Why not read in phrases?

The student who reads one word at a time will have read 27 different ideas by the time he finishes a 27-word sentence. He may forget what the beginning is about by the time he reaches the end. If he reads in three-word phrases, he will read only nine ideas. (This is an oversimplification, of course, but the point is nonetheless valid.)

Also, if he reads too slowly for his ability, his mind will wander. He will think about next weekend, or last weekend, while his eyes pass over the words. He will not get much out of his reading. If he reads at his optimal rate, he will be challenged, and his mind will not wander. *After* he finishes his reading, he can think about next weekend.

Teaching Strategies

The following techniques should prove helpful in improving speed of comprehension:

1. When easy and interesting materials are being used, students should be timed periodically when reading them. Questions to be answered should be of a general nature—main idea, sequence, summary, etc.

   Students should compute their rates of reading. To find the words per minute, students are instructed to divide the time it took them to read the passage (time is expressed in minutes and fractions thereof) into the total number of words in the passage. For example, if a student reads a 1000-word passage in 3 minutes 30 seconds, he would divide 3.5 into 1000 to get his words-per-minute count:

$$3.5 \overline{\smash{\big)}\ 1000.0} \quad \frac{286}{} \text{ words/minute}$$

   Students should chart their rates on a graph. Emphasizing improvement is important.

2. *The content area teacher* should teach students to *survey a chapter* before they read it. Thus, they have the framework in mind before they begin to read the complete chapter. Having such an "advanced organizer" facilitates efficient reading.

3. *The content area teacher* should state purposes for reading to direct the students' thoughts. Teachers should teach students to formulate their own purposes also.

4. Exercises designed specifically for improving rate of reading can be used. *Content area passages can be altered slightly* by inserting an irrelevant remark. Below is an example of a type of exercise any imaginative teacher could design. Such an exercise could be given to students about once a week, using ideas from that week's assignments. Probably two or three pages should be used at a time, each one timed individually.

   Directions: Read as rapidly as you can. In each numbered item there is an irrelevant word or phrase. Underline it. When you finish each four-item page, record the last time that was written on the board.*

---

* Most of these examples were written by Iris Morgenstern, graduate student, The University of Texas at El Paso.

1.   (English)

Artistic unity is essential to a good plot. Best writers exercise a rigorous selection: they include nothing that does not advance the central intention of the story nor anything the cat from next door said.

2.   (Science)

Blood-vessel space is controlled by the changing size of the vascular system. This is accomplished by the contractions, relaxations, and night driving phobias of the smooth muscles in the walls of the arteries and veins.

3.   (Art)

The distrust between artist and the public was mutual. To the businessman, an artist was little better than an impostor who demanded ridiculous prices for something that could hardly be called honest work. Among the artists it became a pastime to shock the burghers out of their complacency and butane electrical outlets and to leave them bewildered and bemused.

4.   (History)

Turn back the clock of time to the year 1387. Approaching Tabard Inn in the town of Southwark across the river from London is a band of pilgrims. Traveling on eagleback, they will have a long, slow journey to Canterbury, about 65 miles to the southeast.

Time _____

1.   (Mathematics)

According to the Pythagorean theorem the square on the hypotenuse is equal to the sum of the squares of the legs. When using this theorem, one must be sure to have a right triangle with square legs.

2.   (Science)

Starches and sugars are the chief sources of energy for herbivorous and omnivorous animals. Carnivores, however, do not rely on these foods for their primary energy source, but on protein, fats, and iced cannons.

3.   (Home Economics)

Cabbage held in cold storage shows no appreciable loss of ascorbic acid for one or two months. Some loss occurs by the third month, however. Cabbages taken from the middle of the clock may be held in the refrigerator for a week without appreciable loss of ascorbic acid.

4.   (Home Economics)

Jelly is a product made from fruit juice. An ideal jelly is stiff enough to hold its form when removed from the mold yet sufficiently delicate in texture to quiver and decode a cryptogram. It is transparent and has the characteristic color and flavor of the fruit from which it is made.

Time _____

5. Time students as they underline the words that are the same as the key word. Use content area words.

1) cabinet:	oracle	domain	local	cabinet
2) colony:	tariff	colony	budget	veto
3) repeal:	revenue	ratify	repeal	statute
4) treasury:	treasury	revision	decree	concede
5) impeach:	secede	writ	local	impeach
6) appoint:	regulate	appoint	quorum	senator

•

•

•

20) tariff:	annul	anarchy	budget	tariff

Time _____

6. Time students as they underline a synonym for each key word.

1) adjacent:	bordering	intercepting	equivalent	bisecting
2) symmetry:	secant	balance	common	locus
3) altitude:	radius	degree	height	similar
4) theorem:	tangent	base	coincide	postulate
5) converse:	diagonal	opposite	proof	geometric
6) external:	axiom	outer	polygon	altitude

•

•

•

20) midpoint:	center	degree	radius	perimeter

Time _____

7. Time students as they underline an antonym for each key word.

1) consonant:	vowel	phoneme	morpheme	grapheme
2) debate:	argue	speak	agree	read
3) résumé:	partial statement	complete statement	axiom	synopsis
4) predicate:	adjective	verb	noun	subject

5) prefix: root   suffix   vowel   noun

●

●

●

20) salutation: closing   beginning   middle   letter

Time _____

8. Students can use cards or envelopes to cover successive lines of print. The student reads the lines just before they are covered. Each student moves his own card down the page as rapidly as he can force himself to read.

9. The teacher gives the student class time for free reading of interesting material. Students are encouraged to read rapidly.

10. Timed exercises, such as the SRA *Rate Builders* and the McCall-Crabbs *Standard Test Lessons in Reading* are useful in English and reading classes.[3] For good results, about four or five of these exercises should be used at least once every week.

MECHANICAL DEVICES, OR THE MYSTERIES OF SOME READING CENTERS

There are a number of mechanical devices that have been designed to help students improve their speed of reading. In general, this equipment is expensive, and after summarizing research, Robert Karlin concluded that "It appears that gains in rate of reading can be achieved through programs which include mechanical instruments. . . . It is apparent that instruction which does not favor machines not only can bring about these same gains but also . . . surpass them. Dependence upon expensive equipment to achieve suitable outcomes in reading rates cannot be recommended in view of present knowledge."[4] However, because of their immense popularity among teachers, some of these devices and their uses will be described here.

There are three types of machines: tachistoscopes, pacers, and film or filmstrip machines. (See references at the end of this chapter for trade names and companies.)

Tachistoscopes

Tachistoscopes, also called flashmeters, are designed to flash a single exposure on a screen at a rapid rate—usually between one second and 1/100 of a second (see Figs. 10.2 and 10.3).

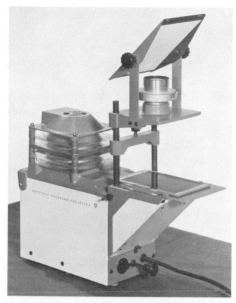

Fig. 10.2 Overhead projector with tachistoscope attachment. (Photograph of Keystone Overhead Projector courtesy Keystone View Company, Meadville, Pa.)

Fig. 10.3 Tach-X Tachistoscope. (Photograph of EDL Tach-X Tachistoscope courtesy Educational Developmental Labs, Huntington, New York.)

Anything might be included in this exposure—from pictures used in visual discrimination for reading readiness to digits to words or phrases. The exposure might look like any of these:

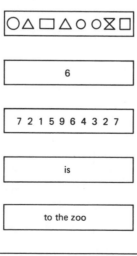

Groups of students can work together for short periods of time using this machine. The teacher usually flashes the exposures using the 1/100-second setting, and the students record what they have seen. After about eight or ten exposures, students check their papers. Then the teacher flashes another series. About 20 or 30 exposures are seen at one sitting.

The object is to increase the eye span and to minimize the time for each exposure, or fixation. Single words and then two-, three-, or four-word phrases can be flashed. Accompanying these, at the same setting, can be digits—three- or four- or five-digit numbers. Sometimes the teacher starts flashing the tachistoscope at 1/25 of a second and works up to 1/100 of a second.

Hand Tachistoscopes

One application of linguistic theory appropriate to the improvement of phrasing and, therefore, to speed of comprehension is related to the use of signal words, or markers. Markers are of various types: noun markers (a, an, the; one, two, three; these, those, etc.), verb markers (is, am, was, were, has been, etc.), phrase markers (of, to, with, from, etc.), clause markers (since, however, nevertheless, etc.), question markers (who, what, where, when, why, which, *even*?). Such markers can be used as cues that a phrase or clause is beginning. Recognizing such markers will help students read in natural English phrases. This is especially appropriate for use in English or special reading classes.

Chalk-board exercises, flash cards, hand tachistoscopes, or mechanical tachistoscopes can be used in teaching this concept.

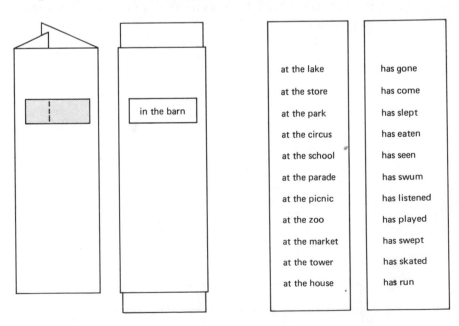

at the lake	has gone
at the store	has come
at the park	has slept
at the circus	has eaten
at the school	has seen
at the parade	has swum
at the picnic	has listened
at the zoo	has played
at the market	has swept
at the tower	has skated
at the house	has run

in the barn

Fig. 10.4 Shadowscope, a pacer. (Photograph courtesy Psychotechnics, Inc., Glenview, Ill.)

Fig. 10.5 Rateometer, a pacer. (Photograph of AVR Reading Rateometer courtesy Audio-Visual Research, Waseca, Minn.)

Pacers

Pacer devices incorporate a shade, metal bar, or light beam that moves down a page to cover successive lines of print at a rate set by the reader (see Figs. 10.4 and 10.5). The student reads *below* the shade or bar or within the light beam. Almost any type of reading material can be used, including workbooks, textbooks, and paperbacks.

The student is instructed to set the device so that it is comfortable for him, and then to set it slightly faster to push himself just a bit. As soon as that rate becomes comfortable, he sets the machine to go faster, etc. Some reading experts recommend that the student alternate pages, reading one page on the machine, the next without it, etc. Or, the student might read one on the machine and two or three without it. This might help to eliminate his dependence on the machine for increased rate.

Films and Filmstrips

Films that are paced so that one phrase at a time is exposed (about three flashes per line) are available with reading material at the high school level (see Figs. 10.6 and 10.7). These films can be used on a regular movie projector.

Machines designed to use filmstrips—with phrases exposed in sequence, with a sliding exposure, or with a full-line exposure—are also available. Filmstrips are available at all reading levels, from readiness through college levels. Workbooks accompanying some of these are very well planned and use a survey technique, programed vocabulary development, and statements of purpose before the film is read. In general, the films contain very high-interest reading materials.

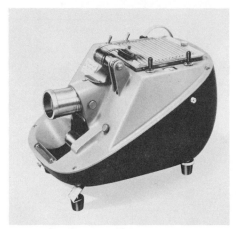

Fig. 10.6 Tachomatic 500 Reading Projector, a filmstrip projector. (Photograph courtesy Psychotechnics, Inc., Glenview, Ill.)

Fig. 10.7 Controlled Reader, a filmstrip projector. (Photograph courtesy Educational Developmental Labs, Huntington, New York)

The purpose of these machines is to increase a student's reading rate by improving his left-to-right eye movements and by increasing the eye span. Such films and machines are frequently misused, however. Often, it is the advertising that leads to such misuse. The teacher who has such materials at his disposal should look carefully at his students to decide who might benefit from their use. How many students read at the same rate? And of these, how many will be likely to progress at the same rate? Instead of using such a device in a group situation, it is probably best to have students work individually, possibly in a small booth.

Such machines, if used properly, may be helpful in a reading program. But their purchase should be low on the priority list. Paperbacks and a variety of workbooks are essential to a successful program. The machines are accessories and may add some variety to an already good program. But they are not essential.

Extreme caution should be taken when working on the improvement of reading rate, especially when using mechanical devices. Frequently, use of these machines leads to the treatment of the symptom rather than the cause of slow reading.

It is true that an occasional student may read slowly just because he has not been trained to use a variety of rates. He may be a science or mathematics major and may not have learned to read other materials more rapidly. If he has no comprehension problems except those caused by a plodding rate, machines may help him a great deal. But most students read slowly because of poor word attack skills, inadequate vocabulary, poor comprehension, mind set, etc. Training their eyes to move more rapidly compounds their problem. The cause must be treated before, or along with, the rate improvement program.

SUMMARY

Most students have the potential to read more rapidly without decreasing their comprehension. However, rate in itself is no virtue. The *mechanics of reading* dictate that the fastest rate of reading that anyone can hope to attain is about 800–900 words per minute. However, the *ability of a person to assimilate ideas* often suggests that rates slower than his own absolute maximum be used for greater thoroughness of understanding.

Students should be taught to read at various rates—at a slow rate for difficult material they are studying carefully, at a medium rate for material of moderate difficulty, and at a faster rate for easy material or when reading for escape. *The difficulty of the material and the purpose for reading it should determine the rate used at any specific time.* Students should also be taught to skim and scan. Techniques that any classroom teacher can use to help his students improve their ability to skim and scan and to read at appropriate rates were suggested.

Mechanical devices—tachistoscopes, pacers, films, and filmstrips—that might be used in special reading classes were also explained. Such machines should be considered as accessories, to be purchased only if a wide variety of paperbacks, workbooks, kits, and other materials is already available in the classroom. On occasion, such machines can be helpful, but there is a real danger of misuse—or using them to treat the symptom rather than the cause of slowness in reading. Of course, whenever we work directly on improving rate, such a possibility exists. When we carefully check comprehension, there is a lesser likelihood of this.

NOTES

1 George D. Spache. "Is This a Breakthrough in Reading?" *The Reading Teacher*, **25** (January 1962): 258–263.

2 Leonard Braam. "Developing and Measuring Flexibility in Reading." *The Reading Teacher*, **26** (January 1963): 247–254.

3 SRA *Rate Builders* from Science Research Associates, Inc., Chicago; McCall-Crabbs *Standard Test Lessons in Reading* from Teachers College Press, Columbia University, New York, 1961.

4 Robert Karlin. "Research in Reading." *Elementary English*, **37** (March 1960): p. 183.

SUGGESTED ACTIVITIES

1. Explain why Spache contends that 900 words per minute is a maximum rate for reading. Compare this rate with claims made by some "speed reading" schools. Explain how you would react to a principal or school board member who was anxious to establish a speed-reading class in your school.

2. Define eye-span, fixation, and saccadic sweep.

3. Design three different exercises or techniques to help students read more efficiently in your content area.

4. Design three exercises for teaching students to skim.

5. Describe the following types of mechanical devices in relation to their uses in a reading program: tachistoscope, pacer, and film and filmstrips. Review the professional literature. Is the purchase of such equipment justifiable? If so, when? If not, why?

6. Give specific examples of instances when each of the various rates (fast, medium, slow, skimming, scanning) is desirable when reading in your content area.

7. Assume that you will have a group of students for a period of one school year. Design a plan for integrating the teaching of the use of efficient rates of reading with the teaching of the content of your course. Precisely when and how will you teach students to scan? Skim? Read rapidly? Read at a medium rate? Read slowly? Make a hypothetical plan, plotting the integration of these skills with the teaching of content over a period of one year.

SUGGESTED ACTIVITY FOR UNIT THREE: DIRECTED READING ACTIVITY

Select a chapter or part of a chapter, a poem, essay, etc., appropriate to your content area. Design a Directed Reading Activity for this section.

1. First and second steps
    a) Show how you would do the first and second steps of the DRA. Give explicit questions and activities.
    b) Share these with your class or with a subgroup in your class. Discuss your ideas (and theirs). Revise your plan if you have gained new insights.

2. Fourth step (third step is silent reading)

   a) Show how you would proceed with step four if you were a classroom teacher. Choose one or the other approach suggested, or a combination. Be sure you can justify your approach in relationship to your reading assignment.

   b) Share your "discussion procedure" with your class or subgroup in the class. Revise your plan if you have gained new insights.

3. Fifth step

   a) Show how the reading activity can be extended. Suggest a variety of readings and/or other possible related activities. Give explicit examples. You may wish to design an Interest Inventory, similar to that given on p. 63.

   b) Share your extension activities with your class or subgroup in the class. Ask for further suggestions. Revise your plan if you have gained new insights.

REFERENCES FOR FURTHER READING

Bond, Guy L. and Miles Tinker. *Reading Difficulties: Their Diagnosis and Correction.* New York: Appleton-Century-Crofts, 1967, Chapter 15.

Ehrlich, Eugene. "Speed Reading Is the Bunk." *The Saturday Evening Post,* June 9, 1962.

Grob, James A. "Reading Rate and Study-Time Demands on Secondary Students." *Journal of Reading,* **14** (January 1970): 285–288, 316.

Hafner, Lawrence E. (ed.). *Improving Reading in Secondary Schools—Selected Readings.* New York: Macmillan, 1967, Section 9.

Harris, Albert J. *How to Increase Reading Ability.* New York: David McKay, 1970, Chapter 18.

Karlin, Robert. "Machines and Reading: a Review of Research." *The Clearing House* (February 1958): 349–352.

Karlin, Robert (ed.). *Teaching Reading in High School—Selected Articles.* Indianapolis: Bobbs Merrill, 1969, Section 9.

Owsley, Clifford D. "Confessions of the World's Fastest Reader." *Saturday Review,* June 9, 1960.

Schubert, Delwyn and Theodore L. Torgerson (eds.). *Readings in Reading—Practice, Theory, Research.* New York: Thomas Y. Crowell, 1968, Section 5.

Spache, George. *Toward Better Reading.* Champaign, Illinois: Garrard, 1963, Chapters 14 and 15.

Witty, Paul. "Rate of Reading—A Crucial Issue." *Journal of Reading,* **4** (November 1960): 102–106, 154–163.

MECHANICAL DEVICES

Tachistoscopes

1. *EDL Tach-X Tachistoscope*
   Educational Developmental Laboratories, Huntington, New York
   Shutter Speed: 1/100 to 1½ second
   Levels: k–adult
   Cost: $210.00   Filmstrips: $62.50 per set

2. *Keystone Standard Tachistoscope*
   Keystone View Company, Meadville, Pennsylvania
   Shutter Speed: 1/100, 1/50, 1/25, 1/10, 1/5, 1/2, 1 second
   Levels: k–adult
   Cost: $370.00   Slide packages: $11.25–$135.00

3. *Rheem-Califone Percepta-matic Tachistoscope*
   Carlton Films, Beloit, Wisconsin
   Shutter Speed: 1/100 to 1/10 second
   Levels: 1–8 grades
   Cost: $135.00   Filmstrips: $30.00 per set

4. *T-ap All-Purpose Tachistoscope Attachment*
   Lafayette Instrument Co., Lafayette, Indiana
   Shutter Speed: 1/100, 1/50, 1/25, 1/10, 1/5, 1/2, 1 second
   Cost: $98.00
   Comments: converts any brand of projector to a tachistoscope

5. *SVE Speed-I-O-Scope*
   Society for Visual Education, Inc., Chicago, Illinois
   Shutter Speed: 1/100 to 1 second
   Levels: 1–6 grades
   Cost: $89.50   Filmstrips: $35.00 per set

6. *Electro-Tach*
   Lafayette Instrument Co., Lafayette, Indiana
   Shutter Speed: 1/100, 1/50, 1/25, 1/10, 1 second
   Levels: 1–college
   Cost: $98.00
   Comments: near-point for individual use

7. *Tachist-O-Viewer, Tachist-O-Flasher*
   Learning Through Seeing, Inc., Sunland, California
   Shutter Speed: 1/40, 1/20, 1/10, 1/5 second
   Levels: 1–12 grades
   Cost: $159.50
   Comments: near-point for individual use; programs mainly phonics and vocabulary; series available for remedial classes

8. *AVR Eye-Span Trainer*
   Audio-Visual Research, Waseca, Minnesota

Levels: 4–13 grades
Cost: $8.95
Comments: manually operated

9. *Phrase Flasher*
The Reading Laboratories, Inc., New York
Cost: $9.95
Comments: manually operated; designed for individual use

Pacers

1. *Shadowscope*
Psychotechnics, Inc., Glenview, Illinois
Cost: $94.00
Comments: uses a light beam

2. *Prep-Pacer*
The Reading Laboratories, Inc., New York
Cost: $35.00
Comments: electrical pacer using disk

3. *AVR Reading Rateometer*
Audio-Visual Research, Waseca, Minnesota
Cost: $33.95 to $39.95
Comments: three models: (a) above fourth grade level, (b) elementary and remedial, (c) advanced

4. *SRA Reading Accelerator*
Science Research Associates, Chicago, Illinois
Cost: hand model—$48.95; electric—$68.95

5. *Reading Pacer*
Genco Educational Aids, Chicago, Illinois
Cost: $79.50
Comments: lesson rolls inserted like film in a box camera

Films or Filmstrips

1. *Controlled Reader, Controlled Reader, jr.*
Educational Developmental Laboratories, Huntington, New York
Level: k–adult
Cost: $290.00   Jr.: $220.00   Filmstrips: $16.00–$62.50

2. *Tachomatic 500 Reading Projector*
Psychotechnics, Inc., Glenview, Illinois
Levels: k–adult
Cost: $325.00

3. *Craig Reader*
Craig Research Inc., Los Angeles, California
Cost: $229.50

UNIT FOUR

UTILIZING SCHOOL-WIDE RESOURCES AND STAFF

Introduction

Unit Four focuses on a broader area than the classroom, for it deals with the knowledgeable use of a school library and its resources, and the designing of a school-wide reading program in which all school personnel can participate.

Chapter 11

USING LIBRARY RESOURCES

Co-authored by
I. Jean Stevens

How are most school libraries organized?
What are the main divisions of the Dewey
decimal system? What kinds of materials
are classified in the card catalog? How
are these materials listed in the card
catalog?

What reference aids are useful for locating
periodical literature? books that might be
used in content-related reading? audio-
visual materials? free or inexpensive
materials useful in the classroom?

INTRODUCTION

Although every classroom should contain some supplementary resources, including a book collection, the school library—sometimes known as the instructional materials center, the multimedia center, or the learning resource center, etc.—remains the hub of research activity, the center in which most reference works are located, and the home of most of the school's resource materials. Students must be taught how to use such a resource center effectively, lest they waste invaluable time and effort in attempts to locate materials and ideas—and possibly fail to fully utilize the available materials. In addition, the use of some reference aids may guide them to request the purchase of materials they would like the library to own.

This chapter has been written to help you understand some of the basics of school libraries. The chapter is divided into two major sections. First, some of the basics of school library organization are explained—the Dewey decimal system and the card catalog. Second, basic reference aids frequently found in school libraries are listed and briefly described. Such reference aids include: reference guides to periodical literature (including general and specialized indexes), reference guides for book selection (according to both student interests and content area categories), desk dictionaries, biographical encyclopedias, general encyclopedias, almanacs, atlases, reference guides to periodicals which review audio-visual materials, and guides to free or inexpensive materials. Concluding the chapter is a list of sources which the teacher may wish to consider for use in teaching students how to use a school library.

If students are going to use multiple materials in the courses they study, it is important that such materials be available to them. And it is important that they know where to locate them.

LIBRARY ORGANIZATION

The Dewey Decimal System

Most school libraries in the United States use the Dewey decimal system to classify all of their nonfiction books. The system is simple for children and young people to understand and should be explained, as needed, to students of all ages.

Libraries that use this system normally shelve their books consecutively, beginning with the series numbered 100–199, followed by the 200s, the 300s, and so on. The only books generally omitted from this sequence are the 000–099 books (Generalities, or Reference Works), partly because many of them

---

Co-author of this chapter is Mrs. I. Jean Stevens, Head, Curriculum Library, School of Education, The University of Texas at El Paso.

are oversize, and fiction, which is usually located in the most accessible spot in the library.

The major divisions of the new Dewey decimal system are as follows:[1]

000–099:	Generalities	500–599:	Pure Sciences
100–199:	Philosophy and Psychology	600–699:	Technology (Applied Sciences)
200–299:	Religion	700–799:	The Arts
300–399:	The Social Sciences	800–899:	Literature
400–499:	Language	900–999:	General History and Geography

Some of the more useful and interesting subdivisions within these major divisions are:

000–099: Generalities
    010: Bibliographies
    020: Library Science
        028: Reading Aids
    030: Encyclopedias
    050: Periodicals and Their Indexes
    070: Journalism, Publishing, Newspapers

100–199: Philosophy and Psychology

200–299: Religion
    220: Bible
    290: Religions other than Christian
        291: Comparative Religion
        292: Classical Mythology
        293: Germanic Mythology

300–399: The Social Sciences
    310: Statistics
    320: Political Science
    330: Economics
    340: Law
    350: Public Administration
    360: Social Pathology and Services
    370: Education
    380: Commerce
    390: Customs
        398: Folklore

400–499: Language
    410: Linguistics
    420: English Languages
        421: Written and Spoken English
        422: English Etymology
        423: English Dictionaries
        425: English Grammar
        426: English Prosody
        427: Nonstandard English
        428: Standard English Usage
    430: Germanic Languages (with the same subdivisions as given under English above)
    440: French Languages
    450: Italian Languages
    460: Spanish Languages
    470: Latin Languages
    480: Classical Greek
    490: Other Languages

500–599: Pure Sciences
    510: Mathematics
    520: Astronomy
    530: Physics
    540: Chemistry
    550: Geology (Earth Sciences)
    560: Paleontology
    570: Life Sciences (Anthropology, Biology)
    580: Botany
    590: Zoology

600–699 Technology (Applied Sciences)
    620: Engineering
    630: Agriculture
    640: Home Economics
        641: Foods
        643: Home
        646: Sewing

649:   Child Care and
Home Nursing
650:   Business
660:   Chemical Technology
700–799:   The Arts
710:   Civil and Landscape Art
720:   Architecture
730:   Sculpture
740:   Drawing and Decorative Arts
750:   Painting
760:   Graphic Arts (Prints)
770:   Photography
780:   Music
790:   Recreation and Performing Arts
792:   Theater (Stage Presentations)
793:   Indoor Games and Parties
796:   Outdoor Sports and Games
800–899:   Literature
810:   American Literature in English
811:   American Poetry
812:   American Drama
813:   American Fiction (Classical)
814:   American Essays
815:   American Speeches
816:   American Letters
817:   American Satire and Humor
818:   American Miscellaneous Writings

820:   English Literature
821:   English Poetry
822:   English Drama etc. (as under American Literature)
830:   German Literature
840:   French Literature etc. (as under Language 450–490)

900–999:   General History and Geography
910:   General Geography and Travel
912:   Atlases
920:   General Biography and Genealogy
930:   History of the Ancient World
940:   History of Europe
942:   England
943:   Germany
944:   France
etc.
950:   History of Asia
960:   History of Africa
970:   History of North America
971:   Canada
972:   Mexico and Middle America
973:   United States
980:   History of South America
990:   History of Other Areas
999:   Extraterrestrial Worlds (New to this edition of Dewey)

Variations:

B, 92, or 921:   Biography (Individual)
F . . . . :   Fiction
SC . . . . . . :   Story Collection

The teacher who knows this system, or who has it accessible for reference, can easily guide students to sections in the library which will be most helpful to them for certain assignments. Certain relationships should become apparent. For example:

in English class:

420:   English Languages
820:   English Literature
942:   English History

in Spanish class:

460:   Spanish Languages
860:   Spanish Literature
946:   Spanish History

in Drama class:

812:	American Drama
822:	English Drama
832:	Germanic Drama
842:	French Drama
852:	Italian Drama
862:	Spanish Drama

in History (900–999):

942:	English History
943:	German History
944:	French History
Even 510.09	History of Mathematics
520.9	History of Astronomy
530.09	History of Physics

If Sarah, for example, wishes to find books on English drama, she should be told to go to books numbered 822. And Michael, who has an insatiable interest in English history, should be led to look in the 942s. Alyce, who has a budding interest in sculpture, should look for her books in the 730s. And Alberto, a lover of botany, will find his favorite books numbered 580.

More detailed information about the Dewey decimal classification is available through many sources. Most common is the abridged edition of the current *Dewey Decimal Classification and Relative Index* (see note 1 at the end of the chapter). The subject cards found in a card catalog and the subject index in a book catalog also lead the user to the classification number.

The Card Catalog

The card catalog of a school library is an index to the entire collection of resources housed in the library. Besides containing the usual subject, author, and title cards for books in the library, the catalog also contains cards for the school's filmstrips, films, records, tapes, pictures, and information found in vertical and picture files. These cards guide the user to the desired sources of information.

Since there are so many ways of classifying nonprint materials, no attempt is made here to explain any one scheme. However, catalog cards for printed materials all follow a general pattern, as shown in Fig. 11.1. An explanation of the various items is given in Fig. 11.2. For example, variations of the author card are indicated in the "tracings." They are *subject cards* and *title cards*— and possibly joint-author cards and illustrator cards.

Frequently, the librarian types her own cards, using an abbreviated form, such as that shown in Fig. 11.3. Abbreviated subject and title cards are shown in Figs. 11.4 and 11.5, respectively.

All such cards are filed alphabetically in the card catalog by the first line. The Dewey decimal system classification number indicates the section of the library in which the book is located. For the book shown in Fig. 11.2, for example, that section is 973—United States history. Within this section, all

```
Call
Number   Author, Surname first
              Title..............................
         ......Publisher, date.
              paging  illustrations

              Notes..............................

              contents..........................


              tracings
```

Fig. 11.1   Skeleton author card, showing location of items.

books are classified according to the authors' last names. Thus, a book by Borrowman would be found before this book by Clark, and a book by Curti would be found after it. Alphabetizing by author within a Dewey number is the rule, except for individual biography (combined with autobiography), where the subclassification is by subject (the person written about).

Media cards usually are similar to book cards. They are often color-banded, a different color being used for each media: filmstrips, records, tapes, etc.

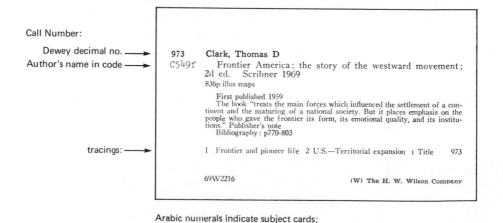

Call Number:

Dewey decimal no. ⟶
Author's name in code ⟶

```
973      Clark, Thomas D
C549f       Frontier America; the story of the westward movement;
         2d ed.   Scribner 1969
         836p illus maps

            First published 1959
            The book "treats the main forces which influenced the settlement of a con-
         tinent and the maturing of a national society. But it places emphasis on the
         people who gave the frontier its form, its emotional quality, and its institu-
         tions." Publisher's note
            Bibliography: p770-803

         1  Frontier and pioneer life  2 U.S.—Territorial expansion  1 Title    973


         69W2216                                    (W) The H. W. Wilson Company
```

tracings: ⟶

Arabic numerals indicate subject cards;
Roman numerals indicate title card and
all cards other than subject cards, e.g.,
joint author card, illustrator card, etc.

Fig. 11.2   Completed author card, with explanation of items.

```
973
C549f    Clark, Thomas D
             Frontier America; the story of the
         westward movement.  2d ed.    Scribner,
         1969.
             836p.  illus. maps.




             1. Frontier and pioneer life. 2.
         U.S.-Territorial expansion.  I. Title.
```

Fig. 11.3 Librarian's abbreviated author card.

```
973         FRONTIER AND PIONEER LIFE
C549f    Clark, Thomas D
             Frontier America; the story of the
         westward movement.  2d ed.    Scribner,
         1969.
             836p.  illus. maps.

         973         U.S.-TERRITORIAL EXPANSION
         C549f    Clark, Thomas D
                     Frontier America; the story of the
                 westward movement.  2d ed.    Scribner,
                 1969.
                     836p.  illus. maps.
```

Fig. 11.4 In abbreviated subject cards, the subject may be typed in either color or capital letters, to distinguish it from a title card.

```
973         Frontier America
C549f   Clark, Thomas D
            Frontier America; the story of the
        westward movement.  2d ed.    Scribner,
        1969.
            836p.  illus. maps.
```

Fig. 11.5   Librarian's abbreviated title card.

REFERENCE AIDS

Reference Guides to Periodical Literature

Although there is a Dewey number for periodicals and their indexes (050) and for newspapers (070), these numbers merely help the reader locate periodicals, newspapers, and indexes, not desired articles within these. The indexes, themselves, must be used for the location of articles.

There are several indexes, or reference guides, to periodical literature which are sometimes found in school libraries. *The Readers' Guide to Periodical Literature* and the *Abridged Readers' Guide* are the most common of such indexes. Others, listed below, may be found in some school libraries and are commonly found in local libraries.

Indexes to general and nontechnical magazines

1. *The Readers' Guide to Periodical Literature,* 1900–. New York: H. W. Wilson.

   An index to the contents of about 160 popular magazines, published twice monthly, September to June, and monthly in July and August. Cumulated volumes, which include all information from a number of issues combined into one alphabet are available periodically.

   Each magazine article in the 160 magazines indexed is entered under both the author's name and the subject, and sometimes also under the title.

   For teaching the use of *The Readers' Guide to Periodical Literature* (or the *Abridged Readers' Guide*): *How to Use the Readers' Guide to Periodical Literature.* New York: H. W. Wilson, revised edition, 16 pages, 1970. This pamphlet is designed for teaching the use of the *Readers' Guide* to secondary and elementary school students. Class-size sets are free.

2. *The Abridged Readers' Guide to Periodical Literature*, permanent volumes available from 1948–. New York: H. W. Wilson.

An index to the contents of about 44 magazines of general interest, especially suitable for use in elementary and junior high schools and other small libraries. It uses the same format as the *Readers' Guide* and is published monthly except in June, July, and August. The September issue includes indexing for these summer months. Cumulated volumes are available yearly.

Specialized indexes

1. *Applied Science and Technology Index*, 1958–. New York: H. W. Wilson.

A subject index to about 225 periodicals in such fields as aeronautics and space science, chemistry, construction, earth science, electricity, engineering, industrial arts, machinery, mathematics, physics, transportation, etc. Published monthly, except July, and with annual cumulations.

2. *Art Index*, 1929–. New York: H. W. Wilson.

An author and subject index to about 185 periodicals and museum bulletins, domestic and foreign. Includes such subjects as: archaeology, architecture, art history, crafts, fine arts, industrial design, interior decoration, photography and films, landscaping, etc. Published quarterly, with annual cumulations.

3. *Biological and Agricultural Index*, 1964–. New York: H. W. Wilson.

An index to about 190 periodicals in such fields as: agricultural chemicals, economics, engineering, research, bacteriology, biochemistry, botany, conservation, ecology, forestry, marine biology, nutrition, veterinary medicine, etc. Published monthly, except August, with annual cumulations.

4. *Business Periodicals Index*, 1958–. New York: H. W. Wilson.

A subject index to about 170 periodicals in such fields as accounting, advertising, automation, banking, communications, finance, investments, insurance, labor, management, taxation, specific businesses, etc. Published monthly, except August, with annual cumulations.

5. *Education Index*, 1929–. New York: H. W. Wilson.

A subject index to about 240 educational periodicals, yearbooks, monographs, books, proceedings, etc. Published monthly, except July and August, with annual cumulations.

6. *Social Sciences and Humanities Index*, 1965–. New York: H. W. Wilson.

An author and subject index to about 200 periodicals in such fields as anthropology, archaeology, classical studies, area studies, economics, folklore, geography, history, language and literature, music, philosophy, political science, religion, sociology, theater arts, etc. Published quarterly, with annual cumulations.

Indexes to newspapers

1. *The New York Times Index*, September 1851–. New York: New York Times.

    A subject index to articles that have appeared in the *New York Times*. The brief summaries of these articles and dates of events may help students locate similar articles in local newspapers. It is published semimonthly, with annual cumulations.

2. *The Christian Science Monitor Index*, January 1960–. Boston: Christian Science Publishing Society.

    A subject index to articles that have appeared in the *Christian Science Monitor* issued monthly, with semiannual and annual cumulations.

Selection aids for periodical literature

In addition, there are several sources designed to help an individual or a library select periodicals to be purchased for school use.

1. Dobler, Lavinia and Muriel Fuller. *World Dictionary of Youth Periodicals* (Third Enlarged Edition). New York: Citation Press, 1970.

    A graded and annotated index to periodicals from around the world of interest to young people. American periodicals are classified by subject. Others are classified according to the country that publishes the periodical.

2. Katz, Bill. *Magazines for Libraries*. New York: R. R. Bowker Co., 1969.

    A subject and annotated index to periodicals for school libraries of all levels, including college level.

3. Scott, Marian H. *Periodicals for School Libraries*. Chicago: American Library Association, 1969.

    An alphabetical and annotated index principally to American periodicals suitable for school libraries. It includes a subject index.

Reference Guides for Book Selection

Most school libraries contain reference guides to help in the selection of books according to student interests and content area categories. The use of such reference aids by teachers and students should lead to desired reading materials. In many cases, the use of such guides may lead to the purchase of certain books by the library. Among the most useful of such guides are:

Bibliographies for book selection—classifications by student interests[2]

1. Emery, Raymond and Margaret Houshower. *High Interest—Easy Reading for Junior and Senior High School Reluctant Readers*. Champaign, Illinois:

National Council of Teachers of English, 1965.

Book titles are listed by subject, e.g., adventure (science, sea, historical, mystery, sports, western, etc.), animals (dogs, horses, etc.), family life, teenage adjustment, folk tales, vocational, etc. Each listing is briefly annotated.

2. New York Public Library. *Books for the Teen Age*. New York: The New York Public Library, annually.

Books are arranged by subject, with brief annotations on newer titles. It covers a wide range of interest and readability levels.

3. Nicholsen, Margaret. *People in Books*. New York: H. W. Wilson, 1969.

Individual and collective biographies for all ages are indexed by subject. In many cases, grade-level ranges are suggested.

4. Reid, Virginia M., ed. *Reading Ladders for Human Relations*, 5th ed. Washington, D.C.: American Council on Education, 1972.

Book titles are listed in four sections, each related to extending sensitivity toward people, their values, and their ways of living: creating a positive self-image, living with others, appreciating different cultures, and coping with change. Each listing is annotated, and books are listed within a section in order of maturity and reading difficulty.

5. Roos, Jean Carolyn. *Patterns in Reading*, 2d ed. Chicago: American Library Association, 1961.

Book titles in each of some 70 interest areas are listed in order of difficulty. Each listing is annotated. Among the interest areas are: adventure, Africa, Alaska, American Indians, artists, ballet, Biblical days, Civil War times, conquering handicaps, Mexico, Revolutionary days, scientific challenge, scientific giants, sea adventure, theater, etc.

6. Spache, George. *Good Reading for Poor Readers*, rev. ed. Champaign, Illinois: Garrard, 1968.

Books of high interest and low reading level are listed by title according to subject. Each listing is annotated. Subjects such as the following are included: adventure, Africa, animals, aviation, China, folk tales, humorous tales, Mexico, music, mystery, Revolutionary period, etc. A listing of adapted and simplified materials is also included, as well as textbooks, workbooks, games, series books, magazines, newspapers, and book clubs.

7. Spache, George. *Sources of Good Books for Poor Readers*. Newark, Delaware: International Reading Association, 1969.

A brief compilation of sources of materials for poor readers.

8. *The Reader's Adviser*, 11th ed., 2 vols. Winifred F. Courtney, ed. New York: R. R. Bowker Co., 1969.

The best books from around the world in almost every field of human knowledge are indexed by subject. Annotations are included.

9. Strang, Ruth, Ethlyne Phelps, and Dorothy Withrow. *Gateways to Readable Books*, 4th ed. Bronx, New York: H. W. Wilson, 1966.

Books for adolescents with reading problems (high interest, low reading level) are arranged by subject. The estimated grade level of difficulty is included, as are annotations. Some of the subject categories are: adventure, animal life, aviation, biography, careers, folk tales and myths, health and safety, history and geography, hobbies, humor, music and art, poetry and drama, science (various fields), sports, transportation and communication, young people here and abroad, etc. Also included are listings of books in series, adapted versions of books, magazines and newspapers, and simplified dictionaries.

Bibliographies for book selection—classifications by content areas

Mathematics

1. National Council of Teachers of Mathematics. *The High School Mathematics Library*, 3d ed. Washington, D.C.: National Council of Teachers of Mathematics, 1967.

Materials are arranged by subject according to mathematical categories. Brief annotations are included.

Science

1. American Association for the Advancement of Science. *The AAAS Science Book List*, 3d ed. Washington, D.C.: American Association for the Advancement of Science, 1970.

Materials are arranged by subject according to the Dewey decimal system. The range of difficulty and interest is from grade 7 to young adult.

Social studies

1. National Council for the Social Studies. *American History Booklist for High Schools: A Selection for Supplementary Reading*. Washington, D.C.: National Council for the Social Studies, 1969.

Materials are arranged chronologically and are briefly annotated.

2. National Council for the Social Studies. *Reading Guide in Politics and Government* (Bulletin #38). Washington, D.C.: National Council for the Social Studies, 1966.

Materials about American government are indexed by subject; those about foreign governments are indexed by country. Lengthy annotations are included.

3. National Council for the Social Studies. *World Civilization Booklist: Supplementary Reading for Secondary Schools*. Washington, D.C.: National Council for the Social Studies, 1968.

    Materials are arranged by time periods, and within that, by topics and geographic areas. In the second part of the volume, books are listed alphabetically by author and are annotated. A general estimate of age/maturity level for the materials is given.

4. U.S. Office of Education. *Books Related to the Social Studies in Elementary and Secondary Schools*. Washington, D.C.: U.S. Government Printing Office, 1969.

    Materials are indexed according to geographic areas and are briefly annotated. This is one of a series from the Educational Materials Center. Inexpensive and interesting.

Books and reading—about the adolescent reader

The books listed in this section, in contrast to those listed in the preceding sections, contain more conversation about why certain books are useful, about how to use books with young people, and which books should be given to young people.

1. Burton, Dwight L. *Literature Study in the High School*, 3d ed. New York: Holt, Rinehart and Winston, 1970.

    Designed for English teachers, this book explains how to teach the literature that appeals to young people. Representative books are listed according to genre and are briefly annotated.

2. Carlsen, G. Robert. *Books and the Teen-Age Reader: a Guide for Teachers, Librarians, and Parents*, 2d ed. New York: Harper & Row, 1972. Also in paperback, Bantam H3468.

    A solid source, this book explains the stages of reading development and gives an ample number of examples (classified by genre), each annotated, of books that appeal to teenagers and young adults.

3. Fader, Daniel and Elton McNeil. *Hooked on Books: Program and Proof*. New York: Putnam, 1968. Also in paperback, Berkley S1508.

    A teaching method that worked with delinquent boys who could read but would not is explained. Illustrative lesson plans are given, and a reading list of 1000 paperbacks of appeal to young people is included.

4. Fader, Daniel. *The Naked Children.* New York: Macmillan, 1971.

   The author tried his program (as explained in *Hooked on Books*) at Garnet-Patterson Junior High School in Washington, D.C., with mixed success. He presents a good case for teaching English in every classroom.

5. Edwards, Margaret. *The Fair Garden and the Swarm of Beasts.* New York: Hawthorn Books, 1969.

   The author describes how librarians can be trained to help young people get the most out of the library. Of special value is "The Tool Shed: A Practical Appendix," which covers principles of book selection, how to give book talks, and a brief reading list for younger adults to mature adult readers.

6. Pilgrim, Geneva Hanna and Mariana McAllister. *Books, Young People and Reading Guidance*, 2d ed. New York: Harper & Row, 1968.

   A strong part of this book is a lengthy section on adolescent needs in which the authors stress the importance of guidance in reading for growth toward maturity and include discussions of books which can be used toward this end.

7. Rossoff, Martin. *The School Library and Educational Change.* Littleton, Colorado: Libraries Unlimited, Inc., 1971.

   This book illustrates, in a simple way, how supplementary materials can be used in the classroom to increase the level of interest among students.

Desk Dictionaries

Every library and classroom should contain a variety of dictionaries. Usually, the library also will have at least one unabridged dictionary. Among the better abridged dictionaries are the following:

College level

1. *The American College Dictionary.* New York: Random House, 1966.
2. *The American Heritage Dictionary of the English Language.* Boston: Houghton Mifflin, 1969.
3. *Chambers' Twentieth Century Dictionary.* New York: Hawthorn Books, 1965.
4. *Funk and Wagnalls Standard College Dictionary.* New York: Funk and Wagnalls, 1964.
5. *Random House Dictionary of the English Language.* New York: Random House, 1968.
6. *The Shorter Oxford English Dictionary on Historical Principles.* New York: Oxford University Press, 1962. (2 vols.)
7. *Webster's Seventh New Collegiate Dictionary.* Springfield, Massachusetts: G. & C. Merriam Co., 1967.

8. *Webster's New World Dictionary of the American Language*. Cleveland: The World Publishing Co., 1964.

Secondary level

1. *Thorndike-Barnhart Advanced Junior Dictionary*. Chicago: Scott, Foresman, 1968.
2. *Thorndike-Barnhart High School Dictionary*. Chicago: Scott, Foresman, 1968.
3. *The World Book Dictionary* (2 vols.). Chicago: Field Enterprises Educational Corporation, 1972.

General Reference Materials—Biographies, Encyclopedias, Almanacs, Atlases

Other very important reference materials available in most libraries are volumes containing biographies or references to biographical information; encyclopedias, which contain summary statements about a multitude of topics; almanacs, which contain weather forecasts, tide tables, astronomical information, lists, charts, tables of various types; and atlases, which are bound collections of maps. A selected listing of such sources of information follows.

Biographies

1. *The Authors Series*. New York: H. W. Wilson Co.

    A series of volumes titled: *American Authors: 1600–1900, British Authors Before 1800, British Authors of the Nineteenth Century, European Authors: 1000–1900, The Junior Book of Authors* (about authors and illustrators of books for children and young people), *More Junior Authors, Third Book of Junior Authors, Twentieth Century Authors, First Supplement to Twentieth Century Authors*.

    Each volume contains biographies of authors (including pictures), a list of each author's principal works, and brief reference lists to critical sources. The *American Authors: 1600–1900* volume also contains sketches of many statesmen, religious leaders, and educators, in addition to authors.

2. *Concise Dictionary of American Biography*. New York: Charles Scribner's Sons, 1964.

    An abridgement of *The Dictionary of American Biography*. It is a ready reference to outstanding Americans no longer living.

3. *Current Biography* (monthly, with annual cumulations). New York: H. W. Wilson.

    Contains biographical sketches on important contemporary people in all fields. Sources of the information included are newspaper and magazine articles, books, and possibly the biographee himself. References cited are included.

4. Nicholsen, Margaret. *People in Books*. New York: H. W. Wilson, 1969.

A subject index to individual and collective biographies for all ages. In many cases, grade-level ranges are suggested.

5. *Webster's Biographical Dictionary*. Springfield, Mass.: G. & C. Merriam Co., 1970.

Contains very brief biographical data about more than 40,000 prominent people in the world, with emphasis given to British and Americans. Pronunciation of names is included.

Encyclopedias

1. *Collier's Encyclopedia* (24 vols.). New York: Crowell-Collier, 1969. *Collier's Encyclopedia Yearbook* is available annually.

A popular set, with large print.

2. *Compton's Encyclopedia* (24 vols.). Chicago: F. E. Compton, 1972. *Compton Yearbook* is available annually.

A curriculum-oriented set, with a fact index in each volume.

3. *Encyclopedia Americana* (30 vols.). New York: Encyclopedia Americana Corp., 1968. *Americana Annual* available. A set with many articles on America. It has an Index volume.

4. *Encyclopedia Britannica* (24 vols.). Chicago: Encyclopedia Britannica, Inc., 1968. *Britannica Book of the Year* available annually.

A scholarly set. It has an Index volume.

5. *Encyclopedia International* (20 vols.). New York: Grober, 1968. *Yearbook* available.

An especially good set for junior high school. It is tested for readability.

6. *Merit Students Encyclopedia* (20 vols.). New York: Crowell-Collier Educational Corp., 1968. *Merit Students Yearbook* available.

A junior and senior high school set which is curriculum-oriented.

7. *New Book of Knowledge* (20 vols.). New York: Grober, 1968. *Book of Knowledge Annual* available.

A useful set for slow learners in junior and senior high school. Very colorful.

8. *World Book Encyclopedia* (22 vols.). Chicago: Field Enterprises, 1972.

An accurate children's encyclopedia which can be used by all ages. It has an Index volume.

Almanacs

1. *World Almanac and Book of Facts.* New York: World-Telegram, annually. Found in most school libraries—paperback.

2. *Information Please Almanac.* New York: Simon and Schuster, annually. Contains information not found in *World Almanac.*

3. *Statesman's Yearbook.* New York: St. Martin's Press, annually. Contains information about governments of the world.

Atlases

1. *Encyclopedia Britannica World Atlas.* Chicago: Encyclopedia Britannica, 1964.

2. *National Geographic Atlas of the World*, 2d ed. Washington, D.C.: National Geographic Society, 1966.

3. *The World Book Atlas.* Chicago: Field Enterprises Educational Corp., 1972.

Periodicals with Reviews of Audio-Visual Materials

Among the periodicals containing reviews, discussions, and critiques of audio-visual materials are those listed below. Reading appropriate reviews will help to keep teachers up to date and may guide their recommendations for the purchase of current materials. Students, too, may read such reviews and may use them to decide which of the available materials merit their attention.

1. *Audiovisual Instruction.* (Sept.–June). Anna L. Hyer. National Education Association, Dept. of Audio-visual Instruction, 1201–16th Street N.W., Washington, D.C.

   Educational technology for teachers and media specialists. Includes an index to audiovisual reviews in other publications. Reviews films, records, and new equipment.

2. *The Booklist* (twice monthly, September to July, one issue in August). Chicago: American Library Association.

   Reviews of print and nonprint (16-mm films, filmstrips, recordings, etc.) materials recommended for purchase. For all ages.

3. *Education Screen and Audio-Visual Guide* (monthly). Chicago: Trade Periodicals, Inc.

Discusses and reviews media in sections on AV in religion, filmstrips, film evaluations, audio, and local production. A "New Materials" section evaluates films and lists them by subject, giving complete information for purchase.

4. *Media and Methods* (September–May). Philadelphia: Media and Methods Institute, North American Publishing Co.

   Emphasizes creative and practical methods to use with media, including paperbacks, in the secondary school classroom.

5. *School Library Journal* (September–May). New York: R. R. Bowker Co.

   Reviews and criticizes recordings, filmstrips, 16-mm and 8-mm films.

Reference Guides to Free or Inexpensive Materials

Free or inexpensive materials of quality can be used used in various ways in the classroom. Such materials can be used to supplement textbooks and library reading, to give wider scope to a program and thus help develop critical-creative-evaluative reading skills, to illustrate reports and projects, and to brighten bulletin boards.

Among the guides to such materials are:

1. *Educators Guide to Free. . . .* Randolph, Wisconsin: Educators Progress Service.

   Individual guides to such media as free films, filmstrips, guidance materials, health and physical education materials, science materials, social studies materials, tapes, curriculum materials, etc.

2. *Free and Inexpensive Learning Materials* (biennially). Nashville, Tennessee: George Peabody College for Teachers.

   A subject index (paralleling units frequently taught in elementary and secondary schools) to maps, posters, pictures, charts, pamphlets, and other free or inexpensive educational aids.

3. *Selected Free Materials for Classroom Teachers*, 3d ed. Ruth Aubrey. Belmont, California: Fearon, 1969.

   A subject index organized by nationally recognized curriculum topics to free materials useful in the classroom.

4. *Vertical File Index* (September–July). New York: Wilson Publications.

   A subject and title index to selected pamphlets, booklets, leaflets, and mimeographed materials of interest to general libraries.

SUMMARY

This chapter was written in two major divisions. One part was concerned with the organization of a school library; the other part, with various types of reference aids found in many school libraries and some classrooms.

First, the Dewey decimal system was delineated, with main divisions and some major subdivisions given. It is important that the reader note the pattern of this system, for such recognition will make it easily usable. Then, the card catalog was briefly explained, and several kinds of cards—author, subject, and title—were illustrated. The card catalog contains an index of not only all books in the library, but also such other school resources as filmstrips, films, records, tapes, pictures, and information found in vertical files and picture files. The latter types of cards are often color-banded to indicate the specific type of material.

Next, reference aids that many school libraries own were listed and annotated. Guides to periodical literature were given first. The most common of such guides is *The Readers' Guide*, an index to popular magazines, and *The Abridged Readers' Guide*. Specialized indexes, however, are often more valuable if the student is engaged in content area research. Six specialized indexes were mentioned: *Applied Science and Technology Index, Art Index, Biological and Agricultural Index, Business Periodicals Index, Education Index*, and *Social Sciences and Humanities Index*. Although some of these may not be found in a school library, most are found in local libraries, and students should be aware of their existence. Two indexes to newspapers were also included.

Basic reference guides for book selection were also included. Three specific types were mentioned: guides in which classifications are related principally to student interests (probably English and/or humanities), guides in which classifications are related to content area subjects, and guides that discuss the adolescent reader and how to use books with young people. There is a great deal of overlapping among these categories, and most teachers will find all of these guides useful.

Next, popular desk dictionaries and general reference materials (encyclopedic biographies, encyclopedias, almanacs, and atlases) were noted. The concluding sections dealt with periodicals containing reviews of audiovisual materials and guides to free or inexpensive materials.

It is hoped that the classroom teacher will use a variety of materials—multilevel, multiinterest, and multimedia—and that these references will serve as guides to the selection of such materials. Also, it is hoped that students will be made aware of these guides and will use them to find important information.

NOTES

1 Melvil Dewey. *Dewey Decimal Classification and Relative Index*. Lake Placid Club, New York: Forest Press, 1971.

2 See "What Every Professional Reference Library Should Include," a brochure listing timely resources for the location of supplementary reading and audio-visual materials for secondary schools. Urbana, Illinois: National Council of Teachers of English.

SUGGESTED ACTIVITIES

1. List from memory the major divisions of the Dewey decimal system. Give exact numbers of important materials in your content area.

2. Name three types of cards for books commonly found in a card catalog.

3. Using a timely topic in your content area, indicate which *periodical* guide, or guides, would be useful in locating appropriate materials. Using the guides, write a list of at least 12 current articles that relate to the topic.

4. Select a content area topic, or theme, that might interest your students or prospective students. Tell which guides to *book selection* would be appropriate for students to use in making book choices. Use these guides to write a list of 12 appropriate books. If readability levels for the books are given, include them.

5. Design a content area assignment in which students can use periodical literature, books, general reference works (almanacs, encyclopedias, encyclopedic biographies, atlases, dictionaries), and audiovisual aids. Indicate which aids you and they should use to locate such materials and which general reference works might be used. Finally, include an annotated list of appropriate materials for their use.

REFERENCES ON THE USE OF THE LIBRARY AND REFERENCE MATERIALS

Advanced Library Reference Skills (and *Library Reference Skills—elementary level*). Chicago: Reference Divisions, Encyclopaedia Britannica Educational Corp. (An example of a program designed for teaching students how to use various reference materials. Overhead transparencies are included, as well as a teacher guide and student resource books.)

Berner, Elsa. *Integrating Library Instruction with Classroom Teaching at Plainview Junior High School*. Chicago: American Library Association, 1958.

Cleary, Florence Damon. *Discovering Books and Libraries*. New York: H. W. Wilson, 1966.

Cook, Margaret. *The New Library Key*, 2d ed. New York: H. W. Wilson, 1963.

Downs, Robert. *How to Do Library Research*. Urbana, Illinois: University of Illinois Press, 1966.

Gates, Jean Kay. *Guide to the Use of Books and Libraries*, 2d ed. New York: McGraw-Hill, 1969.

How to Use the Readers' Guide to Periodical Literature, rev. ed. New York: H. W. Wilson, 1970. Free class-size sets.

Rossoff, Martin. *The Library in High School Teaching,* 2d ed. New York: H. W. Wilson, 1961.

Rossoff, Martin. *Using Your High School Library,* 2d ed. New York: H. W. Wilson, 1964. (For high school students.)

Santa, Beauel and Lois Hardy. *How to Use the Library.* Palo Alto, Calif.: Pacific Books, 1966.

Teaching Reference Skills with the Random House Dictionary. New York: Random House, 1966 (an example of a teacher's guide produced by a publishing company). A student workbook is also available.

Chapter 12

DEVELOPING A SCHOOL-WIDE READING PROGRAM

Who should serve on a coordinating committee to design a school-wide reading program?

What kinds of decisions and recommendations should a coordinating committee make?

What are the major facets in a school-wide reading program? How is each organized, and how does each operate?

INTRODUCTION

If you have been reading carefully and thinking about what you have been reading, you know that every content area teacher must know what is involved in reading instruction and what he can do to help his students learn better through more efficient and enjoyable reading. Every teacher who uses printed materials must select them on the basis of their appropriateness to the students who will be using them. He must fuse the teaching of reading and study skills with the teaching of content if he is to foster optimal student achievement, development, and interest.

No longer can we justify the contention that "a child learns to read in grades one to three, and thereafter he reads to learn" unless we define reading in the narrowest of terms, e.g., simple decoding. We know now that learning to read, like learning to think and enjoy, is a continuous process which does not begin and end at the elementary level, or any level, for that matter. Note, for example, the popularity of adult reading courses, and note that these are not remedial in nature. Also note the popularity of study skills and college reading courses for all types of readers—good and bad—in high schools and colleges, even in our best universities.

But the content area teacher at all levels has a unique contribution to make. His ability to make that contribution depends on his ability to recognize the kinds of reading and study skills that are necessary for success in reading and studying and enjoying the materials of his field. He must be able to look at his materials to see which skills his students must have to read them with understanding. Then he must know how to teach these skills concurrently with his subject area. Thus, he must know his students in order to know which skills they already have, which skills need reinforcement, and which skills need to be introduced.

The modern teacher cannot defend a lock-step position. He must be aware, alert, and alive to all kinds of students, and his approach must be fluid. Although many teachers accept this challenge, some of them do not know how to achieve such goals. Therefore, a school-wide program involving all students and providing for teacher training is essential.

LEADERSHIP IN THE PROGRAM

To make the attainment of goals a reality, certain considerations must be dealt with first. A major concern is identifying a person who is able to spearhead the program. This is followed by the need to identify faculty members and others who are willing and able to serve on a coordinating committee whose tasks are to share ideas, to determine a workable philosophy about reading instruction and ways of implementing this philosophy, to supply feedback to other faculty members, and to set things in motion.

If you are already a teacher, the present course work should help make you an invaluable contributing member to such a committee. If you are a pre-service teacher, you should anticipate working on such a committee and seriously consider the kinds of school-wide contributions you will be able to make in the future.

Usually, the principal or another administrator takes the initiative in getting the program on its feet. He may hire a reading consultant, who in turn assumes a leadership role, or he may coordinate the program himself and arrange for the services of a reading consultant when necessary.

The reading consultant may serve the faculty as a demonstrator in the classroom, as a leader in in-service work, as a leader in college or university workshops, as a professor of reading education courses, or in any number of other capacities. This person should have completed the recommended re-quirements for a reading consultant as set forth by the International Reading Association. The consultant should be especially well versed in developmental reading and in reading and study in the content areas, and he should be familiar with common remedial reading procedures. He need not be an expert in remedial reading, however, since this is the forte of the remedial reading teacher. The reading consultant may lay the groundwork for a school-wide program, but he definitely needs a coordinating committee to work along with him. This committee should be composed of people with a sincere interest in furthering the goals of reading instruction of various types, but especially of improving such instruction *in all classrooms,* i.e., in all content areas. In addi-tion to the reading consultant, it is desirable to have the following personnel on the coordinating committee:

1. the principal
2. a representative from each department, including nonacademic depart-ments
3. a guidance counselor
4. a school librarian
5. a member of the school board
6. other personnel when needed: the school nurse, director of audiovisual instruction, etc.

DUTIES OF THE COORDINATING COMMITTEE

When the coordinating committee meets, its members must make the basic decisions that will govern the way the program will function. Such decisions normally include the following:

1. *determining a philosophy of reading.* What is reading? How important is it to build interests? What cognitive skills are important? What word-attack skills are necessary? How important is speed of comprehension?

2. *determining ways of diagnosing students' needs in reading skills.* What standardized tests should be given? What informal techniques should teachers use? How can we best train teachers to interpret these instruments and translate student needs to classroom practice?

3. *deciding what kinds of materials teachers should be encouraged to purchase.* Should multiple textbooks be adopted? Should teachers have classroom libraries? Should teachers be allowed to bring or send their students to the library at any time they wish? What supplementary materials should be made available?

4. *deciding on recommendations for school-wide grouping plans.* Should team teaching be used? Should multigrade classes be offered? Should there be achievement grouping?

5. *determining ways of helping teachers group students and individualize instruction in the classroom.* How can teachers best be taught techniques of grouping students according to skill needs, achievement, interests, social needs and desires, etc? How can teachers be taught to use the unit plan, to individualize instruction, etc.?

6. *determining ways of showing teachers how to recognize the need for specific types of skill development and ways of showing them how to satisfy these needs.* How can teachers be taught which skills are important in understanding the materials used by their students? How can teachers be taught to develop these skills?

7. *determining ways of showing teachers the value of the Directed Reading Activity, SQ3R, and building interests, etc.* Can demonstration teaching be done? What else can be done to demonstrate the usefulness of these concepts?

8. *determining how the school-wide reading program can be coordinated and providing for such coordinaton.* Can a plan be made for developing reading skills, *possibly spirally,* from K–12? Can plans be made for developing interest in reading by using a wide variety of techniques? Can a plan be made relating services rendered in special reading classes with those in content area classes?

9. *determining methodology and materials to be used in evaluating the successes and failures of the program.* Who should test? Should standardized and/or informal techniques be used? What should be evaluated, etc.?

10. *determining policies to be used in in-service training.* Should there be released time? Should the whole faculty meet together at times? In departments at times? Who should be invited to guide in-service training?

AN IDEAL PROGRAM

The coordinating committee should attempt to design an ideal program for the school or the school system. Such a program might be three-faceted, providing for:

1. full participation by content-area teachers in the teaching of reading and study skills and the development of interests as they relate to each course of study

2. the development of units designed for the direct teaching of reading skills and the development of interests in English classes

3. special reaching classes.

Let us look briefly at each of these elements.

Participation of Content Area Teachers

Ideally, every content area teacher will do all the right things. He will select materials appropriate to an individual student's reading achievement and, if possible, interests. He will know what skills are necessary for understanding these materials and will teach these skills at appropriate times. He will teach the vocabulary of his field, use the Directed Reading Activity when he should, and get students involved affectively.

The ideal teacher will be aware that teaching such skills is not teaching an additional *something*, but rather "it is a *way* to teach—a way of teaching which advances not only the student's knowledge of subject matter but his ability to learn other subject matter independently and at will. [His] aim, then, [would be] to unify knowledge learning and the skills of acquiring knowledge." [1] The ideal teacher is a paragon of virtue—and, amazingly, there are some of these people around.

But many teachers have never had a reading course, and they are not sure just what they should be doing. Many of these teachers are doing some reading tasks quite well, though they may not know what they are. (Some teachers think that teaching reading is just teaching word attack skills, etc. They are horribly misinformed!)

A good starting point in designing a school-wide reading program in the content areas is to discuss what is meant by reading. Directly before or after this, a survey form, such as the following, might be checked and analyzed. (The higher the score, the better.) Many teachers will find that they are doing more than they realize.

Survey Form*

Please circle 1, 2, 3, or 4 to indicate the frequency with which you use each of the given practices:

1. seldom or never	2. sometimes
3. most of the time	4. almost always

Practices Related to Reading in the Content Areas

1. I know the reading ability of my students from standardized tests, other evaluative materials, and/or cumulative records.   1 2 3 4

2. I know the reading level of the textbook(s) being used.   1 2 3 4

3. The materials used are suited in difficulty to the reading levels of my students.   1 2 3 4

4. Students are sometimes grouped within my classroom for differentiated instruction.   1 2 3 4

5. The course content is broader in scope than a single textbook.   1 2 3 4

6. Adequate reference materials are available.   1 2 3 4

7. Students are taught to use appropriate reference materials.   1 2 3 4

8. An adequate quantity of related informational books and other materials are available for students who read *below grade level, at grade level,* and *above grade level.*   1 2 3 4

9. I take advantage of opportunities that may arise to encourage students to read recreational as well as informational matter.   1 2 3 4

10. I encourage students through assignments to read widely in related materials.   1 2 3 4

11. At the beginning of the year, adequate time is taken to introduce the text(s) and to discuss how it (they) may be read effectively.   1 2 3 4

12. I am aware of the special vocabulary and concepts introduced in the various units.   1 2 3 4

13. Adequate time is given to vocabulary and concept development.   1 2 3 4

14. I know the special reading skills involved in my subject.   1 2 3 4

15. I teach adequately the special reading skills in my subject.   1 2 3 4

16. Provisions are made for checking the extent to which vocabulary, concepts, and other skills are learned, and reteaching is done when needed.   1 2 3 4

---

* This form is modified from Ira E. Aaron, "Check List of Practices Related to Reading in Content Areas." Used with permission of the author.

17. Time is allowed in class for reading pleasurable materials and for the informal sharing of ideas from these materials.   1   2   3   4

18. Provisions are made for checking the extent to which interests have been developed, and continued attempts are made to give breadth and depth to interests.   1   2   3   4

Launching a reading program in the content areas may seem a formidable task, yet in reality it need not be so. With the coordinating committee at work, certain decisions can be made and implemented. It is, of course, important to be patient. A good reading program must evolve; it is not born in a day or even a year or two. It takes time and effort.

One content area program was begun in the following way:[2]

1. Priorities for skill development were established by testing students and analyzing their needs in the school system. In-service meetings were held to instruct teachers about teaching these skills.

2. The responsibility for the teaching of these skills was relegated to specific content area departments at specific times.

3. All content area teachers were encouraged to use the D.R.A.

4. All content area teachers were encouraged to teach the vocabulary necessary for understanding the ideas of their fields at all times.

5. All content area teachers were encouraged to build interests in depth and/or breadth in topics related to their fields at regular times.

A block design was formulated, showing the dates each department was responsible for teaching specific skills. Such a design, showing this program in action, is given in Table 12.1. You might be able to design such a program, or a better one. Why not try?

Other programs have been designed in which all teachers teach the same skills at the same time. For example, during the first month of classes in the fall, all teachers might teach by using the *preview* technique and/or by using SQ3R, or a variation of it. They might stress the importance of book parts by using the table of contents, title page, glossaries, and index. In addition, they might stress how to ask appropriate questions or how to state purposes for reading.

The next month, they might stress outlining and/or other sequential translation activities: writing and reading graphs, maps, and charts in their content area materials. Following this, they might focus on vocabulary development, building interest in reading, using the library, developing interpretive skills, critical-creative-evaluative skills, etc., in any order preferred.

Table 12.1 Design of school-wide reading program

Skill	English	Social Studies	Science	Mathematics	Other (fill in department and month)
SQ3R	November April	September February	October March	January May	
Sequence and main idea	December January	October March	November April	September February	
Interpretations: a) anticipation b) cause-effect c) motives of characters and real people	October (anticipation) February (motives)	December (motives) April (cause-effect)	September (cause-effect) May (anticipation)	November (cause-effect) March (anticipation)	
Following directions: a) literal level; b) critical-thinking level	November April	September February	October March	December May	
Analysis level: a) fallacies of reasoning; b) propaganda analysis; c) syllogistic reasoning; d) fact-opinion	October (propaganda) March (fallacies)	December (fallacies) April (propaganda)	September (fact-opinion) February (syllogistic reasoning)	November (syllogistic reasoning) January (fact-opinion)	
Synthesis level: a) unique communication; b) inductive/deductive reasoning	September May	November February	December March	October April	
Interest: emphasis on building interest, *per se*	September May	November February	December March	October April	
Developing flexibility of rate	whenever appropriate	whenever appropriate	whenever appropriate	whenever appropriate	

The problem with such a pattern, however, is that it may quickly bore students. But it does provide a focus for faculty discussions and for in-service work.

If, however, both teachers and students do a good job of SQ3R—especially the second step, Q, that is, if they ask the right questions—these questions should indicate which skills are necessary for understanding the assignment, and these are the skills that should be taught at that time. Or, if the teacher does a good job of the first two steps of a D.R.A., this should give clear focus to his teaching, for by doing this he will recognize the reading skills and abilities necessary for understanding and responding to the content.

The problem is that many teachers do not recognize the need for these skills, nor do they know how to teach these skills. So the problem is basically one of designing an appropriate in-service program for teachers, one that will increase their awareness of these factors and instruct them how to teach needed skills.

An ideal approach, of course, is to look at the materials and at the students to see which skills the students must be taught in order to understand the materials. This is a method similar to one suggested by Herber.[3] This is the ultimate of a school-wide program and is best left for the second year of the program, unless just one content area is worked on first.

Special Units in English Classes

Certain reading skills might be taught regularly as part of the English program.[4] For example, the multidimensional aspects of words might be explained in English class, as well as much of diachronic linguistics, certain aspects of semantics, and the basic skills of outlining. Yet, surely, English itself, like any other content-area subject, offers ample opportunity for the development of reading skills and interests that relate to the *content* of English. Interpretive skills, application skills, and critical-creative-evaluative reading all have a place ordained by the content of the course. It is important that these skills be taught well when they are needed for the understanding of such content. In addition, the English class is a marvelous place for the development of recreational reading interests—for free reading. Time should be allotted to reading for pure enjoyment, and no book reports should be required for such reading. There should be choral reading. The teacher should read to the class. There should be oral reading of plays. There should be *sharing* of a voluntary type. Units might be designed around themes of interest to the class, or there might be a completely free range in choice of materials. Something *must* be done to develop interest in reading for pleasure.

Special Reading Classes

Special reading classes of various types should be available to all students *on an elective basis—for credit*. The importance of making these classes elective cannot be overemphasized. Reading classes are not dumping grounds for students with complex problems, nor can such classes serve as a panacea. In a sense, a reading course is a skill course, as is a writing course, or even a typewriting course. Although society puts greater value on learning to read well than on learning to write or to typewrite well, success in learning to read will not solve most student problems. Of course, it might help solve them if the cause of the problem was inadequate reading, but this is not always so.

Students, even those in dire need of a reading course, should not be forced to take the course. The course is functioning poorly if such force is necessary. Students who do not read up to their ability level should be *invited* to take a special reading class. If they accept the invitation, they should be allowed to enroll. Other students who wish to take a reading class should also be allowed to enroll.

> When I began one of my high school jobs, my classes were filled with underachievers in reading who had been forced to take my course. It was a mess. Nobody *wanted* to be in the classes. Fortunately, most of the students found that reading class was not all that bad, but it was a difficult beginning for them and for me.
>
> The following semester I decided to accept only those students who personally asked me to be in one of my classes. I ruled out having a mother or father ask me. The school counselor, who gave the school-wide tests, extended the initial invitation to the students. All but two students who had been invited asked to be included, and one could not take reading because of a schedule conflict. My classes were filled, and I found I could take about twice as many students as I had taken the first semester because *they wanted to come*. There was an *esprit de corps*. And why not? There should be, if reading is taught correctly—cognitively *and* affectively.

Before talking about different kinds of reading classes that might be offered, we must first determine what kinds of readers we have. There are two broad categories: those students who read up to capacity, or almost up to capacity, are usually considered to be *developmental readers*. Those students who read well below their potential, or capacity, level are called *disabled readers*. The gap between potential and achievement widens from first grade to twelfth grade for students generally considered disabled.

If a child is reading one-half year below his potential level (see Chapter 1) in grades 1–3, he is considered disabled and in need of special help in reading. In grades 4–6, the difference must be three-quarters of a year; in grades 7 and

8, one year; and in grades 9–12, two years. (Part of the reason for the broader range in the secondary school is that the margin of error of most tests increases as the grade level increases, and such a span is necessary to be certain that there is a real disability.) Disabled readers should normally be encouraged to take remedial reading.

Developmental readers, or those who are making normal progress in reading in relationship to their intelligence, can be classified into three general categories:

1. *accelerated readers*—those students who are reading well above grade level and approximately at potential level. They need a rapidly paced program and should make more than a year's progress in a year's time.

2. *average developmental readers*—those students who are reading up to potential and are reading approximately at grade level. They need an average-paced program and should continue to make about one year's progress each year.

3. *slower than average learners*—those students who are reading well below grade level because they have low potential. They need a slowly paced program, often called an *adapted reading program*. If their I.Q. test scores are accurate, they will never read at grade level if they are socially promoted, even with excellent help from the school and cooperation and effort on their part. Normally, they make less than a year's progress in a year's time.

Ideally, all students who wish to should have the opportunity of enrolling in special reading classes. There should be *remedial reading classes* (though named something else) for disabled readers and *developmental reading classes* of various types for the developmental readers. Or, if the school's philosophy favors heterogeneous grouping, such clear lines need not be drawn.

I've always enjoyed having a few better readers included in classes which were principally remedial. Students enjoyed this, too. Instruction was individualized, so it really didn't matter. Also, if there is only one special reading teacher, such flexibility is needed to accommodate student schedules. These classes might meet daily for a semester or a year.

In addition to remedial and developmental classes in reading, there might be one or two *college prep* reading courses for accelerated readers in their senior year. (Average or slow-learning readers should take developmental reading.) These classes might meet twice a week for a semester or year.

Such a program has worked well for me. In another school, another plan might function better. Perhaps you can design a program you would prefer.

SUMMARY

If a school-wide reading program is to be effective, all teachers must participate. One or several reading teachers cannot accomplish our goals, nor can one department. Furthermore, it is impossible to develop all desirable reading skills and interests at any one (or several) grade level. Learning to read, and to read better, is a never-ending task. And teaching students to improve their thinking skills and interests as they relate to reading materials is an integral part of good teaching in all subjects at all levels.

Designing a school-wide reading program, however, is not a simple task. A school or school system should have a *coordinating committee*, composed of a reading consultant, the principal, a guidance counselor, a librarian, a representative from each department, possibly a school board member, and other specialized personnel. *Duties of this coordinating committee* include determining a philosophy of reading acceptable to the school staff and the community and which relates to the best modern thought in reading education. This committee should also determine ways of implementing this philosophy.

The coordinating committee should develop an "ideal program" for the school or school system. Such a program should be three-faceted and provide for: (1) full participation by all content area teachers in the fusion of reading skills and interests with the teaching of content, (2) additional participation by English teachers in the development of units or lessons designed for the direct teaching of some reading skills and the development of interest in reading, and (3) organization of a variety of special reading classes.

NOTES

1 Jane H. Catterson. "Successful Study Programs." *Perspectives in Reading #4: Developing Study Skills in Secondary Schools*, Harold L. Herber, ed. Newark, Delaware: International Reading Association, 1965, pp. 158–159.

2 *All Teachers Can Teach Reading*, 1951 Yearbook of the Secondary School Teachers Association, Plainfield, New Jersey.

3 Harold Herber. "Teaching Secondary Students to Read History." *Perspectives in Reading #2: Reading Instruction in Secondary Schools*. Newark, Delaware: International Reading Association, 1964.

4 See Margaret Early. "Reading: In and Out of the English Curriculum." *Bulletin of the National Association of Secondary School Principles*, **51** (April 1967): 47–59.

SUGGESTED ACTIVITIES

1. List the important reading skills students should have to facilitate their understanding of your content area ideas. If possible, compare this list with those written by your classmates or colleagues.

2. Plan, if possible, along with your classmates or colleagues, a design for a school-wide reading program for improving reading skills in all content areas. You may wish to design this in steps: first year, second year, third year, etc. What types of special reading classes would you hope to include in a school-wide program? What special personnel?

3. Define, in general terms and by using specific criteria, what is meant by the term *disabled reader*.

4. Define what is meant by *developmental* reading. Compare the approaches and materials teachers should use with the various kinds of developmental readers (slow learner, average learners, accelerated learners).

REFERENCES FOR FURTHER READING

All Teachers Can Teach Reading, 1951 Yearbook. Plainfield, New Jersey: Secondary School Teachers Association.

Artley, A. Sterl. "Implementing a Developmental Reading Program on the Secondary Level," *Perspectives in Reading #2, Reading Instruction in Secondary Schools,* Margaret Early, ed. Newark, Delaware: International Reading Association, 1964.

Artley, A. Sterl. *Trends and Practices in Secondary School Reading.* Newark, Delaware: International Reading Association, 1968.

Beery, Althea, Thomas Barrett, and William Powell, (eds.). *Elementary Reading Instruction: Selected Materials.* Boston: Allyn and Bacon, 1969, Chapter 11.

Bond, Guy L. and Miles Tinker. *Reading Difficulties: Their Diagnosis and Correction.* New York: Appleton-Century-Crofts, 1967, Chapter 15.

Catterson, Jane H. "Successful Study Skills Programs." *Perspectives in Reading #4: Developing Study Skills in Secondary Schools,* Harold Herber, ed. Newark, Delaware: International Reading Association, 1965.

Hafner, Lawrence E., (ed.). *Improving Reading in Secondary Schools, Selected Readings.* New York: Macmillan, 1967, Sections 10 and 12.

Harris, Theodore L., Wayne Otto, and Thomas C. Barrett. "Summary and Review of Investigations Relating to Reading." *Journal of Educational Research*, February or March yearly.

Herber, Harold. "Teaching Secondary Students to Read History," *Perspectives in Reading #2: Reading Instruction in Secondary Schools,* Margaret Early, ed. Newark, Delaware: International Reading Association, 1964.

Karlin, Robert. *Teaching Reading in High School.* Indianapolis: Bobbs-Merrill, 1964, Chapter 14.

Karlin, Robert, (ed.). *Teaching Reading in High School—Selected Articles.* Indianapolis: Bobbs-Merrill, 1969, Chapters 7, 12, and 14.

Marksheffel, Ned D. *Better Reading in the Secondary School.* New York: The Ronald Press, 1966, Chapters 3, 6, and 8.

National Society for the Study of Education. *Development in and Through Reading*, 60th Yearbook, Part I. Chicago: University of Chicago Press, 1961, Chapters 1, 4, and 5.

National Society for the Study of Education. *Innovation and Change in Reading Instruction*, 67th Yearbook, Part II. Chicago: University of Chicago Press, 1968, Chapters 8, 9, and 11.

Olson, Arthur V. and Wilber S. Ames, (eds.). *Teaching Reading Skills in Secondary Schools*. Scranton, Pa.: International Textbook Co., 1970, Sections 1, 2, 8, 10, and 11.

Robinson, H. Alan and Sidney Rauch. *Perspectives in Reading #6: Corrective Reading in the High School Classroom*. Newark, Delaware: International Reading Association, 1966.

Schell, Leo and Paul Burns, (eds.). *Remedial Reading—an Anthology of Sources*. Boston: Allyn and Bacon, 1968.

Strang, Ruth. *The Diagnostic Teaching of Reading*. New York: McGraw-Hill, 1969, Parts 3 and 4.

APPENDIX A

DALE-CHALL READABILITY FORMULA

The Dale-Chall readability formula is widely used for estimating the reading difficulty of printed materials at the fourth grade level and above.[1] Two factors are used to arrive at the score—*sentence length* and *word difficulty*.

It is necessary to refer to the original article for the list of easy words. With certain stipulations, as explained in the article, all other words are hard.

When the reader knows the number of hard words within a 100-word passage (i.e., the percent of hard words) and the number of sentences totally within the 100-word passage, he can use the "Computation Ease" chart on the following page to find the grade level score.[2]

For example, suppose we are using the passage given in Chapter 2 of this book. There are 13 hard words within the 100-word sample: *Southwesterners, situation, area, perfect, skiers, enthusiasts, area, perfectly, groomed, slopes, accommodate, skiers, beginners.* There are three sentences completely *within* the 100 words.

Using the chart, we see that the *raw score* for the passage is 7.4 and that the *grade score* is 9–10.9. This overlaps somewhat with the Flesch score, which was 10–12.9. You may find that you prefer one formula to the other. You may wish to use a formula just to find the *relative difficulty* of materials.

NOTES

1 Edgar Dale and Jeanne Chall. "A Formula for Predicting Readability." *Educational Research Bulletin* (January 21, 1948): 11–20, 28.

2 Karl Koenke. "Another Practical Note on Readability Formulas." *Journal of Reading*, 15 (December 1971): 206.

COMPUTATION EASE DIRECTIONS

To determine both the Dale-Chall raw readability score and the correspondent grade level placement:

1. Count a 100-word sample from the passage selected.
2. Count the number of sentences in the 100 words. Disregard the sentence in which the one hundredth word appears, i.e., count only those sentences which are completely within the 100-word sample.
3. Count the number of words in the 100-word sample which do not appear on the Dale List of 3,000 Words.
4. Lay a straight edge so that it touches (a) the number of sentences as shown on the left-hand column, and (b) the number of "Hard Words," i.e., those words not on Dale's list, as shown on the right-hand column.
5. Read (a) the Dale-Chall raw score and/or (b) the Grade Level at the point where the straight edge intersects the middle column.

Examples:

1. A 100-word sample with ten sentences and ten "Hard Words" has a raw score of 5.7 and a grade level designation of 5.6.
2. A sample with 20 sentences and seven "Hard Words" has approximately a 5.0 raw score and 5-6 grade level designation.

Fig. A.1 "Dale-Chall Readability Formula: A Computation Ease." (From "Another Practical Note on Readability Formulas," Karl Koenke, *Journal of Reading*, **15**, December 1971, p. 206. Reprinted with the permission of Karl Koenke and the International Reading Association.)

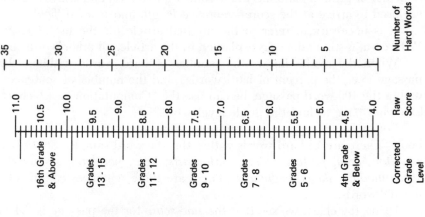

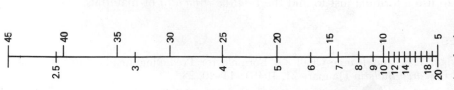

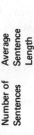

INFORMAL READING INVENTORY— ORAL READING TEST

Sometimes a teacher wishing additional information about the reading achievement of one or more students may have time to administer individual oral reading tests. The kinds of errors a student makes on such a test may give the teacher clues to the type of reading instruction he needs. Such an exam is especially appropriate for students who are reading below about seventh-grade level.

PROCEDURE

The teacher marks off a passage of about 100 words in a book or in a series of multilevel books. Students are asked to read the passage (or passages, beginning with the easiest) orally, individually, and in private with the teacher. As the student reads orally, the teacher records all errors that the student makes. Errors are usually of the following types:

1. mispronunciations—the teacher records the way the student mispronounced the word;

2. substitutions—the teacher writes the substituted word above the word missed;

3. omissions—the teacher circles the word, or words, omitted;

4. insertions—the teacher uses a caret ($\wedge$) and writes in the extra word;

5.   regressions (or repetitions of phrases)—the teacher draws a wavy line under the repeated phrase. A single word may be repeated without being counted as an error if it is finally pronounced correctly;

6.   hesitations—if there is a hesitation of five or more seconds, the teacher writes "H" and then supplies the word.

It is important that the teacher record errors immediately—as they are made—and that he not trust his memory (see p. 297). It is wise to use a passage of exactly 100 words or exactly 200 words so that percentages can be computed easily. The passage need not end at the end of a sentence, though the student should read to the end of the sentence. When the student begins to make an excessive number of errors, i.e., over 6% to 8% errors, the oral testing is stopped.

The teacher's copy of the passage which the student reads orally may look like that shown on p. 297.

INTERPRETATION OF RESULTS

If the student scores 99%–100% correct in oral reading, i.e., up to one error in 100 words, the book is said to be on his *independent reading level.* If he scores 95%–98% correct, i.e., up to one error in 20 words, the book is on his *instructional reading level.* If he makes more than one error in 20 words (94% correct or lower), the book is on his *frustrational reading level.* (Some writers consider 91%–94% correct to be borderline.)

Name: John Sloan

Man is said to be "warm-blooded" because

he maintains a relative (ly) constant body

temperature regardless of the temperature of the

environment. All *mams* mammals and birds

are warm-blooded. All other animals,

including insects, are said to be "cold-blooded"

because their temperature changes with

that of the environment. As body temperature

changes, the rate of activi (ty) changes. You

may have noticed that the chirping rate

of crickets is related to the temperature.

As the temperature drops, their chirp rate

and body motions become noticeably slower.

In late summer, one of the authors took

some data on the chirp rate of tree
    (100 words)
crickets   /   in some honeysuckle, using a

tape recorder to be sure the results could

be reexamined and measured accurately.

	Misp.	Sub.	Om.	Ins.	Reg.	Hes.
	1					
	1					
	1					
					1	
Subtotal:	3				1	

Total = 4

Analysis:

Mispronunciations — 3: word endings

Regressions — 1

Levels	Errors
Independent	0–1
*Instructional	(2–5)
Frustrational	6 or more

MORPHEMES COMMONLY USED IN SPECIFIC CONTENT FIELDS

Table C.1   Morphemes in content areas—some are arbitrarily assigned

Morpheme and meaning	English	Social Studies	Science	Mathematics	General
a (not, without)	aphasia asyllabic athematic atonal	achronological apathetic apolitical asocial	achromatic aseptic asexual atrophy	acentric asymmetric	amnesia amoral atheist atypical
ambi (both)	ambiguous	ambivalent	ambilateral		ambidextrous
anim (life, mind, soul)	animation	unanimous	animal		animosity
ante (before)	antecedent anteclassical	antebellum antedate	anteorbital anterior	antenumber	antechamber antediluvian
anthrop (man, human)	anthropomorphism	anthropology philanthropist	anthropoid		misanthrope
anti (against)	antagonist anticlimax antihero antithesis antonym	antipope antipoverty anti-Semitic antislavery antitrust antiwar	antibody anticatalyst antidote antiperiodic antiseptic	antiderivative antilogarithm antiparallel antisymmetric	antiaircraft antifreeze anti-intellectual antipathy antiperspirant antisocial
apo (off, away from)	apostrophe	apostle apotheosis	apochromatic apogee		apology
arch (chief, principal)	archetype	matriarchy monarch		arch	archangel archbishop

Table C.1   Morphemes in content areas (cont.)

Morpheme and meaning	English	Social Studies	Science	Mathematics	General
arch		oligarchy			architect
auto (self)	autobiography autograph	autocracy autocrat autonomy	autopsy		automatic automobile
bene (well, good)		benevolent	beneficiate		benediction benefactor beneficiary benefit
bi (two)	bilabial bilingual biliteral	bias bicameral bilateral bipartisan biracial	biaxial bicentric biceps bifoliate biped	biangular bilinear bimodal binomial bisect	biannual bicycle bifocals bigamy binocular biplane
biblio (book)	bibliography bibliomania bibliophile	bibliotherapy			
bio (life)	autobiography biography	biogeography biosocial	biochemisty biology		
capt, capit (to take, to seize)	caption	capitulation			
cent (one hundred)		centenary	centipede centrifugal	percent	century

Morpheme					
chrom (color)		chromatic	achromatic, chromosome		monochrome, polychrome
chron (time)	chronicle, chronological	anachronism	chronometer, synchronous		
circum (around)	circumflex, circumlocution	circa, circumnavigate, circumvention	circulation, circuit	circumcenter, circumference, circumradius, circumscribe	circuitous, circumcise, circus
co, con, com (with, together)	coauthor, collaborate	coalition, compatriot	coagulate, cohesive	congruent, correlation	coeducation, colleague
contra (against, opposite)	contradiction, contrast, counterplot	contraband, controversial, counterattack	contraorbital, counterbalance, counterearth		counteract, counterfeit, countersign
cred, credit (to believe, to trust)		accreditation, credentials, credibility, discredit			credo, credulous, incredible
cycle (circle)	cyclorama	encyclical	cyclical, epicycloid	epicycle, cyclone, hemicycle	bicycle
dem (people)		demagogue, democracy, demography, endemic	epidemic		
dia (across, through)	diacritical, dialogue	dialecticism, diatribe	diagnosis, diagram	diameter, diagonal	

Table C.1   Morphemes in content areas (cont.)

Morpheme and meaning	English	Social Studies	Science	Mathematics	General
dic, dict (to speak)	contradiction dictation diction	dictator edict indictment	addictive		malediction predict
duc, duct (to lead)	introduction	production	conductor	deductive reducible	abduction conduct seduce
epi (on, upon, over)	epic epigram epilogue epithet	epidemic	epicenter epidermic	epicycle epicycloid epimorphism	epicure epistle epitaph
eu (well, good)	eulogy euphemism euphony	eugenics euthenics	euthanasia eutrophy		euphoria
fac, fic (to do, to make)	fiction	manufacture	infections	factor	benefactress efficient facile
fin (to end, to limit)	finis definition	finance finalization		infinity	affinity
flex, flect (to bend)	inflection reflexive		deflection reflection		flexible
flu (to flow)	fluency	affluence	fluorescence		effluence influence influx

Morpheme (meaning)					
gamy (marriage)		bigamy misogamy monogamy polygamy	agamic exogamy		
gen (to produce, to beget)		genesis	progenitor		
gnos (knowledge)	cognitive	diagnosis			agnostic prognosticate
graph (to write)	monograph paragraph	demography topography polygraph	electrocardiograph graphite	graph	graphic lithography serigraphy
hemi (half)		hemisphere	hemiplegia	hemispheroid	
hetero (other, different)		heterodox	heterosexual		heterogeneous
hyper (over)	hyperbole hypercritical		hypermorph hypertrophy	hyperbola hypersphere	hyperactive hypertension
hypo (under)	hypothesis	hypocrisy	hypodermic	hypocycloid	hypoacidity
inter (among)	interjection interpretation	interracial interurban	interplanetary interpolar	interaxial interpolate	interrupt intersession
intra (inside)	introduction	intrastate	intracellular		intramural introvert

Table C.1 Morphemes in content areas (cont.)

Morpheme and meaning	English	Social Studies	Science	Mathematics	General
junct (to join)	conjunction	conjoin			adjoining
leg, lig, lect (to choose, to read)	lecture, legend, legible	election, legislative, selectivism			elective, eligible, lectern
log, logy (word speech)	dialectology, trilogy	anthropology, criminology, ideology, psychology, sociology	biology, zoology	logarithm	apology, logic, syllogism
loqu, loc (to speak)	colloquial, colloquy	interlocutory			circumlocution, loquacious
mal (bad, ill)	malapropism	malefaction	malnutrition		maladjusted, malevolence
meter, metr (to measure)	hexameter, metrical, polymeter		barometer, isometrics, metric	diameter, parameter, perimeter, pseudometer	
mono (one)	monograph, monolingual, monologue, monosyllabic	monarchy, monometallism, monopoly, monotheism	mononuclear, monosymmetric	monomial	monocycle, monogamy
mov, mot (to move)	emotion, motivation	demobilize, mobilization, promotion			motor

multi (much, many)	multilingual	multilateral multiparty	multicellular multiped multipolar	multiangular multiplicand multiplication multiplier	multitude
non (not)	nonfiction nonliterate nonobjective nonverbal	nonaggression nonaligned nonpartisan nonviolent	nonconductor nonpolar nonreactive		nonexistent nonflammable nonsense nonstop
pan (all, every, universal)	panorama pantomime	Pan-American pandemic	panchromatic pangenesis		panacea pandemonium pantheism
para (beside)	parable paradox paragraph paraphrase	parachronism paramilitary paramount	paragenesis paramorph paranoia parasite	parabola paraboloid parallel parallelogram parameter	parachute parapet
ped (foot)			biped quadruped		pedal pedestal
phil (loving)	bibliophile	philosophy			philharmonic
phon (sound, voice)	aphonic phonetic				symphonic
poly (much, many)	polyphonic	polyethic	polychromatic	polycentric polygon polyhedron	polygamy
post (after)	posthumous	postwar	postmortem	postmultiply	postdate

Table C.1 Morphemes in content areas (cont.)

Morpheme and meaning	English	Social Studies	Science	Mathematics	General
pre (before)	preface prefix premise preview	preamble prejudice preliterate	preaxial preclinical		preadolescent precaution prefer
pro (forward)	pronoun protagonist	prohibition		protractor	procreate
pseudo (false)	pseudoclassic pseudonym	pseudoaggressive pseudoanarchical	pseudocare	pseudometric	
retro (backward)		retroactive retrocession	retrograde retrorocket		retrospect
rupt (to break)	interruption	corruption disruption	eruption rupture		
scrib, script (to write)	description inscription manuscript scribble	conscription proscribe	prescription	circumscribe	postscript scripture
semi (half, partly)	semiabstract semicolon	semiliterate semipolitical	semiparasitic	semicircle	semiannual semiskilled
spect (to look)	prespective spectacle	inspection retrospective	spectrograph spectrum		expectation spectator

stat (stable)	consistency	resistance statesmanship	astatic	constant	statement status
sub (under, below)	subject	subcontinent subculture		subgroup subinterval	subdivide
super (over)	superlative superscribe	supersede superpatriotic	superego		superabundant superficial superintendent supernatural
syn (together)	synonym syntax	synthesis	syndactyl		syndrome synod synthetic
tang, tact (to touch)	tangible	contingency	contact contagious	tangent	intact tactful tactile
tele (far off)	teleplay	teleology telepathy	telescope		telepathic telephone
theo (god)		apotheosis theocentric theocracy	theomania		atheism polytheism theologian theology
trans (across)	transitive transpose	transaction transcontinental	transference transfusion	transformation transversal	transcend transcript transfer
ultra (beyond)		ultraconservative ultranationalism	ultrasonic ultraviolet		ultramodern

Table C.1 Morphemes in content areas (cont.)

Morpheme and meaning	English	Social Studies	Science	Mathematics	General
uni (one)	unilingual unison	unicameral unilateral	unicellular unifoliate	unimodular	unicorn uniform
val (to be, worth, to be strong)	evaluate	ambivalence devaluation validation	bivalent bivalve	equivalent	validity valuable value
vert, vers (to turn)	advertise conversation converse diversity	controversy diversification reversion subversive	ambiversion converter diversiform irreversible	convergent divergent transversal	aversion conversion convertible divert
voc (to call, to voice)	evocative vocabulary vocal	advocacy provocation revocation			vocalist vociferous

NAME INDEX

SUBJECT INDEX